Coming Back Strong

Distance runners on injury, cross training & rehab

Coming Back Strong

Distance runners on injury, cross training & rehab

Don Kopriva

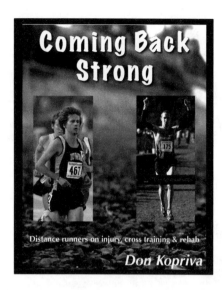

About the cover:
Neither Micah VanDenend (pictured left) nor Dathan Ritzenhein wishes he were on this book's cover, but the two Midwesterners, born 14 months apart, have epitomized elite athletes' striving to "come back strong" despite myriad surgeries and injuries. Their stories are inside.

Copyright © 2010 by Don Kopriva
Covers by Robin Bartlett, Moxie Creative Group
Cover photos courtesy of University of Iowa Sports Information Office (Micah VanDenend); Victor Sailer (Dathan Ritzenhein); Dietrich Wolfframm (author Don Kopriva)

All rights reserved. No part of this book may be reproduced in any form or by any electronic or mechanical means including information storage and retrieval systems—except in the instance of brief excerpts or quotations in reviews or critical articles—without permission in writing from the publisher, WriteOn Communications Solutions.

This book is meant to provide examples of and advice from distance runners coping with and rehabbing from injuries. The publisher is not engaged in offering medical advice. Injured runners are urged to seek the advice of medical professionals, trainers or therapists.

Published by WriteOn Communications Solutions
P.O. Box 3830, Lisle, Illinois 60532
(630) 964-5496
Fax: (630) 964-4996
www.writeoncomm.net

ISBN 978-1-4507-3484-4

Printed in the United States of America by ScotPress Printing, Lombard, Illinois

Acknowledgements

- Micah VanDenend— for his insightful comments from his unique dual perspective as a coach and as an often-injured athlete.
- Dathan Ritzenhein— who, following his first stress fracture, told me how useful a book like this would be to runners and coaches.
- Jim Dunaway— an old and valued friend and one of the sport's greatest writers and greatest treasures, for his always useful professional advice.
- Robin Bartlett— for her terrific cover design and invaluable technical assistance.
- Brandon Bartlett—for his help with the book's web page.
- Rich Elliott— for his editing assistance and professional comments
- Tim Keller —for his help with PayPal and sharing his accounting acumen.
- Dr. Jon Nolan—for supplying the proper medical terms for various injuries.
- Victor Sailer at PhotoRun— for the cover photo of Dathan Ritzenhein.
- The University of Iowa sports information office— for the cover photo of Micah VanDenend.
- Dietrich Wolfframm—for the photo of the author.
- Melna Langham at ScotPress Printing— for her assistance and advice in the printing and publishing process.
- The coaches and experts who so generously offered comments on the nature of injury.

And finally, with gratitude…
To the many fine runners who told of their experiences with injuries, cross training, rehab and recovery.

—Don Kopriva

To my good friends Dathan & Micah

Great runners who personify courage and perseverance in the face of injury and adversity.

Introduction

It has been my great privilege for more than 45 years to write about track and cross country and the athletes who participate in these sports as well as the coaches who work so hard to develop them.

But injury, in one form or another, has a way of affecting even the best of athletes. In fact, many elite runners knowingly push the limits and train right up to that fine line between health and injury. But going over the edge, as so many do in abandoning common sense and caution, is where pain and adversity take over.

In the pages that follow, you will read about the first-hand experiences with injuries that have bedeviled runners, even these elite ones. Profiles in this book are of U.S.-born men who compete or competed in events ranging from the mile/1500 to 10K, although a couple 800 types are also profiled as well as some 5K and 10K runners who've become full-time or part-time marathoners. "Elite," for purposes of this book, includes any men who won NCAA regional or national titles, earned all-America honors or gained places on U.S. Olympic or national teams in track or cross country.

Generally, the profiles are representative of those top men who are active now and likely will be through the 2016 Olympics as well as others recently retired who ran over the past 10-15 years. However, also presented are the injury experiences of some men 20 or more years removed from their competitive days so as give readers a better perspective as to how the treatment of injuries has changed, how coaches' views of injuries have evolved, and how new and improving methods of cross training and rehabbing have put runners back on the track sooner rather than later.

My thanks to the many fine runners who took the time to complete a questionnaire and/or speak with me about their experiences in recovering from their injuries. And good luck to those who read about them; may you never need their advice.

—*Don Kopriva*

Table of Contents

Coaches offer varied views on injuries, cross training, rehab   1 - 10

Athletes' Profiles

1	Ray Appenheimer	11 - 13
2	Jeff Atkinson	14 - 15
3	Chris Bailey	16 - 17
4	Kyle Baker	18 - 19
5	Brandon Bethke	20 - 22
6	Terry Brahm	23 - 24
7	Tim Broe	25 - 27
8	Doug Brown	28 - 30
9	Tom Chorny	31 - 35
10	Mark Coogan	36 - 38
11	Jared Cordes	39 - 40
12	Alan Culpepper	41 - 43
13	Mark Deady	44 - 47
14	Rod DeHaven	48 - 50
15	Chris Derrick	51 - 53
16	Brian Diemer	54 - 56
17	Pascal Dobert	57 - 58
18	Andy Downin	59 - 61
19	Matt Downin	62 - 63
20	Stuart Eagon	64 - 66
21	German Fernandez	67 - 71
22	Darryl Frerker	72 - 73
26	Robert Gary	74 - 75
27	Chris Graff	76 - 77

28	Tim Hacker	78 - 80
29	Brad Hauser	81 - 82
30	Billy Herman	83 - 85
31	Dan Huling	86 - 88
32	Evan Jager	89 - 91
33	Greg Jimmerson	92 - 94
34	Weldon Johnson	95 - 97
35	Tim Keller	98 - 100
36	Bob Kennedy	101 - 102
37	Daniel Lincoln	103 - 104
38	Louie Luchini	105 - 108
39	Eric MacTaggart	109 - 113
40	Paul McMullen	114 - 115
41	Craig Miller	116 - 118
42	Ed Moran	119 - 121
43	John Mortimer	122 - 123
44	Billy Nelson	124 - 126
45	Nathan Nutter	127 - 130
46	Brian Olinger	131 - 134
47	Stephen Pifer	135 - 137
48	Seth Pilkington	138 - 140
49	Steve Plasencia	141 - 142
50	Ken Popejoy	143 - 145
51	Jonathan Riley	146 - 148
52	Dathan Ritzenhein	149 - 152
53	Josh Rohatinsky	153 - 155
54	Chris Rombough	156 - 158

55	Galen Rupp	159 - 161
56	Don Sage	162 - 165
57	Bret Schoolmeester	166 - 168
58	Jerry Schumacher	169 - 170
59	Steve Scott	171 - 172
60	Jeff See	173 - 175
61	Chris Siemers	176 - 179
62	Patrick Smyth	180 - 183
63	Josh Spiker	184 - 185
64	Jim Spivey	186 - 187
65	Matt Tegenkamp	188 - 190
66	Edwardo Torres	191 - 193
67	Jorge Torres	194 - 196
68	Ryan Vail	197 - 199
69	Micah VanDenend	200 - 204
70	Luke Watson	205 - 207
71	Alan Webb	208 - 209
72	Larry Wieczorek	210 - 211
73	Lex Williams	212 - 216
74	Dan Wilson	217 - 219
75	Matt Withrow	220 - 221
76	Rick Wohlhuter	222 - 224
	Appendix A	225
	Appendix B	226
	Appendix C	227

A note about the interview process—
The athletes profiled within responded to a questionnaire and/or were interviewed by the author. Some were contacted as early as 2003, when plans for this book first developed; most others responded in the spring and summer of 2010. Many runners who were contacted some years back may have suffered other injuries and retired since their initial responses; nonetheless, they are included because their experiences with injuries, cross training and rehab remain no less valid. Information is current on most men still competing or more recently retired. The author welcomes updates from any athletes whom he has been unable to subsequently contact or from those who know their whereabouts.

Coaches' views vary on injuries, rehab

"That kid could have been one of the greats if he hadn't been injured so often," more than one coach has lamented.

"I just hate to think about the U.S. national teams I missed making because I was hurt so much," more than one distance runner has said.

Injuries are, unfortunately, part of distance running, especially for elite runners who will push themselves up to and then over that thin edge dividing "healthy" from "hurt," as if daring fate to smite them for seeking perfection.

Alberto Salazar, who coaches some of the finest of America's elite runners with The Oregon Project, contends that the closer you can get to that fine line, the harder you can train without being injured and still recover, the more fit you're going to be.

"You're running against a lot of other people who are flirting with that fine line, too. Not everyone's going to be unlucky," he says. "Some will get very close to it and not get injured and that's who you've ultimately got to compete against.

"People could say, you should never be near that fine line, but to be honest, unless you're so superior to everybody else that you don't need to go near your limits to beat them, you do out of necessity have to go near that line."

Clearly, injuries are the lot of the distance runner, to a greater or lesser degree, regardless of talent or best times, with an Olympic gold medalist as susceptible to a stress fracture as a fun runner.

"Injuries are a necessary evil," says three-time Olympic steeplechaser Doug Brown, a former head track and cross country coach at the universities of Tennessee and Florida.

"They're going to happen, so deal with them."

Renowned Illinois high school coach Joe Newton, with more than a half-century in coaching and in coping with injured runners, echoes Brown.

"Injuries will always be there," says the Elmhurst York High School boys' cross country coach. "You must learn to deal with them and with rehab."

Micah VanDenend, who was a 13:49 5K runner at the University of Iowa but was often sidelined by injury during his high school and college careers, thinks of injuries as unfortunate side effects that most runners will on one or more occasions have to contend with.

"It is important to stay optimistic and confident and to find a way to keep training and to limit the length of time away from actually getting out the door and running," says VanDenend, who is now track and cross country coach at the University of Wisconsin-Parkside.

Indiana University physiologist Robert Chapman, the former cross country coach at IU, remembers Georgia State University physiologist David Martin as saying that "injuries are a mistake in your training plan."

Chapman agrees with that assessment, to a degree.

"As a coach, I control a lot of variables—what surface, how far, how fast, how much rest," he says. "As a general rule, I want to be proactive and try to prevent injuries by manipulating these variables properly, rather than being reactive to an injury that pops up."

Salazar calls injuries "somewhat inevitable," noting that "even when it's just a soreness that the runner feels, I believe that you immediately have to get on it.

"Most injuries don't go from nothing to something big. They're progressive, but when it's been sore for three days it's a lot harder to put the fire out."

Alan Edgecombe, a former Illinois high school coach, also regards injuries as part of the sport.

"As you try to get athletes to reach their full potential, you are pushing them close to the breaking point. The key is to recognize that breaking point for each individual athlete and try to keep him from going past it," he says.

"As a coach, you need to be prepared to deal with injuries. This involves preventive steps, like proper stretching, cross training, and knowing when to tell a runner to stop for the day. And it involves reactive steps, including having medical professionals available who understand athletes' needs and their desire to get back to competition as quickly as possible."

But Edgecombe does have a specific, and somewhat novel, view as to why so many young runners suffer through periods of injury, particularly early in their running careers

"There are injuries today—particularly IT band injuries—in high school runners that are the result of the relative inactivity of today's youth," he contends.

"In the 1960s, children didn't spend hours in front of video games; they were outside playing baseball and riding bicycles," he says. "They were involved in natural cross training, and as a result they were better prepared for a rigorous running training program when they got to high school."

Rich Elliott, author of the authoritative "The Competitive Edge: Mental Preparation for Distance Running" and a former coach, calls avoiding injuries and caring for them ever-present parts of a coach's job.

"My main goal as a coach is to get my runners long stretches of injury-free training and get them to the starting line healthy and ready to race," says Elliott. "Achieving that—without the body-scan device from Star Trek—is a constant challenge."

Andy Preuss, boys' track and cross country coach at Glenbard South High School in Glen Ellyn, Ill., says distance runners seem predisposed to injuries.

"Distance runners seem to be in a high-risk group," says Preuss, who coached Micah VanDenend to two state titles in high school and also dealt with the young runner's first injury as a sophomore.

"One college coach told me there are two types of distance runners—one that has had a stress fracture and the other that will get a stress fracture," he said. "I am not sure that is totally true but high-level distance runners seem to be more at risk."

Runners must learn patience

In spite of themselves, most elite runners have learned to be patient not only with the time it takes to heal but also with the often tedious rehabilitation regimen. But it's tough psychologically, because rehab by nature can be an often difficult and slow process that is alien to the mentality of such highly focused, driven individuals.

VanDenend, who only once in six years at Iowa had a full season of competition, has become an expert on injuries, cross training and rehab (and also on what he calls "pre-habbing") after a seemingly unending series of injuries and surgeries.

"I have heard from a lot of injured athletes who have cross trained for a very long time (months) that there is eventually a breaking point, a point when you feel fed up and feel as if you can no longer continue on cross training," he says.

"I've had these moments—where 20 minutes into a cross training session I have just stopped, taken a shower and gone home. I've reached the point where for a couple days I wouldn't even get on the bike because I could no longer see the purpose. I believe that that is normal.

"But your desire to be great will eventually get the best of you. I can never stay away from the bike/elliptical for too long (more than a couple days) because I always have to prove to myself how tough I am."

The goal—a place on the U.S. Olympic or World team or a medal, a record, pride, ego, something—always drives these runners.

So, while the first rule of coming back strong is patience, tenacity may well be the second.

Two-time Olympian Dathan Ritzenhein, notoriously impatient when he suffered his first stress fracture prior to his sophomore year of cross country at the University of Colorado, has learned through a succession of stress fractures that he can be patient and that he can always recover to run again.

"Each injury I have changed things afterwards," Ritzenhein says. "I think learning from every injury is important. We have left no stone unturned and as the next injury happens, as it most certainly will because that is part of competitive running, I will learn from that one, too, and try to make another change."

Mental aspects

Coaches have mixed views as to whether injuries can be mental in origin.
"I think it is extremely rare when runners dream up an injury. Runners loathe stopping running," says Elliott. "But I do think that emotional stress can lead to injuries."

Newton believes that, "in some cases, injuries are very definitely mental."

But Chapman thinks that only an extremely small percentage might be mental in nature.

"I believe most injuries have a root in a mechanical issue, a structural issue, or a chronic overuse (with distance athletes). There is a difference between being sore and being injured," he says.

"As coaches, we need to help the athlete realize the difference. You can train when you are sore. You need to rest when you are injured."

Edgecombe contends that, absolutely, some injuries are more mental than physical, but that doesn't make them less real to the athlete.

"In a situation where the athlete is 'thinking' himself into an injury, the coach can be a positive or negative force. This situation has to be handled uniquely with each athlete," he says.

"The athlete has to believe that the coach really has his best interest at heart. Some athletes need to be reassured, while others need a kick in the butt."
VanDenend concurs.

"I think that most injuries are rooted in some form of physical discomfort," he says. "However, I also think that our attitudes toward those injuries and how we perceive an injury may sometimes make it worse than it actually is."

Salazar doubts that anyone makes up an injury.

"If you have a real injury and soreness and pain somewhere it isn't in your head," he says. "It may not be as bad as you think. You may be exaggerating it somewhat. Some people can work through some things. Some don't have as high a pain tolerance or threshold."

Preuss thinks it depends on the psychological nature of the injury.

"Athletes and coaches are very aware of injuries and the toll that they take and are very careful," he said. "The athlete and the coach must know the difference between pain and discomfort and injury. Having a highly qualified and trusted athletic trainer is a must. A trainer can help the athlete through any mental barriers they face."

Cross training pluses, minuses

As to rehabbing and recovering, is cross training always the answer?

VanDenend hates it but swears by it. Olympian Matt Tegenkamp has had his share of injuries but doesn't think it does any good. Ritzenhein believes his running career has been saved because of his cross training time on the AlterG, an anti-gravity treadmill that provides weight-bearing therapy.

"There is no form of exercising that is going to keep you in the same kind of fitness as running will," says VanDenend.
"That being said, yes, cross training is certainly effective. Your heart does not know the difference, whether you are running or you are biking, on the elliptical, or aqua-jogging.

"I believe that you can still stay very fit and compete at a high level off just cross training although you will not be nearly as fit as you could be if you were getting out the door and running each day."

Salazar is a strong advocate of immediate cross training, particularly with the AlterG ("It's the closest thing to running.") for those who have access to it, primarily because training on it alleviates weight-bearing stress.

"I believe that the key is to immediately go into some sort of cross training and not try and run through the injury," he says. "Bite the bullet and go into cross training to retain fitness and allow the injury to heal."

"I'm a believer in doing a lot of different cross training things (if you can't do AlterG) because nothing else is (the same as) running," Salazar says. "If you do any one, the more danger is that you're going to build up muscles that will be overdone for running."

Preuss believes in cross training, if it is done correctly.

"There is no substitute for getting your miles in, but everyone is different. If you can lessen the impact you may reduce the chance of injury," Preuss says. "Anything that can get the heart rate up for extended periods has worked for us. The athletes at times get bored but they must understand that it can be beneficial to their health and success."

Others also have their specific reasons for or, kind of, against it, based largely off their experience with physiology or with runners they have coached.

"It depends on the activity," says Brown. "You can't get better as a runner without running so if the cross training activity either involves some type of running, like circuit training, or at least simulates the running motion, then I think there's benefit. I don't like biking, swimming, or weights for distance runners unless it's for injury rehab."

Chapman thinks cross training can be good but sees it as more a way to slow down the loss of fitness an athlete will experience while not running.

"I have always felt the best way to train for running is running—the 'specificity principle,' if you will," he says. "I know there are coaches who integrate cross training into their regular training design. I would rather manipulate other variables, like surface, intensity, recovery, volume, etc. For some, cross training can help them burn both calories and nervous energy.

"Some athletes are poor recuperators, and they need some form of exercise to stay sane," Chapman adds. "In those ways, I think cross training is effective."

However, the Indiana physiologist believes the biggest issue with cross training is trying to get the heart rate high enough. Most runners are unable to get their heart rate high enough while doing prolonged cross training at a gentle pace, something that would mimic a gentle running effort.

"My experience has been that, to get the HR high enough, a fartlek-type session works best," Chapman says. "Whether it is cycling, aqua jogging, etc., some sort of higher intensity 'on' interval, followed by a lower intensity 'off' interval gets HR elevated.

"Because the cross training session is not weight-bearing, the athlete can do a session like this most every day. A fartlek-type session also helps break up the monotony of cross training."

Most coaches cite patience

"I think that I am patient, but my runners may tell a different story," says Edgecombe.

"I once heard of a coach who told a runner to go into the shower room and soak off a cast so that he could rejoin the team. Obviously that isn't the right solution. You have to be very careful today in how you bring an athlete back from injury.

"With high school runners, you cannot go against the wishes of the parents or you might end up with a lawsuit. However, I have had occasions where a parent has wanted me to run their son or daughter in spite of an injury, and I have resisted."

Chapman says he is patient to a fault, noting that "I tend to be overly conservative with athletes who get injured. I would rather they get healthy and back to a full program of training, than some sort of half-assed, day-on, day-off routine that gets dragged out for double the time."

Elliott says that coaches just have to be patient.

"Knowing that injuries are an occupational hazard with runners, I tend to be patient," he says. "That's not to say I don't feel frustration when injuries persist. The frustration comes from feeling I have to get better at (helping runners in) avoiding injuries and better at treating injuries."

VanDenend would rather his athletes face injuries head-on from the start.

"I am aggressive at the onset of injuries. I don't like this sit-and-wait approach that many doctors and trainers take when an injury first occurs. Oftentimes they say 'let's give it a week or two and see if it gets any better,'" he says. "The problem is that when that time passes and the athlete isn't any better we just wasted two weeks."

The UW-Parkside coach thinks it's fine to take a day or two off and see if the symptoms dissipate, but then he wants his athletes to see a physician, begin cross training, get in the ice tub, start taking anti-inflammatories, use the ultrasound, do some strengthening, get the deep tissue work to see if they can beat the injury.

"I feel I am very patient," says Preuss. "If athletes rush back or are not prepared for their return, then their rehab process can really be put on hold. This is where knowing the athlete and trusting the trainer helps. Those relationships will guide you.

"In Micah VanDenend's junior year in cross country, I am sure he wanted to run at sectionals and state. If I asked him to run he would have. We did not let him. I feel that is one of the best decisions I ever made. Who knows what would have happened?"

Return to competition

How do coaches know when a runner is ready to return to training? To racing? His word, your gut instinct, how he looks running, his ability to do some workout?

"I rely mostly on the trainers or doctors," says Brown. "I coach, they treat. Obviously, though, if he's training pain-free and has a full range of motion in the injured area, he's probably ready."

Preuss believes it is important to know and trust your athlete.

"How they look and what they say are critical," he says. "If you know your athlete you can gain a lot of information simply by the questions they ask."

Edgecombe looks at his running motion and posture to help judge whether a runner is recovered.

"Each runner has a very distinctive motion, almost like a fingerprint," he says. "If that isn't right, then something is wrong. I once had an 800-meter runner who was struggling during indoor track. He was leaning back more than usual, even early in his races, which to me indicated a high level of fatigue. I recommended a blood test to his parents."

The physician found an inflammation of the pericardium and immediately put the young man on medication. He was back for outdoor track and anchored the school's 4x800 relay to a state medal.

"Most serious athletes will try to come back too quickly, so I often find myself putting the brakes on in the recovery process," Edgecombe says.

"An athlete's return to racing is based on a combination of things," says VanDenend. "It's always a good idea to err on the side of caution. When you've missed so much time away from running, what's one more week?

"I'd rather give my athlete those extra couple days or that extra week and know that they're ready to get back to training than be kicking myself and wishing I had given them that extra time. We want to make sure that we have whipped this thing before really getting back to work." "

Elliott says all the above-mentioned factors enter into his decision on an athlete's return.

"When first returning to running, we will do a few test workouts before returning to full training. Light jogging, see how the legs react; then light speed work, and see how the legs react. Once a runner can do a hard speed workout without any relapse, he is ready to race."

So, when is the right time to return?

For Salazar, it's an easy decision.

"I think it has to do with pain," he says.
"The key is to monitor that closely to be sure you're not doing too much too soon. It comes down to what are they feeling? I tend to go by that."

Effect on team

Finally, an injury to a team's top runner almost certainly affects the other members of the team to greater or lesser degrees.

Chapman believes an injury can hurt the training part of a team's program more than the competition aspect.

"I think the bigger effect is the loss of a quality training partner more than some psychological effect of a top dog being injured," he says. "The advantage of the training group is the group. Together, they will get more fit and accomplish more than if they did the exact same training separately. So having an athlete hurt lessens the training group effect, and that is the big negative."

VanDenend contends that it's vital to keep injured runners connected to their teammates and the team's goals.

"Whenever you lose any member of your team the dynamics change," he says. "Losing a top runner is never easy because they tend to be the team leaders, if not vocally, then certainly by example. It's very important to keep those injured athletes involved in the day-to-day grind and, if possible, let them travel them to meets. It will do both the injured individual and the rest of the team a lot of good."

Not surprisingly, injuries can be more critical to high school teams that may have only one great runner whose loss to injury can have a negative ripple effect on young runners.
"It can be devastating. This is where solid leadership comes into play," Preuss said. "You need to be strong and keep pushing toward the goals that the team has set."

Edgecombe says athletes are smart enough to know how an individual injury has impacted the team.

"When this occurs, the right approach is to acknowledge the situation and challenge them to achieve to the best of their ability," he says. "It doesn't do any good to pretend you can accomplish unrealistic success, and in the long term it damages the coach's credibility with the athletes. The athletes not only want your respect, they need to be able to respect the coach."

Newton and Elliott see an injury hitting a team's attitude and spirit.

"I tell them that the rest of the team must 'step up,'" says Newton. "I quote Mike Ditka, 'We will run with what we've got.'"

"Injuries can certainly be bad for morale," says Elliott. "The potential is there for discouragement, but that's when you have to keep preaching optimism. But, really, injury is so much a part of the sport that you have to just learn how to roll with it."

Most elite runners do roll with it, recognizing that injury is often the price of running over the edge.

But some elite runners, like recent NCAA 5K champs Chris Solinsky and Bobby Curtis and 2009 USATF cross country runner-up Tim Nelson, have never had season-shortening injuries. They are the lucky ones—and the few.

Ray Appenheimer
Colgate University
5K, XC

"While at times there is rhyme and reason why an injury occurs, injury does not make you a failure or less of a runner. Use the injury as a learning experience."

Ray, briefly profiled
Birth Date and Place: Oct. 18, 1972, Buffalo, N.Y.
Began running: 16 years old; Began running competitively: 16 years old; Retired: Fall 2001
Height/Running Weight: 5'8", 140 lbs.

Colgate University, 1994
College coach: Art McKinnon
St. Joseph's Collegiate Institute., Kenmore, N.Y. (1990)
High school coaches: Mike Diggins, Jim Roland, Matt Hellerer

Current residence: Oberlin, Ohio
Current occupation: Head track & cross country coach, Oberlin College

Personal record: 13:28.99 (2000)

Notable accomplishments
College – Five-time All-American…USA indoor 3,000m Champion… USA Club National XC Champion…Member of USA XC Team (12k)… World University Team at 5,000m and 10,000m… 13:28 for 5,000m

Favorite rehab/cross training workout
I really liked and felt I benefited from this workout in the pool that I did most days: Warm up for ten minutes of easy pool running. Run very hard in the pool for 45 seconds, recovering with 15 seconds of easy pool running. I would repeat this 10 times for one set of ten minutes. I would take two minutes between sets and run up to eight or nine sets. Cool down with ten minutes of pool running. I envisioned this workout being like repeat 300s with a very minimal recovery.

Worst running-related injury
Necrosis of Achilles (dead spot on the left Achilles tendon).

Approximate date of injury, nature of it and was surgery required?
January 2000 – August 2000 (8 months). Necrosis of Achilles; surgery was required.

What flaw led to the injury? Or did you do something that caused it?
Bad blood flow to the Achilles tendon. Also had adhesions removed from the right Achilles two years earlier.

Rehabilitation program that you followed. How long before you resumed "normal" training?
Eight months of rehab. Every morning I would bike for one hour from steady to hard. Every afternoon I would do one to two hours hard in the pool. Plus I'd do 500 sit-ups and 100 pushups daily and lifted three times a week.

Given that running takes a fair amount of time and that cross training for that same time would probably drive you crazy, what did you do to keep busy?
The cross training kept me plenty busy and plenty tired. My philosophy was that if I kept myself exhausted I wouldn't get too depressed. Also, I knew that every minute in the pool and on the bike would accelerate my fitness when I returned to running.

What was the most difficult aspect of being injured? How did you deal psychologically with missing a season?
I was the U.S. champion at 3,000 indoors in 2000 and I crapped out at the Trials that year because of my Achilles. These chances only come along once in a lifetime and I missed mine. That's the hardest part.

What specifically did you learn from being injured?
My friends and family really rallied around me and pulled me through these tough times. Also, being injured made me value each day of healthy running I've had since.

What advice would you give another elite runner who suffers a season-ending injury?
Cross train like a mother. Stay in contact with other athletes, especially those who have been through the same. Having a support network, be it teammates, coaches, physical therapists, whoever, will get you through what can be a painstaking day-to-day existence of cross training.

When you returned to full-time training, did you alter the type of training you were doing?
Yes, I could no longer run in spikes. My track career was over.

What was the result in your first major competition after returning from injury?
10th place, San Francisco Bay to Breakers. First non-Kenyan finisher.

What advice would you give a high school or young college runner regarding injury prevention and/or rehabilitation?
Same as above only don't take the injury personally. While at times there is rhyme and reason why an injury occurs, injury does not make you a failure or less of a runner. Use the injury as a learning experience.

After being injured and coming back, did it change your sense of who you were as a runner? Did you have more patience or did you find yourself training on the edge again?
I became much better at listening to my body and altering my training accordingly. Having a long-term injury has informed how I work with the athletes I coach today. To their benefit, they have a coach who made plenty of mistakes as a runner.

Other thoughts on injury prevention or rehabilitation
One has to possess enough confidence to take a day off when some small pain (a potential injury) crops up. The very best runners I knew and trained with had this capacity. In retrospect, it makes perfect sense—a day off is nothing compared to the time and effort when that little pain becomes something more serious. If you do get injured, take it day by day and do your best to celebrate whatever you accomplished that day. Stay positive, stay focused and understand that everything you do will be paid back to you down the road.

Jeff Atkinson

Stanford University
1500m

"Six weeks to repair <u>with</u> or <u>without</u> any therapy"

Jeff, briefly profiled
Birth Date and Place: Feb. 24, 1963, Manhattan Beach, Cal.
Began running: 14 years old; Began running competitively: 14 years old
Height/Running Weight: 6'1", 150 lbs.

Stanford University, 1986
College coach: Brooks Johnson
Mira Costa High School, Manhattan Beach, Cal. (1981)
High school coaches: Dave Holland

Current residence: Redondo Beach, Cal.
Current occupation: Coach

Personal record: 1500—3:35.15 (1989); Mile—3:52.80 (1988)

Notable accomplishments
High School – 19th at Kinney Nationals (1980)… 3200m school record (9:02.77)
College/Post-Collegiate – Three-time All-American at 1500m (outdoors)…Stanford school record in the mile (3:55.30)…1988 Olympic Trials champ (1500m)… 10th at 1988 Olympic Games (1500m)…U.S. indoor 1500m record (3:38.13)…1989 World Indoor Championships bronze medalist (1500m).

Worst running-related injuries:
Achilles tendonitis, plantar faschitis, knee tendonitis, hamstring insertion under butt ("itis").

Approximate date of injuries, nature of them and was surgery required?
Injuries came yearly, always in the connective tissue, never needed surgery. Each injury lasted about six weeks.

What flaw led to the injuries? Or did you do something that caused it (them)?
Too much, too soon of any kind.

Rehabilitation program that you followed. How long before you resumed "normal" training again?
Rehab a waste of time!!! After six weeks off I began with 1/3 the volume I had been doing.

Given that running takes a fair amount of time and that cross training for that same time would probably drive you crazy, what did you do to keep busy?
Drank beer, watched movies, and played golf.

What was the most difficult aspect of being injured? How did you deal psychologically with missing a season?
Frustration. I planned for the next season. I missed my best chance at the 1992 Olympic Trials with a hamstring injury.

What specifically did you learn from being injured?
Patience in preparation. Do supplemental exercises daily.

What advice would you give another elite runner who suffers a season-ending injury?
Plan for two years in advance and go slowly.

When you returned to full-time training, did you alter the type of training you were doing?
No, just got to "full volume and full intensity" more gradually.

What was the result in your first major competition after returning from injury?
Less than 100% but still okay.

What advice would you give a high school or young college runner regarding injury prevention and/or rehabilitation?
Do supplemental exercise and build slowly.

Other thoughts on injury prevention or rehabilitation.
"Six weeks to repair with or without any therapy"

Chris Bailey
Illinois State University
3K, 5K, 10K, XC

"Gradually increase the amount of mileage you do over the years. Don't do what others are doing (running). Everybody handles different intensities—do what works for you."

Chris, briefly profiled
Birth Date and Place: Aug. 4, 1977
Began running: 14 years old; Began running competitively: 14 years old
Height/Running Weight: 6'1", 135 lbs.

Illinois State University, B.A., 2000 (Education)
College coach: John Coughlan
Westmont High School, Westmont, Ill. (graduated spring 1995)
High school coaches: Steve Wolf

Current residence: Aurora, Ill.
Current occupation: High School Cross Country & Track Coach

Notable accomplishments
High School—Two-time Class A Illinois State Cross Country Champion (1993, 1994)
College/Post-Collegiate—All-American at 10K (1999)…NCAA qualifier at 5K (1999)… NCAA XC qualifier (1998)… 10-time Missouri Valley Conference champion…Region V cross country champion (1998)… 2-time MVC cross country champion.

Worst running-related injuries
Three separate stress fractures over a two-year period.

Approximate date of injuries, nature of them and was surgery required?
November 1995, November 1996, and December 1997. No surgeries were required. Missed 4-6 weeks for each.

What flaw led to the injuries? Or did you do something that caused them?
Increased mileage. I went from 25-30 miles a week in high school to 45-50 miles a week in college.

Rehabilitation program that you followed. How long before you resumed "normal" training?
Nordic Trac for 40-45 minutes twice a day and an additional 45 minutes to an hour of swimming a day. Did this for 4-6 weeks before running again.

Given that running takes a fair amount of time and that cross training for that same time would probably drive you crazy, what did you do to keep busy?
Nothing changed. While teammates were out running, I was cross training.

What was the most difficult aspect of being injured? How did you deal psychologically with missing a season?
Not being able to compete was the most difficult. I used not running as a chance to motivate myself by working that much harder during the cross training.

What specifically did you learn from being injured?
I appreciated competition and took it more seriously. After the injury I ran each competition hard and did whatever I could to win.

What advice would you give another elite runner who suffers a season-ending injury?
Be patient, let the injury heal.

When you returned to full-time training, did you alter the type of training you were doing?
No, I (with my coach) just kept a close eye on how many miles I was putting in each week.

What was the result in your first major competition after returning from injury?
Running 8:19 (3K) at Iowa State and setting the freshman record at Illinois State.

What advice would you give a high school or young college runner regarding injury prevention and/or rehabilitation?
Gradually increase the amount of mileage you do over the years. Don't do what others are doing (running). Everybody handles different intensities—do what works for you.

Kyle Baker

Michigan State University
5K, 10K, Marathon

"Don't be scared to miss one or two days at the onset rather than months down the road. Most things can be taken care of with ice, treatment, and 1-2 days off."

Kyle, briefly profiled
Birth Date and Place: Jan. 21, 1976
Began running: 11 years old; Began running competitively: 12 years old
Height/Running Weight: 6'2", 145 lbs.

Michigan State University, B.A., 1999 (Business Administration)
College coach: Jim Stintzi
Anderson Highland High School, Anderson, IN. (graduated spring 1994)
High school coaches: Robert Jackson and "Buckie" Burkhart

Current residence: East Lansing, Mich.
Current occupation: unknown
Current affiliation or club:
Current Coach: Self coached

Personal record: Marathon— 2:14:13 (debut, Chicago, 2002)

Notable accomplishments
High School –Footlocker XC Finalist (1993).
College/Post-Collegiate – Four-Time Big Ten Track Champion (1997-99)…Four-Time NCAA All-American (1997-99)…Ranked #6 U.S. Marathon list (2002)… Ranked #10 U.S. 10,000m (2002)… #6 All-Time U.S. 20k list.

Worst running-related injuries
IT Band Tendonitis, sciatic nerve (ongoing major discomfort, and Achilles tendonitis.

Approximate date of injury, nature of it and was surgery required?
IT band, August/September 2000. I missed about 30 days. With the sciatic nerve, January 2000, ongoing therapy. The Achilles (most recent), May 2002. Missed about five days over two weeks.

What flaw led to the injuries? Or did you do something that caused them?
IT band resulted from overwork. Achilles injury came from running a 10K on the track and a road 25K within two weeks of each other. The sciatic nerve is the result of scoliosis in the spine and I have a major leg length discrepancy. I constantly needed re-alignment.

Rehabilitation program that you followed. How long before you resumed "normal" training?
For tendonitis, direct contact with ice works best, some ultra sound, up to eight times a day. Ice baths also. With the sciatic, see a D.O. periodically. Physical therapy, took about one month of three times per week to feel almost normal. Every time I race frequently or increase mileage or intensity it hurts.

Given that running takes a fair amount of time and that cross training for that same time would probably drive you crazy, what did you do to keep busy?
Stationary bike, core strength exercises, tons of sit-ups and push-ups.

What was the most difficult aspect of being injured? How did you deal psychologically with missing a season?
Feeling like you're getting behind your competition. Fear of not being "in shape" down the road. Psychologically, you do what you can to recover and be patient. I never missed chance to make a U.S. team.

What specifically did you learn from being injured?
You will come back. Don't try to come back too quickly or soon. Take care of little things early on.

What advice would you give another elite runner who suffers a season-ending injury?
Don't give up; it has happened to everyone. The adversity should make you stronger.

When you returned to full-time training, did you alter the type of training you were doing?
No, but I paid more attention to little aches and pains.

What was the result in your first major competition after returning from injury?
Runner-up, Fall U.S. XC championships in 2000.

What advice would you give a high school or young college runner regarding injury prevention and/or rehabilitation?
Ice!!! More than you think you should. Don't be scared to miss one or two days at the onset rather than months down the road. Most things can be taken care of with ice, treatment, and 1-2 days off.

Brandon Bethke

Arizona State University
Mile/1500, 3K, 5K, XC

"Make sure that you listen to your body and stay on top of anything that starts to hurt. Getting treatment and taking a little time in the beginning will help prevent a more serious injury later."

Brandon, briefly profiled
Birth Date and Place: Jan. 19, 1987; Mission Viejo, Cal.
Began running: 14 years old; Began running competitively: 14 years old
Height/Running Weight: 5'11", 160 lbs.

Arizona State University, B.A., 2010 (Organizational Studies)
College coach: Louie Quintana (ASU); Jerry Schumacher (Wisconsin)
El Toro High School, Lake Forest, Cal. (2005)
High school coaches: Rick Hagin and Martin Pennell

Current residence: Ann Arbor, Mich.
Current occupation: Professional Runner
Current affiliation or club: Arizona State University
Current Coach: Ron Warhurst

Personal records: 1500—3:42.82; Mile—3:59.85; 3K—7:51.54i; Steeple—8:48; 5K—13:27.79

Notable accomplishments
High School—State cross country champion …All-American.
College—All-American in 5K at 2008 NCAA indoor for Wisconsin…won Big Ten titles at 3K, 5K and steeple…transferred to Arizona State after 2008 season…won Pac-10 5K in 2009…earned all-America honors…

Favorite rehab/cross training workout
I don't really do any cross training…I lift weights and if I am injured elliptical with a 15 min warm-up and 1 min hard fartleks for 40 min with a 10 min cool down.

Worst running-related injuries
Stress fracture and femeroacitabular impingement.

Approximate date of injuries, nature of them and was surgery required?
Spring of 2005. I missed 2 months of training for the stress fracture my senior year of high school. Impingement—spring of '08. I missed 3 weeks of training and minimal training starting back up.

What flaw led to the injury(ies)? Or did you do something that caused it (them)?
The stress fracture was a shoe or biomechanical issue and the impingement was something of the same, I am not sure.

Rehabilitation program that you followed. How long before you resumed "normal" training?
I aquajogged for the duration of my injury in high school everyday and sometimes did elliptical training. For the impingement I just took time completely off and did not do any rehab.

Given that running takes a fair amount of time and that cross training for that same time would probably drive you crazy, what did you do to keep busy?
Most of the time there was a TV nearby, I would read a book, or some of my friends were swimming in the pool but all in all cross training is one of the most boring activities for me.

What was the most difficult aspect of being injured? How did you deal psychologically with missing a season?
The most difficult thing about being injured was knowing how easy and fun it is to run when you're healthy, and when you're injured you can't do it. The psychological toll that it took was tough because other people run fast and when you're sitting and watching.

What specifically did you learn from being injured?
How important it is to take my faith seriously. During the toughest times in my life my faith in Jesus Christ has guided me and helped me deal with things when they were not going well.

What advice would you give another elite runner who suffers a season-ending injury?
Don't get too down on your situation; you know at some time you will be able to be back running again.

When you returned to full-time training, did you alter the type of training you were doing?
I was doing a little bit less than I was before, but after a little while it was back to the usual again.

What was the result in your first major competition after returning from injury?
I can't really remember…it was just the start of a new season. I improved and was excited about how I did.

What advice would you give a high school or young college runner regarding injury prevention and/or rehabilitation?
Make sure that you listen to your body and stay on top of anything that starts to hurt. Getting treatment and taking a little time in the beginning will help prevent a more serious injury later.

After being injured and coming back, did it change your sense of who you are/were as a runner? Did you have more patience or did you find yourself training on the edge again?
Maybe for the first little bit that I came back I was more tentative, but other than that I am just more educated about how my body feels when it comes to the beginning of an injury.

Terry Brahm

Indiana University
800, 1500, Mile, 3K, 5K

"Take the time to evaluate 'why?' Use the time to take a break mentally from the rigors of running. Keep fit by cross training. Know that your time will come."

Terry, briefly profiled
Birth Date and Place: Nov. 21, 1962, St. Meinrad, Ind.
Began running: 12 years old; Began running competitively: 12 years old; Retired: 30 years old
Height/Running Weight: 5'10", 139 lbs.

Indian University, B.A., 1986 (Special Education)
College coach: Sam Bell
Heritage Hills High School, Lincoln City, Ind. (1981)
High school coaches: Greg Hale

Current residence: Indianapolis, Ind.
Current occupation: Teacher

Personal records: 800--1:49.9; 1500—3:35.85; mile—3:54.56; 2 mile—8:21; 3K—7:43; 5K—13:28

Notable accomplishments
College/Post-Collegiate – Five-time Big Ten champion… NCAA 5,000 champion (1986)… six-time All-American… silver medalist in 1986 Goodwill Games (5,000m)… bronze medalist at World indoor championships (1987)… 1988 Olympic Team (5,000).

Worst running-related injuries
Strain of right TFL, Bursitis of foot, evulsions of left ankle, hamstring strains, and Achilles tendonitis.

Approximate date of injuries, nature of them and was surgery required?
Strained right TFL in the spring of 1982. Had bursitis and evulsions of left ankle in 1986 and dealt with Achilles tendonitis and hamstring strains all of the time. Never needed surgery.

What flaw led to the injuries? Or did you do something that caused them?
Intense training indoors.

Rehabilitation program that you followed. How long before you resumed "normal" training?
I took a long time off with no training. I did pool workouts, rode the bike, and lifted weights 5-6 days a week during time off.

Given that running takes a fair amount of time and that cross training for that same time would probably drive you crazy, what did you do to keep busy?
My most serious injuries came while in college, so the act of being a student took up the time and kept me from going crazy. I also spent time on the bike, in the pool, and in the weight room if the injury allowed it.

What was the most difficult aspect of being injured? How did you deal psychologically with missing a season?
The most difficult aspect was not being able to contribute and missing opportunities. To deal with it mentally I focused on rehab and cross training the same way I approached running. This allowed me to mentally adjust and gave me the benefit of cardiovascular fitness.

What specifically did you learn from being injured?
Patience, the need to train progressively over time. The need for injury prevention, i.e., stretching, icing, good shoes, proper training, and diet.

What advice would you give another elite runner who suffers a season-ending injury?
Take the time to evaluate "why?" Use the time to take a break mentally from the rigors of running. Keep fit by cross training. Know that your time will come.

When you returned to full-time training, did you alter the type of training you were doing?
I was more aware of the law of progressive overload and that there was a time for each type of workout.

What was the result in your first major competition after returning from injury?
Sub-par performance, but overall fitness was good.

What advice would you give a high school or young college runner regarding injury prevention and/or rehabilitation?
Ice your lower legs in an ice whirlpool after a hard workout. Get good shoes. Stretch, strength training and intelligent training.

Tim Broe

University of Alabama
3K, 5K, Steeple, XC

"Every cross training program should be tailor made for each individual's likes and dislikes. You have to find variety and find something that you enjoy and feel comfortable doing."

Tim, briefly profiled
Birth Date and Place: June 20, 1977, East Peoria, Ill.
Began running: 13 years old; Began running competitively: 13 years old; Retired: 2010
Height/Running Weight: 5'11", 155 lbs.

University of Alabama, B.A., 2000
College coaches: David Troy and Doug Williamson
East Peoria High School, Peoria, Ill. (1995)
High school coaches: Ed McGraw

Current residence: Hanover, N.H.
Current occupation: Professional Coach

Personal records: 1500—3:38.43 (2004); Mile—3:59.67i (2000); 3K—7:39.23i (2002); Steeple—8:14.82 (2001); 5K—13:11.77 (2005)

Notable accomplishments
College/Post-Collegiate— 12-time All-American…NCAA steeplechase champ …three-time U.S. XC 4K champ…two-time U.S. indoor 3K champ…World Champ Team (2001)…4th at 2000 Olympic Trials …11th in 2004 Olympic Games 5K…3-time U.S. outdoor 5K champ (2003-04-05)

Favorite rehab/cross training workout
40 mile bike ride…with 4x8 mile hard surges

Worst running-related injury:
Broke sesmoid bone in left foot in a steeplechase accident, followed by a bone bruise in my right knee caused by trying to return too quickly.

Approximate date of injury, nature of it and was surgery required?
Broke foot on June 20, 2002, did not run for 7 months. Resumed training Jan. 1, 2003.

What flaw led to the injury? Or did you do something that caused it?
Steeple accident caused foot problem

Rehabilitation program that you followed. How long before you resumed "normal" training?
Did no rehab for foot. Took a break after an intense spring and traveled. Finally had a cortisone shot on Dec. 22. For the knee problem, I biked on stationary and did leg strengthening exercises.

Given that running takes a fair amount of time and that cross training for that same time would probably drive you crazy, what did you do to keep busy?
During first injury I traveled and did nothing athletic. I really started to go nuts with the knee problem so I started lifting weights every day which helped get rid of excess energy and was something I had not done in four years.

What was the most difficult aspect of being injured? How did you deal psychologically with missing a season?
The most difficult part was doing all the right rehab and it was not getting any better. Watching everybody else running and I could do nothing but wait. The doctors could find nothing wrong and that drove me nuts, not knowing what was wrong.

What specifically did you learn from being injured?
First, you must do cross training to keep some level of training. Second, pay attention to every pain, don't just ignore it and hope it will go away. Finally, be patient when you start back or you will end up with another injury. TAKE YOUR TIME.

What advice would you give another elite runner who suffers a season-ending injury?
It's not the end of the world, although it may seem like it at the time. Sit down and redefine your goals for the next year and try not to make the same mistake twice.

When you returned to full-time training, did you alter the type of training you were doing?
Not really, I just took my time (16 weeks) and made sure that I did not do something stupid to hurt myself again.

What was the result in your first major competition after returning from injury?
I ran 14:00 for my first 5K at the Jesse Owens Classic

What advice would you give a high school or young college runner regarding injury prevention and/or rehabilitation?
Get in the ice tub, don't overstep your boundaries, stay off the pavement, and listen to your body. Don't ignore it.

Looking back, would you change any of your cross training?
Every cross training program should be tailor made for each individual's likes and dislikes. You have to find variety and find something that you enjoy and feel comfortable doing. That way it stays fun and keeps you exercising. Do as much as you emotionally can handle.

After being injured and coming back, did it change your sense of who you are/were as a runner? Did you have more patience or did you find yourself training on the edge again?
I definitely found myself being a lot more cautious. When you miss enough time you really start to value how nice it is to be running pain free. I don't think it changed my sense of who I am as an athlete

Doug Brown

University of Tennessee
Steeplechase, 5K, 10K, XC

"Be patient and give the injury enough time. Then come back slowly. I pushed back too hard too soon ..."

Doug, briefly profiled
Birth Date and Place: March 1, 1952,
Began running: 14 years old; Began running competitively: 14 years old; Retired: 1984
Height/Running Weight: 6'2", 155 lbs.

University of Tennessee, B.A., psychology, physical education (1974)
College coach: Stan Huntsman
Notre Dame High School, Harper Woods, Mich. (1970)
High school coaches: Conrad Vachon

Current residence: Newnan, Ga.
Current occupation: National Accounts Manager, Southwest Recreational Industries

Personal Records: Steeplechase—8:19.2; 5K—13:33.91; 10K—27:54.19

Notable accomplishments
High School—Michigan state XC champion (1969)...2nd in two-mile at Golden West Invitational (8:57.7)...4:11.3 mile
College/Post-Collegiate—Nine-time all-American...two-time NCAA steeplechase champion (1973, 1974)...American record in the steeplechase (8:19.2)... U.S. Olympic team (steeplechase, 1972, 1976, 1980)...U.S. steeplechase champion (1973/AAU; 1980/TAC)

Favorite rehab/cross training workout
While I never did any cross training as an athlete, I did use circuit training in lieu of weights for the athletes I coached and found it to be very beneficial.

Worst running-related injuries:
Planter fascia and Achilles tendonitis.

Approximate date of injuries, nature of them and was surgery required?
Planter fascia (1979-80). I missed six months. Achilles tendonitis (1983). Missed six weeks but it still didn't go away so I continued to run on it. The Achilles tendonitis kind of ended my career. No surgery was needed.

What flaw led to the injuries? Or did you do something that caused them?
Plantar fascia— not really sure. Achilles— overuse/overtraining.

Rehabilitation program that you followed. How long did the rehab take before you resumed "normal" training?
For the plantar fascia I used DMSO for awhile. This temporarily helped. Direct friction massage was what helped the most. I even had needle injections of B-12 and cortisone, again only temporary help. For the Achilles I took 3-4 weeks off. I swam five hard days a week as cross training.

Given that running takes a fair amount of time and that cross training for that same time would probably drive you crazy, what did you do to keep busy?
Worked for a living! Selling lumber in Eugene, Oregon. Lumber wholesaler for Oregon-McKenzie Lumber (1978-1983).

What was the most difficult aspect of being injured? How did you deal psychologically with missing a season?
Felt worthless. I drank a lot more beer. But, I was fortunate in that I attended three trials ('72, '76, '80) and made the team each time.

What specifically did you learn from being injured?
Patience

What advice would you give another elite runner who suffers a season-ending injury?
Be patient and give the injury enough time. Then come back slowly. I pushed back too hard too soon with both injuries.

When you returned to full-time training, did you alter the type of training you were doing?
Not really, but I was more aware of preventive strategies.

What was the result in your first major competition after returning from injury?
Won USATF and was 2nd at the Olympic trials (1980). Finished 11th in USATF final in 1983 (8:33). I retired shortly afterwards.

What advice would you give a high school or young college runner regarding injury prevention and/or rehabilitation?
Patience, rest, and work the rehab. Listen to your trainer/doctor provided they are qualified; if they are not qualified, find someone who is. Be consistent and persistent with the rehab. As hard as that can be at times, it WILL pay off.

Looking back, would you change any of your cross training?
I would definitely incorporate circuit training into my training like I did with my athletes when I was coaching.

After being injured and coming back, did it change your sense of who you are/were as a runner? Did you have more patience or did you find yourself training on the edge again?
I no longer took training pain-free for granted. Though I still trained on the edge, I was at least more cognizant of preventive strategies.

Other thoughts on injury prevention or rehabilitation.
Come back slowly. Be consistent and persistent with rehab. Ease back to 100%.

Tom Chorny

Indiana University
Steeplechase, 3K, 5K, XC

"Sit back and understand what it was caused from and don't do that again, or learn how to prevent it. Next, try to look at it from a 'bigger picture' view."

Tom, briefly profiled
Birth Date and Place: Nov. 23, 1976; Muskegon, Mich.
Began running: 11 years old; Began running competitively: 12 years old
Height/Running Weight: 6'0", 145 lbs.

Indiana University, B.S., 1999 (Geology)
College coach: Sam Bell (3 years) Robert Chapman (2 years)
Fruitport High School, Fruitport, Mich. (1995)
High school coaches: Randy Johnson

Current residence: Bloomington, Ind.
Current occupation: Professional Distance Runner and Network Marketing
Current affiliation or club:
Current Coach: self-coached (Advisor: Ron Helmer)

Personal records: 1500—3:47.x (2000); Mile—4:07.5i (2000); 3K—7:55.23i (2004); Steeple—8:22.16 (2001); 5K—13:53.62i (2001)

Notable accomplishments
High School – All-state honors (1992)… state XC champ (1993, 94)… State 3200m champ (1994, 95)… Footlocker finalist (1994).
College/Post-Collegiate – NCAA All-American in steeplechase (1997, 1999)… All-American in XC (1999)…10th in steeple at U.S. Olympic trials (2000)…NACAC (2000) Champion 3K Steeplechase… U.S. 3K steeple champion (2001)… World Championship team (2001)… Goodwill Games (2001)… Pan Am Games (2003)

Favorite rehab/cross training workout
Not a fan of cross training, 1) Biking on the road, 2) Stationary Bike—fartlek 1min on/1min off

Worst running-related injuries
Stress fracture in the right femur, Stress fracture in left distal/medial tibia, Osteatis Pubis

Approximate date of injuries, nature of them and was surgery required?
Stress fracture in femur occurred in May 1998. It felt like a groin strain but kept getting worse. When it became too sharp to run on I got a bone scan, missed three months. Tibia fracture occurred in July 2001. It was sore to touch on the bottom side of the ankle. I kept running; it got to the point when I knew it was a stress fracture. I missed 5 months. No surgery was required. In 2004, I developed Osteatis Pubis. Was checked twice for a sports hernia, both negative. Pubic symphysis joint was inflamed and sore to touch. Groins on both sides were sore and tight. Left pubic bone was swollen, but no stress fracture. Hips were hyper-mobile and were constantly out of balance. Couldn't roll over at night without waking myself up in pain. No surgery was required. I did NOT take the cortisone injections that were offered.

What flaw led to the injuries? Or did you do something that caused it them?
Both stress fractures started as minor pain and I kept running on them. Over weeks, the pain got sharper and more intense even while not running. I now believe both were caused by lack of arch support in my left shoe (inside leg on the track) but my left foot has too much movement in the heel bone which causes the talus to drop which reduces my own body's structural support of my arch. I believe the osteatis pubis developed as a result of lateral weakness and too much uncontrolled (too fast) downhill running.

Rehabilitation program that you followed. How long before you resumed "normal" training?
Before diagnosis (of femoral stress fracture), I tried biking and pool running. I actually rode a bike to warm up for a race during this time. Needless to say that was my last race of the season. Then I took time off. During this time off, I was taking a very intense geology field course in the Rockies of Montana. The hiking was intense and it was everyday. In my mind, it was really not much rest, but it healed very well and I started normal (somewhat) training in August.

For the stress fracture in my tibia, I took time off. I ran on this one too long. The injury was so sensitive that I could not bike or swim. Walking hurt, so I wore a boot for a few weeks. After two months of not running, out of frustration I tried to run again... not good, the pain was still pretty intense, so I took another month. Out of necessity I started training again in January (five months). The pain stuck around for the rest of the year.

Everything I read about osteatis pubis said that 50% of the time it was career-ending for athletes, so after the 2004 Olympic trials, which went horribly, I bought a basketball because it was something I gave up almost 10 years earlier and I missed it. I was angry with the injury and figured I wouldn't give up the things I loved anymore. Every step and defensive shuffle hurt beyond explanation. I played pick-up games 3-4 times a week until I noticed that the pain started to ease. I played hard defense and as I got stronger, I realized that my lateral weakness was going away. I added in more lateral drills and stability exercises and months later started to train again, eventually going on to run more miles and more intensity than I'd ever been able to handle before.

Given that running takes a fair amount of time and that cross training for that same time would probably drive you crazy, what did you do to keep busy?
During femoral stress fracture, I took an intense geology field class. Lots and lots of hiking (when no one was looking I jogged a little). For the tibia I could not do anything active, so I substitute taught a lot and started to read some books. I gained 25 pounds, got up to 170. So I must have been eating. I dreamed about running and build up a hunger to be the best that I could be. With the osteatis pubis, I had given up on running and was struggling with the decision to retire. I worked a lot during this time and ultimately basketball saved me.

What was the most difficult aspect of being injured? How did you deal psychologically with missing a season?
In the season of the femoral injury I had run my steeple PR and was extremely determined and confident about winning both Big Ten and NCAA. I was so confident, so not getting my chance was very disappointing. I also missed out on my first U.S. Championships (at age 21). I was lucky that my geology class was so intense because it kept my mind off of running for awhile.

It was difficult to deal with the tibia injury because I had just run 8:22.16 and I felt I was ready for 8:15. I got my first trip to Europe... Nice, Stockholm, Oslo, plus the World Champs and Goodwill...and I knew I was running on a stress fracture. I put off the X-ray until after the Worlds. I made the trips for the experience.

At this point in my career I've missed many seasons due to injuries, but after considering retirement from the sport in 2004, I did some soul searching and made a decision that I was not done until I was done. I have no idea what that will look like or feel like, even now, but I hope that I will recognize when it's time.

What specifically did you learn from being injured?
Patience... maybe it was someone else's time to shine, and more patience. But most importantly, running is not something with which to waste your time. Understand your goals. Understand why you run, and if you're going to do it, do it 100%, in every way.

What advice would you give another elite runner who suffers a season-ending injury?
Sit back and understand what it was caused from and don't do that again, or learn how to prevent it. Next, try to look at it from a "bigger picture" view. What is the reason for this injury? Why me? What am I supposed to learn? Use this time to figure out why you run and if you should continue. I feel that some guys run because they are good and not because they want to. If you're going to half-ass it, and not live the life to go along with it, you will only set yourself up for more disappointment, and I say this from experience. Surround yourself with people who understand your goals and will help you and encourage you to stay on track.

When you returned to full-time training, did you alter the type of training you were doing?
In the 1997-98 season I was running 70-80 miles a week. So post-injury I never got above 55 miles per week. This was from August-June. Extremely gradual build up. I did not want this injury to come back. I redshirted 1998 XC. I was very slow to get into workouts. I did at least two months of just low mileage. On 55 miles a week, the hard workouts were intense and not long. Off of this training I ran PR's across the board (3k, steeple, 5k). Coming back from the Tibia stress fracture I had gained 25 pounds. It took four months to take this off. I built up mileage quickly and sacrificed strength training to try to whip my self into shape. It didn't work. I only raced five times and only ran 8:38.

What was the result in your first major competition after returning from injury?
I competed in indoor track and I ran PR/s in the 3k and mile (8:06 and 4:09) after redshirting the 1998 cross country season. Coming back from the tibia fracture I ran the 2002 U.S. Open. It was a windy race and I ran 8:49. I was not satisfied; I knew I would not be 100% that season.

What advice would you give a high school or young college runner regarding injury prevention and/or rehabilitation?
Prevention. You are not too good to stretch and actually work on your flexibility. Use light strength training to help prevent injury. I use medicine ball for core body strength and body weight for legs. Do Planks and Bridges and work on your balance.

Rehabilitation. Most importantly, listen to your body. If you aren't ready to start training hard yet, don't. Don't rush things. Second, find someone who has had the injury and find out what they did.

Looking back, would you change any of your cross training (more or less of one, more varied)?
I am not a fan of cross training at all, but it is a necessary part of being an athlete. I should have done more cross training throughout my career. It would have saved me the hassle and pain of getting back in shape. If at all possible, find something you enjoy, find someone to cross train with and don't waste your time. Get a book on tape to listen to while you're on the bike. Learn a new language, improve your communication skills, learn how to be healthier… there are many things to put on your ipod.

After being injured and coming back, did it change your sense of who you are/were as a runner? Did you have more patience or did you find yourself training on the edge again?
If you don't come back as a different runner, with a different understanding or attitude, you risk repeating the same mistakes that led to the injuries in the first place. You must be more cautious about when you increase the intensity, when you 'go to the well' in a workout, and when you add on a few more miles. If you're smart, you won't come back stronger, but you'll come back with the ability and the understanding on how to be stronger. And yes, this usually comes with more patience. It's that understanding and ability to be train smarter and stronger that allows you do train on the edge again. The difference is that you will be able to recognize where that edge is.

Other thoughts on injury prevention or rehabilitation
It is important to have a strong core. This doesn't mean to do sit-ups. You have core muscles throughout your body, so work your abs and your back, but also work your lower legs by working on balance. Work your glutes and hip flexors.

It is also helpful to have someone to work on your body to help it stay balanced. If you can find a Muscle Activation Technique (MAT) specialist, and Active Release Technique (ART) specialist and a massage therapist who you can see regularly or when needed, then you'll be much better off in the end.

Mark Coogan

University of Maryland
Steeplechase, 5K, Marathon, XC

"Try to find a rehab place that understands how important running is to you, that it is part of your life and you will do anything it takes to get back. Then, they will treat your injury a bit more seriously, I think."

Mark, briefly profiled
Birth Date and Place: May 1, 1966; New York, N.Y.
Began running: 14 years old; Began running competitively: 14 years old; Retired: 2002
Height/Running Weight: 5'10", 140 lbs.

University of Maryland, B.S., 1988 (Economics)
College coach: Charles Torpey
Bishop Fechan, Attleboro, Mass. (1984)
High school coaches: Keith Gobin and Bob L'Homme

Current residence: Hanover, N.H.
Current occupation: Assistant women's track and cross country coach, Dartmouth College

Personal records: Mile—3:58; 2 Mile—8:21; 5K—13:23; Steeple—8:26; Marathon—2:13

Notable accomplishments
High School – Kinney XC finalist
College/Post-Collegiate – All-American in the steeplechase…eight-time world xc…5k world champs (1995)…Silver medalist at Pan-American (1995)…Olympic qualifier (1996)…3rd at Olympic trials in the marathon (2000)… Once drank 15 beers with Tim Hacker and Rod DeHaven in my back yard at age 35.

Favorite rehab/cross training workout
I would just get into the pool and crush myself run for upwards of two hours. Or I would jump on the elliptical and go as hard as I could holding dumbbells in my hands.

Worst running-related injury
S.I. joint problems. Rotation of the hips (this would lead to hurting the hamstrings and lots of inflammation in the S.I. joint.

Approximate date of injury, nature of it and was surgery required?
July/August 1994, June/July 1992 and March/April 2000. I missed about two months of training and four months of racing. No surgery was needed.

What flaw led to the injury? Or did you do something that caused it?
I think it comes from overuse and slipping on dirt. Track running causes the S.I. joint to rotate out of position. I also had to run a lot on soft surfaces and did interval training to be an Olympian.

Rehabilitation program that you followed. How long before you resumed "normal" training?
Get rid of inflammation by getting the joint into its correct position. Strengthen the areas around the S.I. joint with exercises and weights. Make sure to have proper balance in hips.

Given that running takes a fair amount of time and that cross training for that same time would probably drive you crazy, what did you do to keep busy?
Six to eight beers a day, ten while in Wisconsin (joking). I have kids, but the injury drove me crazy. I was not much fun to be around.

What was the most difficult aspect of being injured? How did you deal psychologically with missing a season?
I missed being ready for the 1992 trials with torn hamstring which I now think came because of a bad S.I. joint. I also had my S.I. joint shot up with lidocaine in 2000 Olympic trials in Pittsburg because of the bad inflammation. I couldn't even put on a pair of pants. I still came in third though.

What specifically did you learn from being injured?
At my age when I get fit, I need to race because I am a bit fragile now that I am older.

What advice would you give another elite runner who suffers a season-ending injury?
Take a total rest and make sure your injury is gone and you corrected the problem that gave you the injury.

When you returned to full-time training, did you alter the type of training you were doing?
No, I didn't because it worked for me. I did try to take care of the S.I. joint with massage and exercises though.

What was the result in your first major competition after returning from injury?
Second place at Pan Am Games.

What advice would you give a high school or young college runner regarding injury prevention and/or rehabilitation?
Try to find a rehab place that understands how important running is to you, that it is part of your life and you will do anything it takes to get back. Then they will treat your injury a bit more seriously, I think.

Looking back, would you change any of your cross training?
I liked how I trained but having someone look over my training programs would have helped me.

After being injured and coming back, did it change your sense of who you are/were as a runner? Did you have more patience or did you find yourself training on the edge again?
You have to train on the edge if you want to be good. This is even more true if you don't use drugs.

Jared Cordes

University of Wisconsin
3K, Steeplechase, 5K, XC

"Don't ignore little aches and pains that aren't normal. Take care of them immediately. Good flexibility helps prevent the majority of running injuries. During rehab, try and set short- term goals for your rehab or cross training exercises to keep yourself motivated."

Jared, briefly profiled
Birth Date and Place: July 22, 1977, Wabash, Ind.
Began running: 13 years old; Began running competitively: 13 years old
Height/Running Weight: 6'0", 150 lbs.

University of Wisconsin, 2001 (Agricultural Economics and Agronomy)
College coaches: Jerry Schumacher, Ed Nuttycombe, and Martin Smith
Northfield High School, Wabash, Ind. (1996)
High school coaches: Richard Leming and Dennis Walker

Current residence: Madison, WI.
Current occupation: Assistant Agronomist- Kaltenberg Seeds, Runner

Personal Records: 1500—3:44; Mile—4:03; 3K—8:05; Steeple—8:27; 5K—14:02

Notable accomplishments
High School—2nd in state XC (1994)...2nd at state in 1600 (1995, '96)...3rd in state 1600 (1995).
College/Post-Collegiate— XC All-American (21st)...indoor All-American at 5K (8th) ... outdoor track All-American in the steeple (5th, 9th)... fall USATF XC champion (2001, 2002)... 40th at World XC championships (2002)...5th in steeplechase at USATF outdoor championships.

Worst running-related injury
A broken bone in my right foot.

Approximate date of injury, nature of it and was surgery required?
It happened when I was running on trails in November 1999. I stepped on a rock or something with the ball of my foot. Surgery was not required. I had eight weeks of no running and missed entire indoor season.

What flaw led to the injury? Or did you do something that caused it?
It's possible that my shoes were not supportive enough to be running trails. I was also not paying close enough attention to the trail where I was running.

Rehabilitation program that you followed. How long before you resumed "normal" training?
I used an aqua jogger for eight weeks, then gradually started running. I ran every other day for only 3-4 miles the first week, then every day after that.

Given that running takes a fair amount of time and that cross training for that same time would probably drive you crazy, what did you do to keep busy?
I just ran in the pool for an hour a day, which was the same amount of time I would have spent running. I guess it did drive me crazy; it was a very frustrating eight weeks.

What was the most difficult aspect of being injured? How did you deal psychologically with missing a season?
Luckily for me, I only missed an indoor season, which is a low priority anyways. The hardest part was returning to competition and not being able to compete at the level I knew I was capable of.

What specifically did you learn from being injured?
If someone cross trains diligently, and can maintain their motivation, then you really don't lose a lot of fitness.

What advice would you give another elite runner who suffers a season-ending injury?
Find some other way to exercise to maintain your fitness, so that running again won't be as difficult of a transition.

When you returned to full-time training, did you alter the type of training you were doing?
No. I did not.

What was the result in your first major competition after returning from injury?
It was a steeplechase race. I had competed at the NCAA championships the previous year and had run 8:45. This time I ran 8:58 and got beat by my teammate, who was running his first steeplechase ever, by 10 seconds. The winner of the race ran 8:40. That was a humbling experience.

What advice would you give a high school or young college runner regarding injury prevention and/or rehabilitation?
Don't ignore little aches and pains that aren't normal. Take care of them immediately. Good flexibility helps prevent the majority of running injuries. During rehab, try and set short term goals for your rehab, or cross training exercises, to keep yourself motivated.

Alan Culpepper
University of Colorado
5K, 10K, Marathon, XC

"Assess what went wrong as to prevent it from happening again. If it was due to overuse then take notes in your training log so it doesn't happen again."

Alan, briefly profiled
Birth Date and Place: Sept. 15, 1972; Ft. Worth, Texas
Began running: 13 years old; Began running competitively: 15 years old; Retired: 2009
Height/Running Weight: 6'1", 135 lbs.
Retired: 2008

University of Colorado, B.A., 1996; (Sociology and Geography)
College coach: Mark Wetmore
Coronado High School, El Paso, Texas (1991)
High school coaches: Sam Walker (Club Coach)

Current residence: Lafayette, Colo.
Current occupation: Owner, Solepepper Sports – Specialty Shoe Store

Personal records: 1500—3:37.7 (1998); Mile—3:55.15 (1999); 5K—13:25.7 (2005); 10K—27:33.6 (2001); Marathon—2:09.41 (2002)

Notable high school, collegiate and post-collegiate accomplishments
High School—five-time Texas state champ...XC All-American.
College/Post-Collegiate—eight-time All-American...NCAA 5K champ (1996)...three-time XC USATF national champ (1999, 2003, 2007)... USATF 5K national champ (2002)... USATF 10K national champ (1999)... U.S. Olympian at 10K (2000); U.S. Olympian in marathon (2004)... American debut marathon record 2002 (Chicago) 2:09:41...twice finished in top 5 at the Boston Marathon

Worst running-related injuries:
Stress fracture, IT Band, and Achilles Tendonitis. Quad Tendonitis

Approximate date of injuries, nature of them and was surgery required?
Stress fracture, March 1995. IT Band began September 1991, and the Achilles occurred both in January 1996 and again in April 2001. Over did it in training and caused the quad tendonitis (2004).

What flaw led to the injuries? Or did you do something that caused them?
Practicing steeple chase during winter months caused stress fracture. The increase in mileage and intensity as a freshman in college caused IT Band injury. Doing intervals in spikes prematurely caused Achilles issues.

Rehabilitation program that you followed. How long before you began "normal" training?
For the stress fracture I took some complete rest and then very slowly built up my mileage over many months. With the IT Band I used ice, massage, rest, pool running. This lasted six months before I was training normally. I did massage, acupuncture, ice, and anti-inflamatories for the Achilles. It was a number of months before pain was totally gone.

Given that running takes a fair amount of time and that cross training for that same time would probably drive you crazy, what did you do to keep busy?
My only main injuries occurred during college so I went about daily college life. Not running my entire freshman year led to me learning to pay the guitar, which I still play today.

What was the most difficult aspect of being injured? How did you deal psychologically with missing a season?
The worst part of an injury is not knowing what the problem is and getting poor advice as to get better. The time off really didn't bother me because I was young. If you are in college, don't be afraid to seek outside opinions aside from school doctors and trainers.

What specifically did you learn from being injured?
You have to be very proactive about seeking good advice and very diligent about your treatment. I have learned that many injuries can be prevented by taking care of them early. Most injuries source is in the feet or hips. Go to the source don't just treat the area that hurts.

What advice would you give another elite runner who suffers a season-ending injury?
Assess what went wrong as to prevent it from happening again. If it was due to overuse then take notes in your training log so it doesn't happen again.

When you returned to full-time training, did you alter the type of training you were doing?
No. I have just learned to be careful and cautious during certain times of the year, i.e. building up my mileage after a long break, during early spring when I first start doing track workouts and begin wearing spikes, and when I am doing full volume I am also careful.

What was the result in your first major competition after returning from injury?
I was only a sophomore in college so nothing special.

What advice would you give a high school or young college runner regarding injury prevention and/or rehabilitation?
I would suggest seeing a physical therapist over anyone else. By keeping your hips and back in alignment you can prevent many injuries. Also, make sure you are in the right shoes; custom inserts help many people.

Other thoughts on injury prevention or rehabilitation.
I see a massage therapist and physical therapist regularly. I am a big advocate of preventive action and being very proactive as soon as something begins to hurt. I have been blessed to be relatively injury free for my entire post-collegiate career.

Mark Deady

Indiana University
1500/Mile, XC

"Take the recovery slowly. A season or two seems like a long period of time when you're missing it, but it's better to take extra time to make sure the injury is healed and (you can) get back into competitive shape."

Mark, briefly profiled
Birth Date and Place: Oct. 2, 1967, Schenectady, N.Y.
Began running: 11 years old; Began running competitively: 11 years old; Retired: 25 years old
Height/Running Weight: 6'3", 155-160 lbs.

Indiana University, B.S., 1990 (Criminal Justice)
College coach: Sam Bell
Adlai E Stevenson High School, Prairie View, Ill. (1985)
High school coaches: Fred Cremer and Bill Dawson

Current residence: Carmel, Ind.
Current occupation: Senior Field Vice President, Mutual of America

Personal records: 1500—3:35.83 (1988); Mile—3:58.65i (1991)

Notable accomplishments
High School—1600 state champ (1985) …runner-up in state 1600 (1984)
College/Post-Collegiate – All-American…U.S. national team…1988 U.S. Olympic team (1500)…advanced to 2nd round of 1500…

Favorite rehab/cross training workout
Swimming, weight lifting, basketball (not for rehab) in "off season"

Worst running-related injuries
Overuse related injuries to both Achilles tendons. Stress fractures.

Approximate date of injuries, nature of them and was surgery required?
The tendons were an overuse injury developed over time. The onset of severe pain was around December 1987 to January 1988. Surgery was performed on both Achilles tendons in early 1989 and again on left tendon in fall of 1989. Although I was able to

sporadically compete, I wasn't able to put in the training necessary to get back to pre-surgery form.

What flaw led to the injuries? Or did you do something that caused them?
Heavy mileage, skinny calf muscles, and in all likelihood tight turns on indoor tracks.

Rehabilitation program that you followed. How long before you resumed "normal" training?
Heavy cross training, e.g., biking, swimming, pool running, weight lifting. I did this every day until able to resume "normal" training. Just guessing, 8-10 weeks post-surgery.

Given that running takes a fair amount of time and that cross training for that same time would probably drive you crazy, what did you do to keep busy?
Cross trained! Now I know what drove me to my current (crazy) state of mind.

What was the most difficult aspect of being injured? How did you deal psychologically with missing a season?
The most difficult aspect of being injured was the frustration of not being able to compete and, once back in competition, not being able to win.

As for psychologically dealing with it, I just mentally prepared for when I would make it back to elite competition. It never entered my mind that I wouldn't make it back so my thoughts were consistently on doing whatever I needed to do to be successful when I did.

Although I made the Olympic team in 1988, I felt then, and do now, that the 1992 Games would have been my best shot at a gold medal. So, my thoughts were only on what I needed to do to win a gold medal in Barcelona. Things just didn't work out that way.

What specifically did you learn from being injured?
It sucks! It did then and it still does.

What advice would you give another elite runner who suffers a season-ending injury?
Take the recovery slowly. A season or two seems like a long period of time when you're missing it but it's better to take extra time (even more than what the doctor tells you) to make sure the injury is healed and get back into competitive shape.

When you returned to full-time training, did you alter the type of training you were doing?
Other than not being able to train at the level that I had previously, no. I wasn't able to make it back to consistent high level training and never got to the point where we could work on the subtleties of a training program.

What was the result in your first major competition after returning from injury?
I ran on the winning 4x800 relay at the Big Ten indoor championships in 1990. Three other guys carried the load.

What advice would you give a high school or young college runner regarding injury prevention and/or rehabilitation?
With regard to injury prevention, always wear good, appropriate shoes. If resources are limited, then buy cheap shorts/shirts/sweats and make sure you have high quality shoes. Also, take the time to warm up, stretch and strengthen the muscles that you'll be using. Cross training, even when you are not injured, is a great way to avoid getting injured in the first place.

As for rehab, take it slowly, but work out (cross train) intently. Don't waste the time.

Looking back, would you change any of your cross training?
No. There is no way of knowing if I would have been able to return to the level of competitive running that I had achieved pre-injury by adjusting the post-surgery routine. That said, I probably should have followed my own advice and taken the recovery more slowly. The post-surgery training/cross-training routine was a good one, but I may have started back too soon.

After being injured and coming back, did it change your sense of who you are/were as a runner? Did you have more patience or did you find yourself training on the edge again?
What made me, and I believe makes most competitive athletes rise to a certain level of success, is a personality trait to push the limits constantly. Taking time off and resting can be counter-intuitive.

It's a fine line between working hard enough to be successful and working too hard and getting injured (or coming back from an injury too soon). It's a balance an athlete has to find and it's safe to say that too often an elite athlete will only see the balance after he or she has gone too far in one direction or the other.

I am currently recovering from a ruptured plantar fascia and find myself just as impatient and frustrated as 20 years ago. However, in my older (hopefully wiser) condition I'm taking the recovery more slowly.

My intensity level hasn't changed much…only the results. I still go all out every time I train or compete. Backing off or slowing down is not something I've ever been able to do well, but I continue to pay a price for it.

Other thoughts on injury prevention or rehabilitation.
Answering this the way I should would be hypocritical. Injury is just an inherent risk in training to compete at an elite level in any sport. Managing to train at the appropriate level and avoiding major injuries is part of the competition.

If an injury does occur, take the recovery slowly, but work as hard or harder at cross training as you would if you weren't injured. Try to stay as close to competition shape as you can while recovering.

On a related note, young athletes today are tempted with all sorts of magic potions and quick fixes that claim to be able make them compete at an elite level or to get them back on the track or playing field sooner, and a very few even work—in the short-term. In the long run, however, they may (and probably will) regret doing so. Toe the line, but don't go over it.

Rod DeHaven

South Dakota State University
1500, 5K, 10K, Marathon

"Consistency in training and stretching will go a long way toward preventing major injuries in most cases."

Rod, briefly profiled
Birth Date and Place: Sept. 21, 1966; Sacramento, Cal.
Began running: 10 years old; Began running competitively: 10 years old
Height/Running Weight: 5'8", 135 lbs.
Retired: 2004

South Dakota State University, B.S., 1989 (Computer Science)
College coach: Scott Underwood
Huron High School, Huron, S.D. (1984)
High school coach: Roger Loeckev

Current residence: Brookings, S.D.
Current occupation: Track & Cross Country Coach, South Dakota State University

Personal records: 1500—3:40.17 (1989); 5K—13:40 (1995); 10K—28:06 (1995); Marathon—2:11.40 (2001)

Notable accomplishments
High School – South Dakota High School Athlete of the year (1984)
College/Post-Collegiate – Olympic Trial marathon champion (2000)…U.S. Olympic team (2000)…Three-time U.S. half marathon champ…#1 ranked marathoner by Track & Field News (2001)…16-time NCAA D-II All-American…D-II indoor NCAA 1500 champ (1985) … South Dakota Collegiate Athlete of the Year (1987).

Worst running-related injury
Sustained my worst injury during early stages of 2002. What started as a sore plantar fascia progressed to nerve problem near the inner tip of the ankle bone. Like most injuries it only bothered me when I ran which made it difficult to diagnose.

Approximate date of injury, nature of it and was surgery required?
January 2002—pronation problem eventually cured by physical therapy and orthotics. No surgery was required. I have been lucky that I have never gone under the knife. Missed approximately five months of sustained training.

What flaw led to the injury? Or did you do something that caused it?
The injury was most likely brought on by too much too soon. I had taken a month off after Chicago in the fall of 2001 and when I started back up I was inconsistent in my training. Once I made a full commitment to training I piled on the miles too quickly and alas I was hurt.

Rehabilitation program that you followed. How before you resumed "normal" training?
I struggled with a conservative treatment program after a bone scan did not reveal a stress fracture in the ankle. After switching to a different PT, I began a program of neural flossing and balance exercises. I also tried to increase my fitness with pool running of 30-4 minutes in addition to my 20-30 minute run.

However, I was not able to resume full training until being fitted and receiving orthotics. Their effect was almost immediate. I was able to run pain-free for 45 minuets. I still had problems with my ankle depending on what surface I would run on. Uneven trails and grass were particularly troublesome. Finally, after nine months, I was running without pain under all circumstances.

Given that running takes a fair amount of time and that cross training for that same time would probably drive you crazy, what did you do to keep busy?
I have three young kids and a job. I have plenty to keep me busy.

What was the most difficult aspect of being injured? How did you deal psychologically with missing a season?
It was difficult missing the Boston Marathon. I had run well there the year prior and I was coming of a PR at Chicago. So I thought that I could do well again. My busy schedule made it fairly easy to miss the race without a lot of psychological damage.

What specifically did you learn from being injured?
At my advanced age I need to be careful with the breaks I take after marathons and that consistence in training will be my best defense against injury.

What advice would you give another elite runner who suffers a season-ending injury?
Believe that you'll come back stronger .

When you returned to full-time training, did you alter the type of training you were doing?
Nothing drastically different. It just took a while to get back to a fitness level that was comparable to my pre-injury level.

What was the result in your first major competition after returning from injury?
8th in the Bix 7 mile road race in a slow time; I was beaten by a gentleman I normally wouldn't lose to.

What advice would you give a high school or young college runner regarding injury prevention and/or rehabilitation?
Consistency in training and stretching will go a long way toward preventing major injuries in most cases.

Chris Derrick
Stanford University
3K, 5K, 10K, XC

"At the end of the day you have to have the awareness and maturity to read your body and know when you need a day (or many) off in order to train injury- free."

Chris, briefly profiled
Birth Date and Place: Oct. 17, 1990; Albany, N.Y.
Began running: 13 years old; Began running competitively: 13 years old
Height/Running Weight: 6'2", 156 lbs.

Stanford University, B.A., 2012 (Economics)
College coach: Jason Dunn
Neuqua Valley High School, Naperville, Ill. (2008)
High school coaches: Paul Vandersteen and James Janota

Current residence: Palo Alto, Cal.
Current occupation: Student-Athlete
Current affiliation or club:
Current Coach: Jason Dunn

Personal records: 1500—3:42.43 ('10); 3K—7:56.3i ('09); 5K—13:29.98 ('09); 10K—29:08.33 ('09)

Notable accomplishments
High School—State XC champ (2007)...NTN XC champ (2007)...2nd at Footlocker (2007)...13:55 5k.
College—Five-time All-American...3rd at NCAA XC (2009)...3rd in NCAA 5k (2009), 4th in 2010...former American junior record holder at 5k.

Favorite rehab/cross training workout
Eccentric calf raises were the best rehab exercise I did for rehabbing my injury. I tried for 3 sets of 10-15 3 times a week during my injury and well after it. As far as exercising went I preferred aqua jogging (with a flotation belt) as I felt the motion best mimicked running. I didn't really like the bike or the elliptical, the former because it gets uncomfortable to sit on a bike for that long and the latter because it just feels restrictive and awkward.

Worst running-related injury:
Achilles Tendonosis/ paratendonitis

Approximate date of injury, nature of it and was surgery required?
December 2009- March 2010. Inflammation of the tendon sheath in right Achilles combined with some tendonosis. No surgery required.

What flaw led to the injury? Or did you do something that caused it?
I have not identified a specific cause. It began after doing a tempo run a little too hard over the winter (my first workout back). My calves were very tight and I did not really stretch them much and the next day I had some pain about halfway through my run.

Rehabilitation program that you followed. How long before you resumed "normal" training?
I tried to cross train for an hour a day when I was not running. I also got treatment at least once and sometimes twice a day. At first treatment mostly consisted of anti-inflammatory procedures with some light thera-band exercises. After I began seeing a physical therapist I got scraping done 3 times a week and began to incorporate eccentric calf raises. It was around a month of treatment before things subsided to the point that I could train again.

Given that running takes a fair amount of time and that cross training for that same time would probably drive you crazy, what did you do to keep busy?
I actually found that I was busier while injured because I was spending an hour or two a day in either physical therapy or the training room. That combined with cross training and school took up a lot of time.

What was the most difficult aspect of being injured? How did you deal psychologically with missing a season?
I would say that the hardest part was the uncertainty. My injury was such that I had no real date at which I could expect to be healthy, I just had to wait and see. That really wore on me for a while. When it never actually felt good that made me feel as though I would never be truly healthy again, even though it was only about 2 months or so before I was able to proceed with confidence. I also struggled with watching my teammates go away to meets and being left back on campus with only one or two guys.

What specifically did you learn from being injured?
First, that I was not invincible. Secondly, that I needed to be less of a slave to the OCD impulse to have a great training log and take days off when I needed them. In this respect I learned a lot from my teammate Elliott Heath.

When you returned to full-time training, did you alter the type of training you were doing?
More building up, more slowly and cautiously.

What was the result in your first major competition after returning from injury?
Won "The Big Meet" 3K in 8:03.

What advice would you give a high school or young college runner regarding injury prevention and/or rehabilitation?
You need to know your own body and know when things don't feel right. Your coach will always want you back as soon as possible and part of you will want to be back as well. Your trainers or doctors will probably be more conservative than you will want to be. At the end of the day you have to have the awareness and maturity to read your body and know when you need a day (or many) off in order to train injury-free.

Looking back, would you change any of your cross training?
I would have biked less (it stretched the Achilles a bit) and focused more on the pool.

After being injured and coming back, did it change your sense of who you are/were as a runner? Did you have more patience or did you find yourself training on the edge again?
Yes. It was my first major injury. I had thought I was kind of indestructible. I recognize now that I need to be more intelligent and patient.

Brian Diemer

University of Michigan
Steeplechase, XC

"Don't give up! It's never over. Even if the season is shot, it will develop you in important ways for next time."

Brian, briefly profiled
Birth Date and Place: Oct. 10, 1961, Grand Rapids, Mich.
Began running: 14 years old; Began running competitively: 14 years old; Retired: 1996
Height/Running Weight: 5'10", 145 lbs.

University of Michigan, B.S., natural resources environmental design (1983)
College coach: Ron Warhurst
South Christian High School, Grand Rapids, Mich. (1979)
High school coaches: Paul Oosting

Current residence: Grand Rapids, Mich.
Current occupation: Cross Country and Track Coach at Calvin College, Grand Rapids

Personal records: Steeple—8:13.16 (1984)

Notable accomplishments
College/Post-Collegiate—NCAA steeplechase champion (1983)…bronze medal in steeple, 1984 Olympic Games, 7th in 1992 Olympics …4th in 1987 World Championships, 5th in 1991…Big Ten Medal of Honor (1983)…voted men's Olympic track team captain in 1992.

Worst running-related injury:
I developed a stress fracture in my sacrum after an intense training period of averaging 85 miles a weeks, with high intensity (Ron Warhurst Style) coupled with doing lots of hurdle drills. I think the day that did the most damage was a cold spring day in Michigan when I did hurdle drills. My flexibility was terrible and nothing was working well. I should have bagged the drills and waited for a better day. I came down wrong a few times off the hurdles, twisting and jarring. The next day, I ran 14 miles on a hilly trail run with lots of downhill jarring. The following day I could hardly walk, let alone run.

Approximate date of injury, nature of it and was surgery required?
Stress fracture and muscle spasms to protect the fracture occurred April 15, 1992. I did not need surgery.

What flaw led to the injury? Or did you do something that caused it?
Stupidity on my part. I knew my body was fatigued and not flexible. I should not have tried to push through the drill, at least not when it was 40 degrees out. It was plain stubbornness to get my miles in the next day. I have realized from coaching that this is the main problem with athletes getting injured. They keep pushing through something that they should pay attention to and address.

Rehabilitation program that you followed. How long before you resumed "normal" training?
A typical day for the first three weeks would have been 45 minutes of intense interval training in deep end of the pool with "wet belt" at 4:00 pm. I'd then do 30 minutes of tempo run effort (steady state) on my Schwinn aerodyne bike at 7:00 pm. The following day I would switch the sessions and do 30 minutes in the pool and 45 minutes on the bike. The next couple weeks I did the same thing but added 1-4 miles of running at 5:45-6:00 pace. I had incredibly fast tempo because of the quick leg movement in the pool. The key was these short amounts of training time. This allowed me to focus with incredible intensity and I could visualize myself running in the trials and Olympics.

Given that running takes a fair amount of time and that cross training for that same time would probably drive you crazy, what did you do to keep busy?
Life! Running a business kept me busy. I was able to do some physical labor as well without hurting my back so I stayed fit and strong. My wife Kerri and my kids helped keep life in perspective.

What was the most difficult aspect of being injured? How did you deal psychologically with missing a season?
Seeing my dreams swirl down the toilet was the hardest part. I was set up for greatness. I was the strongest I had ever been. I had confidence from finishing 5th in Tokyo (World Championships) and now my hurdle technique was coming together. 1992 was going to be my year. As for the psychological aspect, every day when I looked in the mirror, I knew that I didn't give up that day. I worked my butt off at something every day so I could look at myself in the mirror with confidence.

What specifically did you learn from being injured?
The power of an intense focus and desire. Increase visualization. I realized that my real strength came from my heart and desire. When something important was seemingly taken away from me…the Olympic trials, I found out how badly I wanted to be able to "toe the line" at the trials. My heart told my brain to find a way to get the job done. My brain, which usually likes to be in charge, took on its appropriate role as a servant. The brain channeled all my energies to the body parts to get the job done. My brain focused itself with visualizing myself being in the race and winning. It also showed a picture of me being in Narbonne, France at the U.S. training camp.

What advice would you give another elite runner who suffers a season-ending injury?
Don't give up! It's never over. Even if the season is shot, it will develop you in important ways for next time.

When you returned to full-time training, did you alter the type of training you were doing?
Slowly phased away from the cross training and into more running. I balanced my energy levels and fatigue levels with the types of training, i.e., I listened to my body, unlike how I got myself into this predicament.

What was the result in your first major competition after returning from injury?
One and a half weeks after that I was able to run 3:57 in the 1500 at North Central College; Ouch! Two weeks later I ran 7:58 in the 3K at Indianapolis, which was a good confidence builder. Then I raced three weeks later and finished first at the Olympic Trials in New Orleans with a time of 8:16.

What advice would you give a high school or young college runner regarding injury prevention and/or rehabilitation?
Listen to your body. Take care of the injuries before they become more serious. Other than that I would say again, don't give up! It's never over. There are more ways than one to get the job done. Even if the season is shot, it will develop you in important ways for next time. Sometimes, going through an injury crisis is good for developing patience and perspective. We've all heard about and believe that it can build character. These lessons prepare us for future challenges and for life. I wouldn't trade the development that I have been forced to make.

Looking back, would you change any of your cross training (more or less of one, more varied)?
No—except I would have not let Calvin College drain the pool by 12" a day in my last week of training in order to clean it.

After being injured and coming back, did it change your sense of who you are/were as a runner? Did you have more patience or did you find yourself training on the edge again?
First things first. Recovery and healing. Don't be stubborn and stupid. Take care of the issues and then get back on the road to greatness.

Pascal Dobert

University of Wisconsin
Steeplechase, XC

"Listen to your body. Be patient. Add prehabilitation to your training (stretching and strengthening)."

> **Pascal, briefly profiled**
> Birth Date and Place: April 8, 1974, Washington, D.C.
> Began running: 15 years old; Began running competitively: 15 years old
> Height/Running Weight: 6'1", 150 lbs.
>
> University of Wisconsin, B.S., 1997 (Natural Resources)
> College coach: Martin Smith
> Walt Whitman High School, Bethesda, Md. (1992)
> High school coaches: Kerry Ward
>
> Current residence: Portland, Ore.
> Current occupation: Sports Marketing Manager, Nike
> Personal records: Steeple—8:15.77 (2000)

Notable accomplishments
College/Post-Collegiate— Five-time All-American...10th at U.S. Olympic Trials (1996)...3rd at U.S. nationals, World Championship team member (1997)...1st at U.S. nationals (1998) ...4th at Goodwill Games (1998)...7th at World Cup (1998)...1st at U.S. nationals and World championships team member (1999)...1st at U.S. Olympic Trials (2000)...16th at Olympic Games (2000).

Worst running-related injuries
Broken left ankle in 1997 and left Achilles tendonitis and right ankle tendonitis in 2001.

Approximate date of injuries, nature of them and was surgery required?
Broken left ankle in 1997, missed three months. Left Achilles tendonitis and right ankle tendonitis in 2001 caused me to miss four months. No surgery was required.

What flaw led to the injuries? Or did you do something that caused them?
I severely twisted my ankle on a rock while running and the ankle broke. The tendonitis was caused by general weakness in the area.

Rehabilitation program that you followed. How long before you resumed "normal" training?
For the ankle, I did no cross training but did ankle rehab exercises to strengthen the ankle after the fracture had healed. Duration was about two months. I basically began rehab when I was able to run again. For the Achilles, I did some biking on a road bike, but nothing structured. I began rehab strengthening exercises two weeks after sustaining injury. Still continue strengthening exercises as part of training.

Given that running takes a fair amount of time and that cross training for that same time would probably drive you crazy, what did you do to keep busy?
I actually feel that cross training takes more time than running! But, since I didn't do a lot of that, I used the time to remodel parts of my house and also catch up on projects I didn't have the time or energy to do while training.

What was the most difficult aspect of being injured? How did you deal psychologically with missing a season?
I felt very frustrated and useless. I tried to think about the future and use the time for my body and mind to totally rest. I had already made U.S. teams mentioned above.

What specifically did you learn from being injured?
I need to listen to my body. I also needed to add strengthening and stretching to the vulnerable/injury prone areas of my body.

What advice would you give another elite runner who suffers a season-ending injury?
Take this opportunity to do some things you wouldn't do if you were training and competing.

When you returned to full-time training, did you alter the type of training you were doing?
Yes. Just the stretching and strengthening.

What was the result in your first major competition after returning from injury?
3rd in Canberra steeplechase.

What advice would you give a high school or young college runner regarding injury prevention and/or rehabilitation?
Listen to your body. Be patient. Add prehabilitation to your training (stretching and strengthening).

Andy Downin

Georgetown University
1500, 3K, 5K, XC

> **Andy, briefly profiled**
> Birth Date and Place: May 12, 1973, Denton, Texas
> Began running: 14 years old; Began running competitively: 14 years old; Retired: 33 years old
> Height/Running Weight: 5'10", 143 lbs.
>
> Georgetown University, B.A., 1996 (English and Psycology)
> College coach: Frank "Gags" Gagliano
> Duxbury High School, Duxbury, Mass. (1991)
> High school coaches: Chuck Martin and Mark Dunn
>
> Current residence: Eugene, Ore.
> Current occupation: race director, Eugene Marathon
>
> Personal records: 1500—3:36.70 (2001); Mile—3:56.25 (2001)

Notable accomplishments
High School—Mile state champ (1989)…Two-mile state champ (1990-91)…Gatorade Athlete of the Year NE states region (1991).
College/Post-Collegiate—Four-time XC All-American…two-time indoor All-American…outdoor All-American…6th in 1500 in both 1996 and 2000 Olympic Trials….USA 1500 champion (2001)…2nd at U.S. XC 4k (2001)…19th World 4K XC (2001)…7th USA XC 4K (2002.

Worst running-related injuries
Chronic right Achilles tendonitis and pubitis (inflammation/tendonitis of the pubic region).

Approximate date of injuries, nature of them and was surgery required?
Right Achilles soreness (1995-2002)…Right compartment syndrome surgery (1998)…Left arch/Achilles soreness (2000-2002)…Pubitis (April-July, 2002)…Sore hip/glute. Missed about a year because the injury wasn't getting better.

What flaw led to the injuries? Or did you do something that caused them?
Number 1 reason, I feel, for most injuries is some sort of over training of some sort. For my Achilles it was years of anaerobic abuse, i.e., track workouts with not enough rest time

and base to build more aerobic strength and to properly build strength in the hamstring, calf and foot.

Rehabilitation program that you followed. How long before you resumed "normal" training?
A lot of ice. Electric stimulation. Ultra sound. I went on a stretching kick and weight training. All I really needed was rest for a few weeks, to take a step back and start from square one again, jogging very easy.

Given that running takes a fair amount of time and that cross training for that same time would probably drive you crazy, what did you do to keep busy?
I worked. This last injury this summer, I learned everything I could about what I had done wrong and how I could make sure it didn't happen again. I never gave up on solutions, which is something I had done in '98 with my Achilles injury.

What was the most difficult aspect of being injured? How did you deal psychologically with missing a season?
For me it was missing the chance to defend my U.S. 1500 title. I was out to show it wasn't a fluke, and that was part of the reason I over trained. I also missed the opportunity to go to Ireland for the World Cross Country Championships that I had qualified for. Again, my way of dealing with it was to put all my energy in following all the options to get healthy again and to constantly be reading up on the right ways to train to avoid injury. I learned so much during that time.

What specifically did you learn from being injured?
I learned how to measure my body while training, to avoid over training. I started using a heart rate monitor and started taking off weeks every three weeks to allow the body to recover. Also, I began to listen to the body's aches to be able to tell the severity of the problem. In that time, I also learned about a lot of alternate therapies that are out there. I tried to check into every option of therapy I heard about.

What advice would you give another elite runner who suffers a season-ending injury?
Keep the focus on your long term goals. And if you don't have one, set one. Never give up on finding what your problem is and, more importantly, what caused it. Don't hesitate to get a second or third opinion from someone who might tell you something different from what the first person told you, even if you think you are on the right path. Never assume that you can diagnose something yourself. At least ask the opinion of a coach or close friend.

When you returned to full-time training, did you alter the type of training you were doing?
I completely changed my training. Took another step conservative and started wearing a heart rate monitor to watch how tired my body was. Worked off days and weeks into my training.

What was the result in your first major competition after returning from injury?
In 2000, after two years off, I finished 2nd at the USA winter XC Champs. In 2003, I am still coming back and waiting to race.

What advice would you give a high school or young college runner regarding injury prevention and/or rehabilitation?
Listen to your body and take easy days easy. Rest. Eat well. And limit outside stress. I see college kids get away with beating up their bodies and worse, building bad habits while they're young, but it will catch up to them. If you are going to invest your time in doing something, do it right.

Other thoughts on injury prevention or rehabilitation.
I know that hindsight is 20/20, but I feel that I could have been a lot better through college and after if I just knew in college what I know now. Unfortunately life doesn't work that way. I feel most of my problems started in college and I am paying for it now. All the scientific literature is out there. Read up on how to train the body and mind. Talk to as many runners and coaches as possible and absorb what they know. Take pieces from everyone and devise your own plan to stay healthy and have a long career.

I know many athletes feel at the mercy of their coach. Learn to accept your coach's training and control the things you can control, i.e., diet, sleep/rest, the pace of your easy days, stress. I know an athlete who felt he was overtraining on his college team. He went to his coach and asked to try and run his off days a lot easier. He cut a deal with his coach to try it out for two months. It paid off and he started beating the guys on his team who had been kicking his butt.

Matt Downin

University of Wisconsin
3K, 5K, 10K, Marathon

"Relax, let your body heal itself and find the things you need to do in the future to avoid any injuries. Don't get into a cycle of injuries that will stop long-term success."

Andy, briefly profiled
Birth Date and Place: Feb. 10, 1977, Marlton, N.J.
Began running: 14 years old; Began running competitively: 14 years old
Height/Running Weight: 5'10", 140 lbs.

University of Wisconsin, B.A., 2000 (Economics)
College coach: Jerry Schumacher
Pinkerton Academy, Derry, N.H. (1995)
High school coaches: Mike Clark and Chuck Martin

Current residence: Corvallis, Ore.
Current occupation: Runner
Current affiliation or club: Strands.com/Mizuno
Current Coach: Mike Dilley
Personal records: 3K—7:54.04 (2002); 5K—13:40.37 (1999); 10K—28:08.04 (2004); Half-marathon—1:05.44 (2006); Marathon—2:14:28 (2005)

Notable accomplishments
High School—Footlocker XC Champ (1994)...Penn Relays 3K champ (1995)
College/Post-Collegiate— 4th place at NCAA XC championships (1998, 1999)...8th at USATF track championships 5K (1999)...7th in 10k Olympic Trials (2000)...6th USATF championships 10K (2001)... World XC championships team member (2001, 2002)... USATF fall national XC champ (2000, 2006).

Worst running-related injuries
Achilles tendonitis and strained muscle in my back.

Approximate date of injuries, nature of them and was surgery required?
Achilles tendonitis has been chronic since high school all the way to current. This comes and goes and is aggravated by training. No surgery needed. Back strains in spring of 2001. No surgery.

What flaw led to the injuries? Or did you do something that caused them?
The Achilles was a result of bio-mechanics and overtraining. The back strain came from hard effort over 10k.

Rehabilitation program that you followed. How long before you resumed "normal" training?
For Achilles, back off on intensity and volume, ice heavily, find flat, soft running surfaces. Some pool running and biking until I feel improvement. Then I get back to normal training in usually ten days or so. Also, ankle strengthening and lower leg flexibility work coming off injury.
For the back strain, no time off. No cross training. Needed to increase flexibility and core strength to recover.

Given that running takes a fair amount of time and that cross training for that same time would probably drive you crazy, what did you do to keep busy?
Cross trained harder than running would have been. Also, time spent in training room building strength and flexibility.

What was the most difficult aspect of being injured? How did you deal psychologically with missing a season?
I missed almost a whole track season. I was less than full strength. It's hard given the number of years you can do this.

What specifically did you learn from being injured?
The need to take care of your body. I have learned many important daily rehab things that must be done in order to stay healthy.

What advice would you give another elite runner who suffers a season-ending injury?
Relax, let your body heal itself and find the things you need to do in the future to avoid any injuries. Don't get into a cycle of injuries that will stop long-term success.

When you returned to full-time training, did you alter the type of training you were doing?
Not the type of training but daily rehab work.

What advice would you give a high school or young college runner regarding injury prevention and/or rehabilitation?
Use many different methods to stay healthy. There is no telling what will work for you. Conventional medicine, holistic medicine, stretching, yoga, massage, strengthening, acupressure, etc.

Stuart Eagon
University of Wisconsin
3K, 5K, 10K, XC

"When things don't work out I don't freak out as much anymore, because I know that I am going to make smarter decisions that will allow me to be more competitive and healthier throughout my career."

> **Stuart, briefly profiled**
> Birth Date and Place: April 18, 1986; Portland, Ore.
> Began running: 13 years old; Began running competitively: 14 years old
> Height/Running Weight: 6'5", 157 lbs.
>
> University of Wisconsin, B.A., 2009
> College coach: Jerry Schumacher
> Beaverton High School, Beaverton, Ore. (2004)
> High school coaches: Jim Archer, Jim Crawford & Alberto Salazar (during offseason)
>
> Current residence: Portland, Ore.
> Current occupation: volunteer work
> Current affiliation or club: Nike Oregon Project
> Current Coach (indicate if self-coached): Jerry Schumacher
>
> Personal records: 3K—7:54.09i (2007); 5K—13:38.30i (2009); 10K—28:47.04 (2006)

Notable accomplishments
College/Post-Collegiate – Seven-time All-American…two-time NCAA team champions… 9th in 10k USATF Championships (2006).

Favorite rehab/cross training workout
I believe that stationary biking is the most effective time of cross training if your injury will allow for it. I've done countless workouts in the pool (20-30x1 min with 20 seconds rest would be one example) and it has never been nearly as effective as long hard bike rides. Two consistent 45 minute to hour-long bike rides a day are what have always worked best for me (so, 90 min—2 hours a day). If you want to throw in some long intervals, 5-10 minute intervals with a minute rest can be effective as well, but I prefer just lots of consistent riding at a normal (running) heart rate

Worst running-related injury(ies):
Worst injury is probably a grade 4 stress fracture on my right tibia that resulted from overcompensation for a severe right ankle sprain (that removed my calcaneus' ability to evert) I've had approximately five stress fractures and stress reactions on my left tibia as a result of a osteochondral fracture (never caused pain, caused severe restriction, and compensation issues that led to stress fractures) underneath my kneecap, that I ran through for approximately 5+ years.

Approximate date of injury(ies), nature of it/them and was surgery required?
Had (successful) surgery to repair Osteochondral fracture/reattach bone on Nov. 5, 2009. Stress fractures in March 2007, 2 (one each leg) in March 2008, August 2008, February 2009, September 2009.

What flaw led to the injury(ies)? Or did you do something that caused it (them)?
See above. Tibia was forced to absorb extra impact as a result of stiff legged running on right leg [no range of motion or ability to squat on left leg.] Tibia on right leg absorbed pounding as a result of calcaneus not moving correctly.

Rehabilitation program that you followed. How long before you resumed "normal" training?
Last 6 months for me have been slow recovery following arthroscopic knee surgery. Progressed into more challenging PT over the last 10 weeks, started more aggressive PT after 10-12 weeks following surgery…

Started biking 2 weeks following surgery, progressed into more biking over the course of the 6 weeks that followed.

Given that running takes a fair amount of time and that cross training for that same time would probably drive you crazy, what did you do to keep busy?
I always cross train for the same amount of time as I run or even more.

What was the most difficult aspect of being injured? How did you deal psychologically with missing a season? What specifically did you learn from being injured?
My best years are still ahead of me, and even if I never get to where I would like to be, I always look at it as learning. It's a very important educational process for us as athletes; sometimes the only way we can truly learn our body is through first-hand experience.

What advice would you give another elite runner who suffers a season-ending injury?
Always look at the big picture; don't get caught up in individual races. Making World Championship and Olympic teams, or at the very least putting yourself in the position to do so (when healthy) is what's most important. It's all practice until that point; in our sport if you're not 100% there's no sense in trying to push through the pain and compete.

When you returned to full-time training, did you alter the type of training you were doing?
Reduced volume, supplemented cross training as a form of replacement for running (to make up for less aerobic training [with less running).

What was the result in your first major competition after returning from injury?
In 2009, 13:38 5K (2nd fastest by American in indoors in '09) and 6th at U.S. Road 5K Championships in 14:06.

After being injured and coming back, did it change your sense of who you are/were as a runner? Did you have more patience or did you find yourself training on the edge again?
Over the past three years (since February 2007) my view of running and athletics has completely changed. I no longer am dependent on running as my identity, I'm just thankful for the privilege to compete at 100%. When things don't work out I don't freak out as much anymore, because I know that I am going to make smarter decisions that will allow me to be more competitive and healthier throughout my career.

German Fernandez

Oklahoma State University
1500, Mile, 3k, 5k, XC

"Just be patient. Try not to get too anxious or emotional about your injury or the recovery because being in a hurry can cause you to make poor decisions that can lead to more missed time."

German, briefly profiled
Birth Date and Place: Nov. 2, 1990, Watsonville, Cal.
Began running: 14 years old; Began running competitively: 14 years old
Height/Running Weight: 6'1", 135 lbs.

Oklahoma State University
College coach: Dave Smith
Riverbank High School, Riverbank, Cal. (2008)
High school coaches: Bruce Edwards and Johnny Vizcaino

Current residence: Stillwater, Okla.
Current occupation: Student-Athlete
Current affiliation or club: Oklahoma State University
Current Coach: Dave Smith

Personal Records: 1500m—3:39.00 (2009); Mile—3:55.02i (2009); 3K—7:47.97i (2009); 5K—13:25.46 (2009)

Notable accomplishments
High School—Six-time state champ...state record-holder at 1600 and 3200...3rd at Footlocker championships...NTN 2-mile champ...High school national record at 3K, 3200, 2-mile.
College/Post-Collegiate—Five-time Big 12 champion...NCAA outdoor 1500 champ (2009)...25th at IAAF world junior XC championships (2008)...11th at IAAF world junior XC championships (2009)...two-time USATF junior XC champion (2008, 2009)...5th in 5K at U.S. championships (2009).

Favorite rehab/cross training workout
I like running on the Alter G treadmill because it is the closest thing to running I can do while cross training. It is good because I can gradually increase the percentage of body weight I am running at until I am back to full strength and I like seeing that progression. I

also like the bike a lot. My high school coach, Bruce Edwards, had me spend time on the bike even as preventive training every once in a while so it is something I am used to.

We have a couple of different types of electronic bikes and also spin bikes in the track cardio room at OSU. When I use the electronic bikes I usually do one of the preprogrammed hill sessions. On the spin bike, I do fartleks or tempo type workouts.

Coach Dave Smith doesn't want us to have easy days when we cross train on the bike so I always have some type of workout that really gets my heart rate up.

Worst running-related injuries
My worst injury was a torn meniscus but that wasn't from running; I did it playing basketball. My worst running injury has been associated with my Achilles/plantaris tendons. I have had issues with that part of my leg several times starting in my senior year of high school.

Approximate date of injuries, nature of them and was surgery required?
The torn meniscus was late in my sophomore year and I had to have arthroscopic surgery to fix it. My Achilles first bothered me after world juniors my senior year. It was basically tendonitis and just required time off. I missed some time training and missed the Arcadia meet. I also hurt my plantaris tendon at nationals my freshman year in college. That was more of an instant thing and I felt a pop when it happened, which was very painful.

What flaw led to the injuries? Or did you do something that caused them?
I am not sure if there was a flaw. The Achilles tendonitis came after running at world juniors in Scotland and that was a really wet, muddy, soft course and it was really hilly, terrain, conditions I wasn't really used to, so that might have had something to do with it. I came back from Scotland and it started to feel stiff not long after. I kept trying to run on it and it just got worse, so my coach had me take about 10-12 days off and skip Arcadia.

My plantaris rupture kind of came out of nowhere. I just stepped funny and felt a pop and then shooting pain.

Rehabilitation program that you followed. How long before you resumed "normal" training?
I was on the bike every day when I took my time off in high school. I would bike 1-3 times per day. In college, after NCAAs, I couldn't walk for a few days and I was in a boot and on crutches for a little over a week. I was supposed to take a week completely off, but after a few days I went down to our cardio room and used the arm cycler for workouts. After a few days of that, I got bored and started light biking with my boot on. Then, I started rehab strengthening, icing, e-stim and all that stuff. Eventually, I moved to the bike full time without the boot and finally to the Alter G. I went to the pool every once in a while, too. We tried to mix it up to keep me from getting stale. I did rehab everyday and some type of intense cardio 1-3 times per day.

Given that running takes a fair amount of time and that cross training for that same time would probably drive you crazy, what did you do to keep busy?
At OSU I actually have cross trained more than I would have run. (Coach) Dave (Smith) has us go 1.5-2.0 x the time we would spend running depending on what mode of cross training we are using. I would get 90 minutes to 3 hours of cross training per day.

What was the most difficult aspect of being injured? How did you deal psychologically with missing a season?
I hate not being able to run with the guys every day. It is hard when you are sitting in the training room and everybody else is going out for a run. Of course, missing big competitions is tough, especially when you feel like you are fit and ready to race. In high school, I missed the Arcadia meet which, at the time, seemed like a really big deal. We had been pointing for that meet for a year and I really didn't want to miss it.
I kept telling my coach that my leg didn't hurt because I was afraid he wouldn't want me to risk it. The week of the race he had me do some strides and I had just a very slight limp that I couldn't hide from him. When he saw that, he told me I wasn't going to run. That was tough to handle but in hindsight was the best decision.

In college, I really only missed about 10 minutes of the season because the injury happened at the end of the national championship race. But it was a terrible way to end what was, to that point, a great season for me and our team. It was difficult not to look back on the season and have all my feelings shaped by that last 10 minutes. Another tough aspect was waiting two months to get back out there and get that bad taste out of my mouth. It was pretty tough to deal with the first week, but after that it became motivation to train even harder and come back even stronger.

Every day, when I was cross training, I just kept seeing myself in some big race, trying to kick to the finish. I focused on how I wanted to feel when I returned to competing and that kept me motivated and kept my effort level at a very high intensity.

What specifically did you learn from being injured?
The most important thing I have learned from each of my injuries is that the time away from running isn't necessarily a bad thing. Every time I have been injured and forced to spend time cross training instead of running, I have had PRs soon after returning to running. After my knee surgery, I came back and ran 9:06 for 3200 which was a PR off little training. The 3:56 at Arkansas was about 6 seconds faster than my 1600 time from high school converted to and it came after a month off and only a few weeks of running.

What advice would you give another elite runner who suffers a season-ending injury?
Just be patient. Try not to get too anxious or emotional about your injury or the recovery because being in a hurry can cause you to make poor decisions that can lead to more missed time. Remember that your training and your development are part of a process. There will be bumps in the road and there will be frustrating times, but even those times are important to becoming a better runner.

The forced time off can be good for your development and can make you even hungrier to succeed in the future. Learning to deal with the disappointment of losing an important meet or a season prepares you to deal with adversity in future races and seasons and even in other areas of your life.

When you returned to full-time training, did you alter the type of training you were doing?
I haven't altered a lot but I did carry on the rehab for my injuries well past the point of recovery. I added some of the strengthening and flexibility aspects of the rehab into my daily routine and I am still doing them today. I have also been careful to schedule occasional days off running and have been more careful to take breaks from running after my competitive season is over.

What was the result in your first major competition after returning from injury?
The first major competition after my injury was a shock to me. It was about two months after I was hurt at the NCAA championships and I had only been back to running for a few weeks. My mileage was still at a moderate level and I wasn't back to running every day, yet. I was still mixing in cross training with running to keep myself aerobically fit but trying to protect my leg. We really hadn't done any intensity so I wasn't expecting any big results.

Dave entered me in the mile in a field that had some great guys in it including my teammate, John Kosgei, and Dorian Ulrey from Arkansas. The plan was to just get back to racing and to see where I was in terms of fitness. We were kind of hoping for a 4:03-4:05 and maybe finishing in the top 3 or 4. I went out in the back and after 400 started to feel pretty good. There was a rabbit and he was pushing a good pace up front and as people started to drop off I just kept going around them. In the last 400 I was surprised by how good I felt. My legs just seemed really fresh. When I finished and saw the clock said 3:56 I couldn't believe it. I thought there had to be some kind of mistake.

What advice would you give a high school or young college runner regarding injury prevention and/or rehabilitation?
For prevention, don't be afraid to take time off when you have little nagging aches and pains. My coach always tells us that 6 days off now is better than 6 weeks off later. I think that is really a good way to look at it even though it is hard to force yourself to take a couple of days off in the middle of a season when you feel like you are really fit. As far as rehab, as I said before, just take it slow. Stay calm and patient in your return. Focus on the big picture and understand that your injury and recovery are part of the process. See yourself five years down the road and realize that getting there includes going through times like you are having now.

After being injured and coming back, did it change your sense of who you are as a runner? Did you have more patience or did you find yourself training on the edge again?
Being injured always makes me really thankful when I am healthy. I don't take my health for granted and try to do all the little things right to prevent future injuries. It is hard to be patient and when I am healthy, I have to consciously remind myself to scale it back sometimes.

Darryl Frerker
Illinois State University
1500, Mile

"Educate yourself about the injury, stay positive and be patient with cross training/rehab/training."

> **Darryl, briefly profiled**
> Birth Date and Place: Oct. 23, 1963, Breese, Ill.
> Began running: 12 years old; Began running competitively: 14 years old; Retired: 33 years old
> Height/Running Weight: 5'6", 125 lbs.
>
> Illinois State University, B.A., 1987 (Social Work)
> College coach: John Coughlan
> Highland High School, Highland, Ill. (1982)
> High school coaches: Steve Moore
>
> Current residence: Maryville, Ill.
> Current occupation: Boys' & Girls' Cross Country Coach & Boys' Track Coach, Collinsville High School, Collinsville, Ill.
>
> Personal records: 800—1:49.6 (1992); 1500—3:37.85 (1995); Mile—3:57.1 (1991)

Notable accomplishments
High School—2A All-State (1982)
College/Post-Collegiate— NCAA qualifier (1985)...NCAA All-American in mile (1987)...U.S. Olympic trial qualifier (1988)...ranked #1 in U.S. and #5 in world in indoor mile run (1991)...U.S. Olympic trials finalist (1992)...Participated on five U.S. teams (1988-94)...U.S. National Qualifier (1988-95).

Worst running-related injuries
Plantar fascia and stress fractures.

Approximate date of injuries, nature of them and was surgery required?
January 1993, arch muscle, no surgery. October 1982, left shin, no surgery.

What flaw led to the injuries? Or did you do something that caused it?
Lack of summer training before freshman year at ISU. The stress fracture was from running barefoot on a beach.

Rehabilitation program that you followed. How long before you resumed "normal" training?
Had orthotics made for the arch. No cross training done for stress fracture. Six weeks off and then "normal" training resumed.

Given that running takes a fair amount of time and that cross training for that same time would probably drive you crazy, what did you do to keep busy?
I was fortunate to be healthy (few and minimal injuries) and did not have to cross train for extended periods of time.

What was the most difficult aspect of being injured? How did you deal psychologically with missing a season?
Not running, feeling like I let the team down. I knew I had a fifth year to use. Stay positive and work through it.

What specifically did you learn from being injured?
That I really don't want to be injured. Train smarter, listen to my body, be patient, sacrifice activities that may be detrimental.

What advice would you give another elite runner who suffers a season-ending injury?
Educate yourself about the injury, stay positive and be patient with cross training/rehab/training.

When you returned to full-time training, did you alter the type of training you were doing?
No, but I listened to my body more closely and backed down, cross trained as needed, and pushed when appropriate.

What was the result in your first major competition after returning from injury?
High learning curve—it was my first indoor race/season ever. It was all new and I was a meek freshman.

What advice would you give a high school or young college runner regarding injury prevention and/or rehabilitation?
Prevention: Be smart about your training. Learn your body and what it can truly handle. Cross training will help save the pounding.
Rehab: Hang in there, it won't last forever. Do it! It will help sustain conditioning.

Other thoughts on injury prevention or rehabilitation.
Consistent hydration, proper warm up and cool down, stretch well before and after activity, weight lift appropriately, good nutrition habits.

Robert Gary
Ohio State University
Steeplechase, XC

"Don't come back until you're 100% healthy. Running with a slight hitch or any slightly altered form can lead to injuries which can be worse than the original."

Robert, briefly profiled
Birth Date and Place: April 5, 1973
Began running: 4 years old (soccer); Began running competitively: 16 years old; Retired: 32 years old
Height/Running Weight: 5'9", 135 lbs.

Ohio State University, B.A., 1996 (English Education)
College coach: Mark Croghan, Lee LaBadie
Evanston High School, Evanston, Ill. (1991)
High school coaches: Rick Peterson and Willie May

Current residence: Columbus, Ohio
Current occupation: Head Track and Cross Country Coach at Ohio State University

Personal record: Steeplchase—8:19.46 (1996)

Notable accomplishments
High School—All-American in soccer…ranked 2nd in mile among preps…
College/Post-Collegiate – Big Ten steeple champ… All-American in XC, indoor, and outdoor track…held Big Ten 3K record-holder (7:52)…qualified for 11 national teams in XC at 4K, 12K or both…made 11 straight U.S. steeple finals….U.S. Olympian in steeplechase (1996 and 2004).

Worst running-related injuries
Partial tears throughout my right Achilles.

Approximate date of injuries, nature of them and was surgery required?
December 1998 and May 1999. Surgery was strongly recommended by two very good doctors/surgeons.

What flaw led to the injuries? Or did you do something that caused them?
Very tight calves throughout career and speed work/hurdling.

Rehabilitation program that you followed. How long before you resumed "normal" training?
One, Massage therapist/chiropractor, manually breaks up scar tissue almost daily (4-5 days a week) for fourteen straight weeks and then two days a work for eight weeks. Two, religiously swam with ice wrapped around my legs.

Given that running takes a fair amount of time and that cross training for that same time would probably drive you crazy, what did you do to keep busy?
First, it sucks. But you get into a routine and then you go about it with the same discipline you do regular training. I have never thought it hard to get out there every day or to do all the little things. Second, since so much of my rehab is in the pools (no impact) I actually spent more time when I'm injured training. I rarely run doubles; I always cross train twice a day.

What was the most difficult aspect of being injured? How did you deal psychologically with missing a season?
The good thing about track is that there are so many great things to train for. The World Champs are almost as big a deal as the Olympics and then throw in the World Cross and there's always something to shoot for.

What specifically did you learn from being injured?
Do not train until you can truly train. Training at 50% never turns to 60, 70, 80, 90 and 100%. You should either cross train or train how you normally would.

What advice would you give another elite runner who suffers a season-ending injury?
Do not test it all the time. A lot of injuries are due to overuse and testing this or that body part before you are very, very sure you're healthy seems to put you back at square one.

When you returned to full-time training, did you alter the type of training you were doing?
I did more stretching and was more patient with tightness or heaviness. I always try to set myself up for different training phases. If I'm going to start doing quarters in a couple weeks I'll start doing some easy 150's or 200's beforehand. I used to go from 3x3 miles on grass to 10x400. This is not a good idea.

What was the result in your first major competition after returning from injury?
I opened my season (four weeks out of water) with my fastest steeple opener ever. I went on to finish 2nd at U.S. Champs and had my best-ever summer in Europe.

What advice would you give a high school or young college runner regarding injury prevention and/or rehabilitation?
Don't come back until you're 100% healthy. Running with a slight hitch or any slightly altered form can lead to injuries which can be worse than the original.

Chris Graff

St. John's University
5K, 10K, Roads

Advice to those who are hurt: *"None. If they want to walk away, it is a respectable decision. Being hurt is the worst."*

Chris, briefly profiled
Birth Date and Place: Oct. 5, 1975, Brooklyn, N.Y.
Began running: 13 years old; Began running competitively: 13 years old
Height/Running Weight: 5'10", 132 lbs.

St. John's University (1998)
College coach: Jim Hurt
Oceanside High School, Oceanside, N.Y. (1993)
High school coaches: Ken Hendler

Current residence: Palo Alto, Cal.
Current occupation: Athlete
Current affiliation or club: Nike Farm Team

Personal Records: 1500—3:46; 5K—13:37; 10K—28:03.11 (2004); Marathon—2:18.44 (2003)

Notable accomplishments
College/Post-Collegiate – 5th USA Track Championships 10k (2002)…1st Stanford Invite 10k (2002)…8th USA Track Championships 10k (2001…10th Cherry Blossom 10 mile (47:19)…10th Olympic Trials 5k…22nd Olympic Trials 10k…Sydney Olympic A Standard…8th USATF national xc championships (1999)…World XC team member (1999)…Qualified to World University Games (1999)…11th at USATF national outdoor 10k (1999)…Army ten miler champion (1999)…6th fasted American five mile road time (1998)…Two-time NCAA All-American…Big East 10k Champ (1998)…Four-time All-East award winner.

Worst running-related injuries
Recurring hamstring strains.

Approximate date of injuries, nature of them and was surgery required?
Winter 2000 through Spring of 2001. I missed up to three weeks. No Surgery needed.

What flaw led to the injuries? Or did you do something that caused them?
Strength imbalances between right and left legs. Left leg is weaker thus breaks down, or left leg is weaker and right leg over compensates and breaks down.

Rehabilitation program that you followed. How long before you resumed "normal" training?
Phil and Jim Whartons active isolated stretching and strength program, taught to me by Tom Nohilly. A program designed for me to strengthen my abductors, adductors, hammys and lower abs. Within a few months I could run normally and I do the routine currently (and always will) to maintain hip alignment and balance left to right.

Given that running takes a fair amount of time and that cross training for that same time would probably drive you crazy, what did you do to keep busy?
Went to practice, hung out with coach. When I was hurt I would do nothing for a day or two, then coach would snap me into it and I would lift, get therapy, bike (outside) for twice as much time as I run.

What was the most difficult aspect of being injured? How did you deal psychologically with missing a season?
I had the 10K time for 2000 but wasn't healthy. It was awful. I wanted to quit. I left running alone until I was ready (about six weeks). Centrowitz wouldn't let me off the hook that easy.

What specifically did you learn from being injured?
The effect that everything has on running. The wholeness of the body.

What advice would you give another elite runner who suffers a season-ending injury?
None. If they want to walk away, it is a respectable decision. Being hurt is the worst.

When you returned to full-time training, did you alter the type of training you were doing?
I do the same running, but I stretch, lift, drills, etc.

What was the result in your first major competition after returning from injury?
USATF 10K—not that fit but got 8th.

What advice would you give a high school or young college runner regarding injury prevention and/or rehabilitation?
Light weights on legs, hips and stretching will go a long way.

Tim Hacker

University of Wisconsin
1500, 5K, XC

"Follow rehab carefully, take your time, and follow your gut. Returning one or two days early can often result in another week setback whereas if you wait that extra day, you will be fine."

Tim, briefly profiled
Birth Date and Place: Dec. 27, 1962, Milwaukee, Wis.
Began running: 15 years old; Began running competitively: 15 years old; Retired: 37 years old
Height/Running Weight: 5'8", 142 lbs.

University of Wisconsin, B.A., 1986 (Biochemistry)
College coaches: Dan McClimon, Martin Smith
Memomonee Falls High School, Menomonee Falls, Wis. (1981)
High school coach: Bob Rymer

Current residence: Madison, Wis.
Current occupation: Scientist at the University of Wisconsin

Personal records: 1500—3:34.66 (1987); Mile—3:55.2 (1989); 5K—13:35

Notable accomplishments
High School—Two-time state XC champ...3rd in FootLocker...
College/Post-Collegiate – NCAA XC Champ (1985)...U.S. XC Champ (1997)...U.S. 5K champ (1989)...3:34.66 1500 was sixth best performance at the time...fifth in 1500 in 1984 U.S. Olympic Trials....four-time XC All-American...five-time Track All-American.

Worst running-related injuries
Plantar fasciitis, osteocondrotin desicans (dead bone ahead of femur), and various pulled muscles.

Approximate date of injuries, nature of them and was surgery required?
Plantar fasciitis in 1983 cost me six months of training but no surgery required. Had again in 1987 this time lost six months of training and had surgery. Had osteocondrotin in 1999, this ended my running career. I dealt with a number of pulled muscles. These were usually short but often happened late in the season thereby ending the season.

What flaw led to the injuries? Or did you do something that caused them?
Plantar fasciitis was caused by weak moral fiber or high arches, tight and stiff feet and calves. Nothing caused the Osteocondrotin.

Rehabilitation program that you followed. How long before you resumed "normal" training?
I did various PT type exercises for the plantar fasciitis. I ran in water and biked. This lasted about two months before I gave up. I then rested until I healed. Likewise, I also did various PT type exercises, ran in water, and biked for the osteocondrotin. I also used the elliptical trainer. This lasted about a year. With the muscle pulls I generally either did nothing due to the nature of the pull or I biked or ran in the pool as the injury permitted. I generally did this until I was able to run again.

Given that running takes a fair amount of time and that cross training for that same time would probably drive you crazy, what did you do to keep busy?
Generally, the cross training and rehab took longer than the running which really drove me nuts. As I got well past college, I often did not have enough time to do both full rehab and cross training, so I did a little of both. Even in college, I never had trouble filling my time. As I got older I liked the time "off" and caught up on unfinished projects, etc.

What was the most difficult aspect of being injured? How did you deal psychologically with missing a season?
I hated seeing people winning races I thought I could have won. Usually, stopped following results and got busy with other projects and interests. I probably did miss several chances to make Olympic or World teams, but I always thought even if healthy I may not have made the teams. I have convinced myself that I am very lucky to get as far as I did in running, that I did not want more. Moreover, I always had great family/friend support to help me realize that there is more to life than running.

What specifically did you learn from being injured?
I learned that I am addicted to running. I am grumpy when not running. People still like me, even if a am not an athlete.

What advice would you give another elite runner who suffers a season-ending injury?
Enjoy the weekends off. Find a new outlet, start a new project, become two-dimensional. Formulate a plan for next season and get a plan for getting healthy. Take your time—coming back too fast often leads to another injury.

When you returned to full-time training, did you alter the type of training you were doing?
Usually I didn't change the training I was doing because my injuries were mostly not overuse type stuff. Generally as I got smarter, I listened to my body closer, kept a closer check on aches and pains. Finally, in my last couple years I ran and trained totally on feel, not worrying about millage, etc. If I was feeling fresh I ran hard, and if tired, I rested.

What was the result in your first major competition after returning from injury?
Usually pretty poor. Six months of injury might equal 9-12 months of training to get back to full form.

What advice would you give a high school or young college runner regarding injury prevention and/or rehabilitation?
Listen to your body. Write down everything until you really understand what your body does and feels like. This may take 5-7 years until you really understand it (or less if you're much smarter than I am). What makes great runners great is that they push hard no matter what. Great… but be smart about it. Follow rehab carefully, take your time, and follow your gut. Returning one or two days early can often result in another week setback whereas if you wait that extra day, you will be fine.

Brad Hauser

Stanford University
5K, 10K, XC

"Be an intelligent trainer and athlete overall. Rest and recovery is just as important as interval training."

Brad, briefly profiled
Birth Date and Place: March 28, 1977, Danville, Pa.
Began running: 12 years old; Began running competitively: 15 years old; Retired: 31 years old
Height/Running Weight: 6'2", 150 lbs.

Stanford University, B.A., 1999 (Human Biology)
College coach: Vin Lananna
Kingwood High School, Kingwood, Texas (1995)
High school coaches: Zoe Simpson

Current residence: Mountain View, Cal.

Personal record: 5K—13:27.31 (2000); 10K—27:58.02 (2002)

Notable accomplishments
High School – Three-time state champ
College/Post-Collegiate – Twelve-time All-American…Five-time NCAA Champ…10k World track Champs (1999)…12k, 4k World XC Champs (2000, 2001)…Olympic Team (2000).

Worst running-related injury
Tendonitis of both feet. Never properly diagnosed but pain on the insertion of tendons into the metatarsals.

Approximate date of injury, nature of it and was surgery required?
April 2001. Pain was bearable to run on, yet significant enough on every step to cause concern. No surgery was required.

What flaw led to the injury? Or did you do something that caused it?
Not known, possibilities include racing world XC Champs on a horribly muddy course, weakness of musculature in lower limb, or possibly a new training flat.

Rehabilitation program that you followed. How long before you resumed "normal" training?
Pool running for five weeks with frequent massage and icing. There was no improvement with cross training therefore I began to train at a lower volume than usual or about five or six months. I used a temporary orthotic in my training flats. After six months I observed a significant improvement and started training normally. I was running pain free 8-10 months after pain initiated.

Given that running takes a fair amount of time and that cross training for that same time would probably drive you crazy, what did you do to keep busy?
Tried to stay in the same routine with concentration on weights.

What was the most difficult aspect of being injured? How did you deal psychologically with missing a season?
Confidence was the most difficult aspect. I was coming off of an Olympic year and finishing 15th at World XC, probably the most confident of my running career. Missing an entire track season and six good months of training significantly diminished my confidence. I missed a chance at world championship team.

What specifically did you learn from being injured?
Mainly, that it is going to happen if you push yourself to train at the top level. Accepting the fact that you might get injured and have to rehabilitate the injury is a part of being a professional athlete.

What advice would you give another elite runner who suffers a season-ending injury?
Be patient and treat cross training and rehabilitation just like you would treat regular training. Be serious about treating the injury.\

When you returned to full-time training, did you alter the type of training you were doing?
No, I tried to go back to what I knew worked from past seasons.

What was the result in your first major competition after returning from injury?
Extremely poor. I believe that I actually did not finish the race.

What advice would you give a high school or young college runner regarding injury prevention and/or rehabilitation?
Be an intelligent trainer and athlete overall. Rest and recovery is just as important as interval training.

Billy Herman

Northern Arizona University
5K, 10K, XC

"Injuries are humbling. I love what I do as a runner and when I don't get to do what I love to do, it makes you doubt about whether I should be running at all or if I will be able to come back at that level. I learned that you can't rush your training."

Billy, briefly profiled
Birth Date and Place: July 3, 1974, Changua, Taiwan (Parents were teachers/I was U.S. born)
Began running: 10 years old; Began running competitively: 13 years old
Height/Running Weight: 5'9", 132 lbs.

Northern Arizona University (Criminal Justice; Pre Med)
College coach: Ron Mann
Centennial High School (Idaho) (1996)
High school coach: Ron Ascucna

Current residence: San Diego, Cal..
Current occupation: Athlete
Current affiliation or club: U.S. Navy
Current Coach: Joe Uchil

Notable accomplishments
High School—Six-time state champ
College/Post-Collegiate – Four-Time NCAA All-American…Olympic trials Finalist (2000).

Worst running-related injury
Stress fracture to medial tibia on my right leg.

Approximate date of injury, nature of it and was surgery required?
Acquired injury in January or February 2003.

What flaw led to the injury? Or did you do something that caused it?
I came off a great summer, then decided to quit running, took the fall completely off. I was then convinced not to quit and I joined Team USA at Olympic Center. I proceeded to run 100 mile weeks right off the bat. Not too smart. Mostly it was all the weights, plyos, and drills on top of high mileage without building up though many weeks that caused the

stress fracture. I didn't really think that I had a stress fracture for about a month, and then found out after an MRI.

Rehabilitation program that you followed. How long before you resumed "normal" training?
They say it takes twice as long to recover from an injury as it takes to get it. I stopped running for about three months. I then started in on the slowest comeback ever. I started running ten minutes a day under strict supervision of coaches Joe Vigil and Bob Larsen. We were in Mammoth, and the doctor did not want me running too much, but wanted me doing strength building things. So I spend late June, July, and most of August climbing, backpacking, kayaking, and fly-fishing (all the things I love to do). I started normal training in late August when the team all returned to Mammoth for our fall session. I spent all fall building a small base, getting in good workouts, and then slowly adding in my weights. I then added my plyos.

Given that running takes a fair amount of time and that cross training for that same time would probably drive you crazy, what did you do to keep busy?
I was spending whole days just doing the cross training that I love to do. My whole life revolved around being outside and it just so happened that the doctors wanted me doing all the things I wish I had more time to do. So I did all of them for two months! I also have lots of friends here in Mammoth that snowboard professionally. Most of them had lots of time to burn in the summer. Basically, I kept busy. It was hard to watch nationals from the fence and not run for months but my teammates keep me in check and have convinced me that injuries get the fire burning inside and that coming off of and injury can be some of the best running in my career. I'm looking forward to it.

What was the most difficult aspect of being injured? How did you deal psychologically with missing a season?
The most difficult aspect is how you feel out of the loop (in the track world). My teammates saved me. Coach made me watch the steeple at nationals. All these things, teammates, coaches, and the dream of performing better, kept me from losing perspective. Most people look at the short term affects of injuries, but my coaches, teammate, and family kept my perspective on the bigger picture and how this injury might be good for me in the long run. I wasn't missing any teams, just some racing. Through a lot of prayer and faith I made it thorough with everything intact.

What specifically did you learn from being injured?
Injuries are humbling. I love what I do as a runner and when I don't get to do what I love to do, it makes you doubt about whether I should be running at all or if I will be able to come back at that level. I learned that you can't rush your training.

What advice would you give another elite runner who suffers a season-ending injury?
The fall (injury) isn't necessarily the important thing to think about. What's important is how you get up from the injury. Your attitude and perspective of the fall is everything. The choice is yours on how you want to respond. The process of getting better involves learning and growing from our mistakes. The only way to grow is to fall, so that we know

and learn what went wrong, and then grow from it. It's the only way to be better than before.

When you returned to full-time training, did you alter the type of training you were doing?
Caution is the word. We were careful to listen to my body and how it responded to everything that we slowly added back to my training. Doing things too fast, too quick gets you hurt. What's the rush? (As my coach would say)

What advice would you give a high school or young college runner regarding injury prevention and/or rehabilitation?
I use active isolated stretching and icing as preventive things, but never rush things. Time off and patience is the only way to fully recover and then come back slowly. I see so many guys come back too fast or try to rehab in other ways only to keep initiating the problem, making it worse. Take the time your body needs... Listen to it, not your watch.

Dan Huling

Miami University (Ohio)
1500, Steeple, 5K

"Keep your head straight and just tell yourself to be patient. Unless it's a crazy injury you WILL get better and you'll run again."

Dan, briefly profiled
Birth Date and Place: July 16, 1983, North Kingstown, R.I.
Began running: 9 years old; Began running competitively: 13 years old
Height/Running Weight: 6'1", 144 lbs.

Miami University (Ohio), B.A., 2006 (Marketing)
College coach: Warren Mandrell
North Kingstown High School, North Kingstown, RI (1998-99);
Geneva High School, Geneva, Ill. (2002)
High school coaches: Paul Tetrault and Suzy Yaeger

Current residence: Columbus, Ohio
Current occupation: Professional Distance Runner
Current affiliation or club: Reebok
Current Coach: Robert Gary

Personal records: 1500—3:40.20 (2008); Steeple—8:13.29 (2010); 5K—13:24 (2010)

Notable accomplishments
High School – Two-time all-state cross country…all-state track.
College/Post-Collegiate – Four-time all-American…3rd in steeple at U.S. championships (2006)…2nd in steeple at U.S. Championships (2009)…won U.S. steeple title (2010); World Championship Team (2009)…#6 U.S. all-time Steeple.

Favorite rehab/cross training workout
Alter G is my favorite cross training workout. I've never been injured with access to the Alter G but would definitely implement it as much as I could. I've done supplemental running on it thus far

Injuries, I go to the pool and do 10 minute warmup and cool downs. I basically do 2 workouts while in there. One is 20 x 1 minute on 1 minute off with 10 x 30 seconds on. 30 seconds off. The other workout is :15, :30, :45, 1:00, 1:15, 1:30, 1:45, 2:00, 1:45, 1:30, 1:15, 1:00, :45, :30, :15 hard with equal rest in between.

Worst running-related injury
Torn joint capsule on my left big toe. Required surgery and knocked me out for the whole 2007 track season.

Approximate date of injury, nature of it and was surgery required?
April 2007. Surgery was required to pin back the ligament.

What flaw led to the injury? Or did you do something that caused it?
Cortisone shots into the joint in college weakened the ligament and led to a spontaneous rupture that caused my toe to dislocate outward if I tried running hard on it.

Rehabilitation program that you followed. How long before you resumed "normal" training?
I did some physical therapy for a while. It was basic balance things I did for my ankle but also did plantar flexion and dorisflexion of the toe. This was extremely painful. I eventually stopped and started my own program which involved some of the same exercises and also theraband strengthening. Normal training where I was able to get in spikes was in mid-August 2007.

Given that running takes a fair amount of time and that cross training for that same time would probably drive you crazy, what did you do to keep busy?
I'll be the first to admit I get extremely frustrated cross training and often would stop cross training for days on end because I didn't want to and would even convince myself that cross training was pointless and that I could run myself into shape in 4 weeks anyway. You can't do anything in the pool to keep your mind off it, so it's pretty awful the whole time.

What was the most difficult aspect of being injured? How did you deal psychologically with missing a season?
Most difficult part was having my toe hurt every day after surgery for a year and a half and watching all my peers compete and run great times. I think I have a good head on myself so I've always dealt with setbacks pretty well. Running is by no means the end-all, be-all in my life, so I focused my energy on other things. If I were the opposite and running consumed my day-to-day life… I'm sure it's very difficult for people. I think this is why I sometimes stopped my cross training routine. I don't care enough to train really hard unless I'm running.

I thought I missed a great chance to make a World Team in 2007. I was 3rd the year before and when I got hurt was fitter than ever. I feel as if it hurt 2008 as well because I was playing catch-up in the steeple as I hadn't run the event in over 2 years. I got my stride going a week after the trials in 2008 and ran 8:20 three weeks later.

What specifically did you learn from being injured?
I learned patience, obviously, as I'm sure every runner does. Having a relationship with God also played a role. I learned that I had/have to trust that He knows what's best for me. Patience and trust were the two biggest things I think anyone can ever learn from being set back by injury. You're just sitting there, broken, watching everyone else have fun and compete and nothing you do is going to make you're injury go away the next day. It's very easy to give up completely if you have back to back injuries as well.

What advice would you give another elite runner who suffers a season-ending injury?
Keep your head straight and just tell yourself to be patient. Unless it's a crazy injury you WILL get better and you'll run again. The drive you had to get healthy and back running is going to help you get to another level once you're back. NOT A SINGLE RUNNER has had a perfectly smooth trip to the top.

When you returned to full-time training, did you alter the type of training you were doing?
No. I did the same training. Last year in 2009 during April I had a weird little soft tissue injury that put me out a few weeks and learned I needed a more specific core routine that included a lot of glute work.
I have been doing that religiously since then and haven't had any kind of ache or pain.

What was the result in your first major competition after returning from injury?
I ran a big road race on Thanksgiving the next fall. It went mediocre. Felt terrible the whole race, and afterward my toe swelled up like a golf ball because it hadn't been stretched that much since before I got hurt. My first track race was a dismal 8:50 at Mt Sac, an awful event to jump into after 2 years off.

What advice would you give a high school or young college runner regarding injury prevention and/or rehabilitation?
CORE CORE CORE. Unless you have a blunt accident that couldn't have been avoided I believe most injuries come from a weak core that causes deficiencies in your stride. The core I'm talking about isn't situps and pushups but SPECIFIC targeting of important muscles.—your glutes, as I mentioned earlier, as well as your deep abdominal stabilizers. Basically, everything from above your knees to below your back. And when you are doing the drills knowing WHAT and WHY you are targeting the muscle. (side leg raises are pointless if you're doing them incorrectly by targeting your TFL instead of your glute)

After being injured and coming back, did it change your sense of who you are/were as a runner? Did you have more patience or did you find yourself training on the edge again?
Again, I've always been good with dealing with injuries. If something is so alarming that I can't run I've never just run on it. Your body is sending pain signals to your brain for a reason. It's not "tough" to run through a stress fracture, it's just stupid. I've never had a stress fx and I imagine I would still be very tempted to run through it. Of course I think everyone needs to be somewhat on the edge of training but once you have a ache or pain, deal with it for ice for a couple days and if that doesn't take care of it have it checked out or take a few days off. Three days is not going to kill your fitness as much as three months.

Evan Jager
University of Wisconsin
1500, Mile, 5K

"Listen to and know your body. As a runner, you need to know when you can and cannot push your body through aches, pains and potential injuries."

> **Evan, briefly profiled**
> Birth Date and Place: March 8, 1989; Algonquin, Ill.
> Began running: 11 years old; Began running competitively: 12 years old
> Height/Running Weight: 6'2", 147 lbs.
>
> University of Wisconsin
> *(surrendered collegiate eligibility after freshman year to go pro; attends Portland State)*
> College coach: Jerry Shumacher
> H.D. Jacobs High School, Algonquin, Ill. (2007)
> High school coaches: Rob Piercy
>
> Current residence: Portland, Ore.
> Current occupation: Professional Athlete
> Current affiliation or club: Nike
> Current Coach: Jerry Schumacher
>
> Personal records: 1500—3:38.33; Mile—3:54.35; 3K—7:41.78; 5K—13:22.18 (all in 2009)

Notable accomplishments
High School—Footlocker finalist (2005) …4X800 and 1600m state champion (2006) …3rd at Nike Outdoor Nationals two-mile (2006)…cross country state champion (2006) …Footlocker finalist (2006)…3200m state champion (2007).. 3rd in the mile and 4th in the 2 mile at Nike Outdoor Nationals (2007)
College/Post-Collegiate – Two-time All-American as a freshman…8th at NCAA outdoor in 1500 (2008). ..3rd place in 5K at U.S. outdoor championships (2009)…World Championships qualifier (2009).

Favorite rehab/cross training workout
During my most recent injury I either stationary biked or aqua jogged for 60 minutes. There was no particular workout or routine I followed, just 60 minutes straight of hard work.

Worst running-related injury
A stress reaction in the navicular of my right foot which later turned into a stress fracture. That has been the worst in terms of the amount of time I was required to take off running.

Approximate date of injuries, nature of it and was surgery required?
—Winter/Spring, 2003/2004—Stress fracture in the navicular of left foot. No surgery. (Boot for 6 weeks, missed H.S. freshman track season).
—Fall, 2007—Right Achilles tendonitis. No surgery. (2 months, missed college freshman cross country season).
—Winter/spring, 2010—Stress reaction in the navicular of right foot. No surgery. (2 months).
—Spring, 2010—Stress fracture in the navicular of right foot. I had surgery where doctors put two screws in the navicular and shaved off a lesion on the talus bone in the same foot.

What flaw led to the injuries? Or did you do something that caused them?
2004—Added a heel lift in right shoe to compensate for short right leg.
2007—Tried running through Achilles tendonitis.
2010—I think the stress reaction was caused from adding a full foot length lift to my right shoe to compensate for my shorter right leg.

Rehabilitation program that you followed. How long did the rehab take before you resumed "normal" training?
My 2010 injury was the first time I cross trained during an injury. I stationary biked every morning for the last 6 weeks of my injury for 60 minutes a day. I have not started rehab after my surgery yet but I plan to.

Given that running takes a fair amount of time and that cross training for that same time would probably drive you crazy, what did you do to keep busy?
While biking I either listened to my iPod or watched SportsCenter on TV.

What was the most difficult aspect of being injured? How did you deal psychologically with missing a season?
The most difficult part of being injured for me was knowing what good shape I was in before the injury and feeling like all that work I had put in was going to waste.

What specifically did you learn from being injured?
The main thing I've learned from every injury I've had is to enjoy every single day I get to do what I love, which is running.

What advice would you give another elite runner who suffers a season-ending injury?
Missing a season is not the end of the world. Use the missed season as motivation to train hard for the next season; your competitors should be afraid of what you will do after a full year of motivated training.

When you returned to full-time training, did you alter the type of training you were doing?
When I return to training full time I will not alter my training at all. I will merely ease back into training a little bit at a time.

What was the result in your first major competition after returning from injury?
My first major competition after my Achilles injury was also my first race as a collegiate runner and resulted in a win and a PR in the slow heat of the mile at the Meyo Invitational. My first race after my 2010 stress reaction was a 1500; I ran 0.2 seconds off my PR.

What advice would you give a high school or young college runner regarding injury prevention and/or rehabilitation?
Listen to and know your body. As a runner, you need to know when you can and cannot push your body through aches, pains and potential injuries. Another helpful tip I've learned is running on soft surface for a good portion of your runs.

After being injured and coming back, did it change your sense of who you are as a runner? Did you have more patience or did you find yourself training on the edge again?
Being injured has not changed who I am as a runner. I'm still the same person as I train and race with the same drive. I have become very cautious when it comes to Achilles pain because I have dealt with many Achilles problems.

Greg Jimmerson
Stanford University
3K, Steeplechase, 5K, XC

"Don't rush back into training; you'll end up re-injured. Enjoy some time off. Try to figure out the cause of the problem, not just the symptoms, and work to solve that problem."

Greg, briefly profiled
Birth Date and Place: Feb. 1, 1975; Rapid City, S.D.
Began running: 8 years old; Began running competitively: 12 years old
Height/Running Weight: 5'8", 140 lbs.

Stanford University, B.S., 1998 (Product Design)
College coach: Vin Lananna
Stevens High School, Rapid City, S.D. (graduated spring 1993)
High school coach: Greg Forrest Flaagan
Current residence: Los Altos Hills, Cal.
Current occupation: Mechanical Engineer

Personal records: Steeple—8:32.46 (2000); 10K—29:17.15 (2002)

Notable accomplishments
High School—Three-time state XC champ… two-time state 2 mile champ…2nd at Kinney XC Nationals (1992).
College/Post-Collegiate – 4th at NCAA XC (1996)…6th at NCAA XC (1999)…4th at U.S. XC Champs (2001)…6th at U.S. XC Champs (2001)…11th place at U.S. Olympic Trials in Steeple (2000).

Worst running-related injuries
Stress fracture in right navicular bone in November 1996 and plantar fasciitis from April to August in 2001.

Approximate date of injuries, nature of them and was surgery required?
Stress fracture in right navicular bone in November 1996 and plantar fasciitis from April to August in 2001.

What flaw led to the injuries? Or did you do something that caused them?
Navicular fracture occurred during a cross country race on a course with lots of small rolling hills and slants. Plantar problem

occurred due to steeplechase drills and hard landings in the water pit. I didn't do early prevention when it started.

Rehabilitation program that you followed. How long before you resumed "normal" training?
In 1996 I did pool running and exercise bike every day. I usually did about 30-60 minutes in the pool and 30 minutes on the bike. I wore a "boot" for about six weeks and then had a few weeks of walking without the boot before I started running. In 2001 I did no running. I was pool running about five days a week for last four weeks of the break. Average of about 30-60 minuets a day. I had deep tissue massage two times each week and lots of icing and ibuprofen. I taped my foot for several months after I started running again.

Given that running takes a fair amount of time and that cross training for that same time would probably drive you crazy, what did you do to keep busy?
Not much. It pretty much drove me crazy. Sometimes other people were hurt at the same time so we could run in the pool together or bike together. Otherwise I just admired the scenery of the Stanford women's swimmers and divers.

What was the most difficult aspect of being injured? How did you deal psychologically with missing a season?
The worst part was being out of action and watching other teammates running fast and getting good times. It was hard trying to get back in shape and being so far behind everyone else. I didn't really get back to the same fitness for over a year. In 2001, the worst part was that the cross training bore down on me. I was not very motivated to get back into shape, so I didn't. I wasn't in a big hurry.

What specifically did you learn from being injured?
That I hate pool-running and I don't think it really helped me at all. I put on more muscle than I need in my upper body and I didn't get much aerobic benefit. I prefer biking (on a real bike, not a stationary). I also learned that time off can be very beneficial to complete recovery and mental relaxation.

What advice would you give another elite runner who suffers a season-ending injury?
Don't rush back into training; you'll end up re-injured. Enjoy some time off. Some people do well off of pool running and biking and strength work so those are options. Try to figure out the cause of the problem, not just the symptoms, and work to solve that problem. Don't stress too much. It will be hard work, but you can get back to fitness. Come back smart and know your body.

When you returned to full-time training, did you alter the type of training you were doing?
I always advocate taking it slow and not pushing the recovery. I usually altered my training just the same as I would after any long break. I was in terrible shape, so I just took a long time to get back to fitness.

What was the result in your first major competition after returning from injury?
My first race back from my stress fracture was a 5K on the track. I ran over a minute slower than my PR! In 2002, my first race was a 10-mile road race in 49:20 which I was pleased with. I did not try to race before I was ready. I got back in to good fitness before racing.

What advice would you give a high school or young college runner regarding injury prevention and/or rehabilitation?
Talk to someone who has had the same injury. Find out what they did, how well it worked, and how long it took. Don't get down, let it motivate you. I am a believer in orthotics and proper mechanics for injury prevention. Most muscle strains can be prevented or relieved by stretching, massage, icing, and strengthening. I firmly believe in taking enough recover and rest days to avoid overtraining injuries.

Weldon Johnson
Yale University
5K, 10K, XC

"I think that the worst thing for me is when I don't know what the injury is and how to get rid of it. If I'm injured and know what course of action to take, I'm not as depressed because I can focus on the future and focus on where I'll be when I'm healthy."

Weldon, briefly profiled
Birth Date and Place: July 24, 1973; Dallas, Texas;
Began running: 13 years old; Began running competitively: 13 years old; Retired: 31 years old
Height/Running Weight: 6'1", 145 lbs.

Yale University, B.A., 1996 (Economics and History)
College coach: Steve Bartold
St. Mark's School of Texas, Dallas, Texas (1992)
High school coach: John Kellogg

Current residence: Fort Worth, Texas

Personal records: 5K—13:53; 10K—28:06

Notable accomplishments
College/Post-Collegiate – World half-marathon team (1999)...Pan Am Team at 10k (2003)...4th at U.S. nationals 10k (2001 and 2003).

Favorite rehab/cross training workout
I hate cross training but you've got to do it while injured. Pool running, cycling, and Nordic track.

Worst running-related injuries
I had a stress fracture of the fibula in high school. I had a nerve problem in my foot that sidelined me at the end of 2001 and most of 2002 (similar symptoms to plantar fasciitis). A navicular stress fracture ended my career.

Approximate date of injuries, nature of them and was surgery required?
Stress fracture in June 1992 and foot problem from Fall 2001 through July 2002.

What flaw led to the injuries? Or did you do something that caused them?
Not sure. Stress fracture probably because I was still developing. I have no idea what caused the foot problem. I think a lot of navicular stress fractures are caused by poor biomechanics, calf tightness, that then causes people to run differently on their feet.

Rehabilitation program that you followed. How long before you resumed "normal" training?
If possible with some injuries I tried to run. When I couldn't run I would bike or get in a pool or do Nordic Track.

Given that running takes a fair amount of time and that cross training for that same time would probably drive you crazy, what did you do to keep busy?
Although I hated cross training, I tried to cross train as much as I ran with the exception that I did not do doubles. I wanted to make the Olympics so I'd rather be bored than get out of shape and blow my chance

What was the most difficult aspect of being injured? How did you deal psychologically with missing a season?
I think that the worst thing for me is when I don't know what the injury is and how to get rid of it (the foot problem in 2001 and the navicular stress fracture). If I'm injured and know what course of action to take, I'm not as depressed because I can focus on the future and focus on where I'll be when I'm healthy. Navicular stress fractures are often misdiagnosed and can cause residual pain. In my case, the navicular stress fracture went away but I still had pain from inflammation.

What specifically did you learn from being injured?
Every time I'm injured I just think I need to be more proactive when I'm healthy about doing preventative things like massage, stretching, changing shoes, etc.

What advice would you give another elite runner who suffers a season-ending injury?
Just be patient. I'm not sure how I'd react if I couldn't run at all. Luckily with my injury I could still jog most days. But just focus on getting better and the future; dwelling on the past wont help.

When you returned to full-time training, did you alter the type of training you were doing?
No.

What was the result in your first major competition after returning from injury?
1st place at Stanford in the 10K after the foot problem in 2002. I ran 28:50 something and beat future NCAA XC champ Simon Bairu.

What advice would you give a high school or young college runner regarding injury prevention and/or rehabilitation?
Run on soft surfaces as much as possible and ice and be proactive on any minor aches you may have. Be patient with the injury and don't come back too soon, but cross train a lot.

Looking back, would you change any of your cross training?
No.

After being injured and coming back, did it change your sense of who you are/were as a runner? Did you have more patience or did you find yourself training on the edge again?
I generally trained pretty relaxed. The point is not to run as hard as you can each and every run. However, I did a lot of volume and did not change that when I came back.

Other thoughts on injury prevention or rehabilitation.
Don't be afraid to question the doctors and get a second opinion and start from scratch.

Tim Keller

University of Wisconsin
5K, 10K, XC

"Don't ignore the little pains. This is probably the hardest thing since trying to be competitive and listening to your body's little aches and pains don't necessarily coincide. The hard thing is finding the difference between training smart and healthy and training hard and injured."

Tim, briefly profiled
Birth Date and Place: July 16, 1981, West Chicago, Ill.
Began running: 13 years old; Began running competitively: 14 years old; Retired: 26 years old
Height/Running Weight: 5'9", 135 lbs.

University of Wisconsin, B.S., 2005 (Economics)
Arizona State University, M.S., 2009 (Taxation)
College coach: Jerry Schumacher
West Chicago High School, West Chicago, Ill. (2000)
High school coach: Paul McLeland

Current residence: Tempe, Arizona
Current occupation: Accountant

Personal records: 1500—3:47 (2004); 5K—13:47 (2004); 10K—29:09 (2004)

Notable accomplishments
High school—state meet runner-up in 1600 and 3200 in 2001…broke 9:00 for 3200 seven times in 2001…sixth in 2000 FootLocker championships…6th, 2000 FLCC Championships
Collegiate—two-time NCAA all-American…member of three national runner-up teams in XC

Favorite rehab/cross training workout
For cross training, my favorite thing to do was nothing. Let the body recover from the stress that had been put on it. In order not to feel lazy, things I may have chosen to do included ride a stationary bike, elliptical, or aqua jog (i.e., goof around in the pool with my teammates).

Worst running related injuries
Multiple femoral stress fractures

Approximate date of injuries, nature of them and was surgery required?
Had three stress fractures in a year and a half period between 2001 and 2003. Also, Achilles tendonitis, often; Planter Fasciitis, 2006; and IT band tightness, often. Missed 3 months for each stress fracture and weeks here and there for numerous other running & non-running related injuries.

What flaw led to the injuries? Or did you do something that caused them?
Not sure what caused these injuries since they are use related I will say that.

Rehabilitation program that you followed. How long before you resumed normal training?
Steady diet of rest, relaxation, and fun. Anything to keep your mind off the injury is the best possible course in my opinion. Your body needs to get the proper rest which includes both physical and mental when you are injured so there is no use dwelling on it.

What was the most difficult aspect of being injured? How did you deal psychologically with missing a season? Did you miss your best chance to make a U.S. Olympic or World Championship team because of the injury?
Just missing out on being a part of the team.

What advice would you give another elite runner who suffers a season-ending injury?
There really is not much you can do about injuries as they are part of any sport. What you need to do is figure out the best way to try and prevent them in the future because the current injury is here for the time being so enjoy your time off.

When you returned to training full-time, did you alter—either somewhat or drastically---the type of training you were doing?
Increase running slowly probably with an initial run of 5-10 minutes, abs, and core.

What was the result in your first major competition after returning from injury?
Actually after I got my injuries under control I had a fairly successful 2004. I don't specifically remember the first race back but I remember regaining fitness quickly after each injury.

What advice would you give a high school or young college runner regarding injury prevention or rehabilitation?
Don't ignore the little pains. This is probably the hardest thing since trying to be competitive and listening to your body's little aches and pains don't necessarily coincide. In order to be competitive you must push the envelope. The hard thing is finding the difference between training smart and healthy and training hard and injured.

After being injured and coming back, did it change your sense of who you are/were as a runner? Did you have more patience or did you find yourself training on the edge again?
No. I was always a stubborn person.

Bob Kennedy

Indiana University
1500, Mile, 3K,
5K, 10K, XC

"The most important thing when you're injured is getting healthy. Don't stress the things out of your control. Focus on things you can control, like going to therapy and cross training."

Bob, briefly profiled
Birth Date and Place: Aug. 18, 1970, Bloomington, Ind.
Began running: 13 years old; Began running competitively: 14 years old; Retired: 36 years old
Height/Running Weight: 6'0", 147 lbs.

Indiana University, B.S., 1992 (Finance)
College coach: Sam Bell
Westerville North High School, Westerville, Ohio (1988)
High school coaches: Irv Christiansen and Bob Cavin

Current residence: Indianapolis, Ind.
Current occupation: Managing Partner, The Running Company

Personal records: 1500—3:38.2; Mile—3:56.21; 2K—4:59.9; 3K—7:30.84; 2 Miles—8:11.59; 5K—12:58.21 (1996); 10K—27:37.45 (2004)

Notable accomplishments
College/Post-Collegiate—Two-time NCAA XC champ...won 1990 NCAA 1500 and 1991 NCAA indoor mile....multiple all-American ....12th in 5K in 1992 Olympics, 6th in 5K in 1996 Olympics...held U.S. 5K record from 1996-2009... won 1992 U.S. cross title five days after winning NCAA title, only second man to win both in same year...four-time U.S. 5K champ...

Worst running-related injuries
Plantar Fasciitis, bruised and swollen vertebrae, and irritated perennial nerve.

Approximate date of injuries, nature of them and was surgery required?
Plantar fasciitis was Feb 1997, vertebrae in May 2000, and nerve was June 2002.

What flaw led to the injuries? Or did you do something that caused them?
Pronation led to plantar fasciitis. The vertebrae was from being in an auto accident and I still don't know what caused the perennial nerve issue.

Rehabilitation program that you followed. How long before you resumed "normal" training?
With both of my first two injuries I rode the stationary bike twice a day for a total of 90 minutes. I didn't do anything during the nerve injury.

Given that running takes a fair amount of time and that cross training for that same time would probably drive you crazy, what did you do to keep busy?
When injured, cross training and therapy takes about three times longer than running. I had less time for other stuff.

What was the most difficult aspect of being injured? How did you deal psychologically with missing a season?
Not being able to prepare the way you should be preparing as the clock ticks away. Psychologically, I just tried to concern myself with things I could control (cross training, therapy, etc.)

What specifically did you learn from being injured?
Appreciate being healthy and make the most of it.

What advice would you give another elite runner who suffers a season-ending injury?
Get healthy and get ready for next season.

When you returned to full-time training, did you alter the type of training you were doing?
No.

What advice would you give a high school or young college runner regarding injury prevention and/or rehabilitation?
The most important thing when you're injured is getting healthy. Don't stress the things out of your control. Focus on things you can control, like going to therapy and cross training.

Daniel Lincoln
University of Arkansas
Steeplechase, 5K, 10K, XC

"Decide how long you are going to be in the sport and what your goals are. Then, if your goals are missed or cannot be met, pursue another career. But if there is a chance, don't be lazy, do rehab more intensely than training previously."

Daniel, briefly profiled
Birth Date and Place: Oct. 22, 1980, Ruston, La.
Began running: 13 years old; Began running competitively: 16 years old
Height/Running Weight: 6'3", 160 lbs.

University of Arkansas, B.A., 2002 (Biochemistry)
College coach: John McDowell
Arkansas School for Math and Science, Ark. (1998)
High school coaches: Rodney Rothoff

Current affiliation: Nike
Current residence: Portland, Ore.
Current occupation: physician

Personal records: 1500—3:37.50 (2006); Mile—3:57.86 (2004); 3K—7:48.79 (2005); Steeple—8:08.82—AR (2006); 2 Mile—8:13.70 (2006); 5K—13:32.27 (2004); 10K—28:20.20 (2003)

Notable accomplishments
College/Post-Collegiate— Twelve-time All-American…three-time NCAA steeplechase champion….NCAA 10K champ…1st in 2004 Trials steeple…11th in Olympic Games….two-time U.S. steeple champ…

Worst running-related injuries
A strained hamstring and a stress fracture.

Approximate date of injuries, nature of them and was surgery required?
September 1999 for the hamstring. It was an overuse injury and no surgery was required. The stress fracture was in the summer of 2002.

What flaw led to the injuries? Or did you do something that caused them?
Lack of training before the fall cross country season led to the hamstring. Running in old trainers caused the stress fracture.

Rehabilitation program that you followed. How long before you resumed "normal" training?
For both injuries I did pool running and biking everyday.

Given that running takes a fair amount of time and that cross training for that same time would probably drive you crazy, what did you do to keep busy?
Rehab!

What was the most difficult aspect of being injured? How did you deal psychologically with missing a season?
Watching teammates get better while I was missing out.

What specifically did you learn from being injured?
Don't come back off a break too hard and keep fresh shoes.

What advice would you give another elite runner who suffers a season-ending injury?
Decide how long you are going to be in the sport and what your goals are. Then, if your goals are missed or cannot be met, pursue another career. But if there is a chance, don't be lazy, do rehab more intensely than training previously.

When you returned to full-time training, did you alter the type of training you were doing?
No.

What was the result in your first major competition after returning from injury?
Dull legs and a lack of concentration.

What advice would you give a high school or young college runner regarding injury prevention and/or rehabilitation?
Listen to your coaches, don't overdo mileage, and again, keep fresh shoes.

Louie Luchini

Stanford University
5K, 10K, XC

"I also learned, once I was able to start running again, not to come back too quickly. Nothing is more frustrating than injuring yourself while coming back from an injury. Take your time in coming back."

Louie, briefly profiled
Birth Date and Place: May 24, 1981; Bar Harbor, Maine
Began running: 12 years old; Began running competitively: 12 years old
Height/Running Weight: 5'6", 128 lbs.

Stanford University, B.A., 2004 (Human Biology)
College coach: Vin Lannana
Ellsworth High School, Ellsworth, Maine (1999)
High school coaches: Andy Beardsley

Current residence: Ellsworth, Maine
Current occupation: Candidate for State Legislature
Current affiliation or club: unattached
Current Coach: Self-Coached

Personal records: 1500—3:45.39 (2003); 3K—7:56.70i (2003); 5K—13:25.19 (2004); 10K—28:26.61 (2008)

Notable high school, collegiate and post-collegiate accomplishments
High School –2nd at Footlocker Championships (1998).
College/Post-Collegiate – Eleven-time NCAA All-American...2nd place NCAA 5K (2003) Pac-10 5K and 10K champion (2003)...NCAA XC finishes: 12th, 5th, 6th (2001, 2002, 2003) ...member of two XC national championship teams (2002, 2003).

Favorite rehab/cross training workout
Anti-gravity treadmill—favorite because it is the most like running. I would take off some weight and run like normal. Usually do normal distance type of runs.

Pool Running—very monotonous and not my favorite activity, however the one I probably did the most while injured. Usually would do workouts in the pool. Sometimes shorter intervals, like 1 minute hard, 1 min easy, or would do longer repeats, like 3-5 min hard, to emulate 1000 or mile repeats on the track.

Elliptical—good for maintenance type runs. Would often do this for 45 min to 1 hour. Good at getting your heart rate up because it involves both arms and legs. Motion is similar to running as well.

Worst running-related injuries:
Achilles problems—had to have surgery—Haglund's deformity
Various other problems, like IT band problems, bad tendonitis in flexor hallicus.

Approximate date of injuries, nature of them and was surgery required?
2001—Flexor hallicus longus tendinitis—had a cortisone injection.

Achilles—started in 2003, but managed it through the Olympic trials in 2004. I tried to heal by taking lots of time off following, but to no avail. I had surgery on it in 2005. The surgery entailed removing the Achilles, shaving down the calcaneous, and reattaching Achilles. I think the Achilles was also scraped.

During recovery, had an inflamed CC joint in my foot requiring time off and eventually a cortisone injection.

What flaw led to the injuries? Or did you do something that caused them?
Haglund's deformity is what the doctors said created my Achilles problem. It is a ridge formed in the back of the calcaneous, and it frays the Achilles.

Rehabilitation program that you followed. How long before you resumed "normal" training?
Very slow rehab, because I was in a cast for 3 weeks, and then a boot for several months. Perhaps the most difficult part of recovery was regaining muscle. My entire left leg had substantially atrophied. It took a while just to walk somewhat normally after the boot came off, and months later before I could run again.

Most of the early rehab was PT with a goal of regaining muscle. After a month or so, I was in the pool on a daily basis trying to maintain some sort of cardiovascular fitness, unsuccessfully.

Given that running takes a fair amount of time and that cross training for that same time would probably drive you crazy, what did you do to keep busy?
For me, the best way to cross train is with other people. After my Achilles surgery, I would go to the pool every day with my coach, Frank Gagliano, who was rehabilitating a knee injury. That held me accountable and ensured that I would cross train. I knew I would get an earful if I didn't show.

Cross training is very difficult for me mentally, and I generally would burn out after a few weeks or so, and would often end up stopping completely for a while.

What was the most difficult aspect of being injured? How did you deal psychologically with missing a season?
For me, the most difficult part of being injured was that I didn't recover as quickly as I felt I should have.

Psychologically it is very difficult being injured.
I missed my best shot at a U.S. Olympic team in 2004 because of my Achilles injury. My training was really poor that year, but I was somehow still able to run 13:25.

What specifically did you learn from being injured?
One thing I learned after being injured was the importance of cross-training. I have difficulty in actually getting out there and cross training, and many times have pretty much skipped it, which makes coming back that much harder. Even if I wasn't able to get that much cardiovascular benefit, cross training helped me keep my weight under control.

I also learned, once I was able to start running again, is not to come back too quickly. Nothing is more frustrating than injuring yourself while coming back from an injury. Take your time in coming back.

What advice would you give another elite runner who suffers a season-ending injury?
Season-ending injuries are always the toughest to deal with. If I were in that situation, I'd probably take some time completely off, and give myself a longer recovery period afterward. Personally, I'd be unable to cross train vigorously if I knew my season were over.

When you returned to full-time training, did you alter the type of training you were doing?
I think the most important advice is just to pay attention to your body. Often, runners try to train through injury, and end up causing more problems.

What was the result in your first major competition after returning from injury?
It's hard to get the racing feeling back in the first competitions after injury. You have to be patient.

What advice would you give a high school or young college runner regarding injury prevention and/or rehabilitation?
My advice would be the same—listen to your body and be patient. Coaches often will try to ramp your training up too quickly after injury, so you have to be cautious. You shouldn't drastically ramp up training just because NCAAs are coming up in a month. You have to think long-term.

After being injured and coming back, did it change your sense of who you are/were as a runner? Did you have more patience or did you find yourself training on the edge again?
I was probably a little more patient, but no runner that I know takes injuries well, whether it's the first one or after several. It's very hard to deal with.

Most runners naturally want to train on the edge, and it's probably good. If you want to get the most out of yourself, you have to train really hard. Injuries are part of the sport. I probably got a little better at listening to my body.

Eric MacTaggart
University of Iowa
3k, 5k, 10k, XC

"If you are injured and the rehab and treatments you are doing are not helping, find new things to try. A lot of time can be wasted if you just try the same things over and over that just don't work! Be proactive and always be looking for different ways to get healthy."

Eric, briefly profiled
Birth Date and Place: Dec. 16, 1985, Glen Ellyn, Ill.
Began running: 7 years old; Began running competitively: 10 years old
Height/Running Weight: 6'0", 130 lbs.

University of Iowa, B.M., 2009 (Music)
College coach: Larry Wieczorek
Glenbard South High School, Glen Ellyn, Ill. (2004)
High school coaches: Andrew Preuss, Terry Artman

Current residence: Rexburg, Idaho
Current occupation: Music Teacher

Personal Records: 3K—8:08; 5K—14:04; 10K—28:50

Notable accomplishments
High School—3200 meter school record holder (8:55.4) (2004)
College/Post-Collegiate— All-American 10K (2006).

Favorite rehab/cross training workout
I only did cross training when I was injured or when I was coming off an injury. I always preferred pool running over biking, because pool running is not stationary and there is no impact on the legs (great if you have an injury that is irritated by impact).

When I was injured and doing cross training on the stationary bike or in the pool, I would try and follow the normal workout schedule that the rest of the team was doing (usually long runs on Sundays and workouts on Tuesdays and Fridays). Mostly I did intervals/fartleks on the the bike or in ther pool. I think that if you can work hard while cross training, you can still stay in decent shape and keep your overall fitness for when you get back into running.

Worst running-related injury
The one big injury I had in college that really set me back as a runner was my Achilles injury, which occurred in February 2007. I was not back up to normal mileage/training until March 2008. It was around that time that I started to have shin problems, which lasted another month or two.

I had some other small injuries, but I was able to recover from them pretty quickly and get back to normal training within a week or two.

Approximate date of injury, nature of it and was surgery required?
No surgeries were required. I had a cortisone type shot in my Achilles to try and help with that injury, but that probably made it worse rather than help it.

What flaw led to the injuries? Or did you do something that caused them?
As I look back at my injuries, most of them occurred during the winter months. Winters in the Midwest can be very challenging for runners, when your two options are running on the indoor track or running on ice outside (Iowa City does a terrible job of snow removal!).

The team used to change directions on the indoor track to try and work different muscle groups and prevent injury (30 minutes clockwise, 30 minutes counter-clockwise on the indoor track), but I think that it is still hard on your body to be running in 200 meter circles for more than an hour every day. As a result, I had lots of little aches and pains because of running a lot on the indoor track or running outside on slippery surfaces, which set me up to be susceptible to more serious injuries if I wasn't careful.

I think that I should have done more core strengthening exercises, especially during the winter months, to try and make my body stronger overall and ready for the rough surfaces I would be running on.

Rehabilitation program that you followed. How long before you resumed "normal" training?
I worked with our head athletic trainer on the rehabilitation program I would use to get back from a certain injury. Rehab was usually cross training (pool running or stationary biking) and a set of exercises to strengthen various muscle groups (using resistance bands, heel raises, etc).

I also did my fair share of taping, hot packs, and icing (ice cups and cold tubs). This was a rather typical program that didn't vary from what any other athlete would be doing to get back from injury.

The best form of rehabilitation I ever came across was going to see a massage therapist. The massage therapist would do deep tissue work, which really helped with the healing process and getting me back to running. I was out for basically an entire year with my Achilles injury, but once I started going to the massage therapist, I started noticing huge improvements. I think that if I had never gone to see him, my injury would have lasted even longer.

Another form of rehabilitation that really worked for me was the Graston technique, which the head trainer would do a few times a week with me while I was recovering from injury. I even had Graston done while I was healthy, just for prevention.

Given that running takes a fair amount of time and that cross training for that same time would probably drive you crazy, what did you do to keep busy?
Cross training was very difficult for me. I don't think time moves any slower than when you are on a stationary bike or swimming in the pool. I would try and not look at the clock very often and workouts usually went by faster than just "normal runs" where I was just pool jogging for an hour or something like that.

Outside of doing the cross training, I would do rehab exercises and ice close to everyday. I also had other treatments done in the training room, such as Hivamat and ultrasound. I would also go see the athletic trainer in the mornings to get Graston work done or get in some cross training. Overall, I ended up spent just as much time or more time at practice when I was injured as when I was healthy.

What was the most difficult aspect of being injured? How did you deal psychologically with missing a season?
The hardest part about being injured for me was the fact that even if I tried my best and did everything I could to get healthy, I could still fail. In academics and other parts of my life, I knew that if I worked hard I could succeed. With injuries, it is completely unknown and sometimes out of your power, which is extremely frustrating.

One of the hardest parts was telling people bad news whenever they asked about how my running was going. It was hard being the bearer of bad news, especially with my teammates and coach. After being injured for more than a few months, you wonder when or if you will ever be able to run again in college. It was always a stressful time when I was injured in college, worrying about when I would be able to run again.

What specifically did you learn from being injured?
You have an entirely new appreciation for running after being injured for a long time. Just the act of running is great after being out for several months. Those first few trail runs after being out for a long time that are a just a few minutes long can be exciting. I remember being envious of recreational joggers around campus while I was injured. Don't take anything for granted and be grateful for your health when you are healthy. Take advantage of being a healthy athlete!

What advice would you give another elite runner who suffers a season-ending injury?
Find any way you can to help out the team, even when you can't run. Try and stay positive and think of how you plan on getting healthy and prepare for future seasons. Attitude is pivotal when you are injured. It can be very depressing for you and anyone around you if you have a negative attitude.

When you returned to full-time training, did you alter the type of training you were doing?
I think the type of training was similar, but your attitude needs to be a little different. I think that it's easy to get discouraged if you aren't having the same success in workouts that you had before you were injured. You need to have patience, even after you slowly build up your training after an injury. I think it takes a long time to get back to where you were pre-injury, especially if you were injured for several months.

What was the result in your first major competition after returning from injury?
I've had a huge range of how I have run coming off injury. When I was injured for a good part of the season my junior year of high school, I was able to make a big comeback and place 5th in the state meet. I think I was able to do that because I worked hard on the bike and was able to get in a few running workouts near the end of the season to get back into the swing of things. I had a similar experience my sophomore year in college, when I had a little hamstring injury near the end of the season. I went into the NCAA outdoor track meet not knowing how I would do. I ended up running a great race and being All-American in the 10K. When I had more serious injuries (my Achilles injury), my first races did not go very well and were considered "building blocks" toward becoming totally healthy and fit. Again, it's all about patience and keeping a positive attitude when you are coming off injuries.

What advice would you give a high school or young college runner regarding injury prevention and/or rehabilitation?
Prevention is huge. You will most likely make gradual improvements throughout your running career and become a much better runner than if you are always getting set back by injuries. I think that I would have gone on to do some great things in college if I could have avoided my Achilles injury.

To me, prevention is making your body stronger overall. Doing things like push-ups, ab routines, and doing "rehab exercises" when you are healthy will help you stay injury-free. I think keeping a running log is important as well, to make sure you are not doing anything drastic in your training (you don't want to run 50 miles one week and 70 miles the next). You also want to always be listening to your body. If you feel really beat from a workout the previous day, take your recovery day a little easier. If you feel sharp pains anywhere, don't just "run through it" (if it's in a workout)... At least get it checked out to see if it's something you need to worry about.

I think that a lot of injuries are made worse by assuming it will be OK and running on an injury for a week before you start to treat it seriously. In general, if you can start treating an injury right away, it won't linger as long (from my experience).

Looking back, would you change any of your cross training?
I think I would have added in some cross training during the winter months, instead of only pounding out runs on the indoor track or out on the icy roads. I could have become more fit without worrying about running too much indoors or on icy surfaces.

After being injured and coming back, did it change your sense of who you are/were as a runner? Did you have more patience or did you find yourself training on the edge again?
I think injuries hurt my confidence as a runner. It takes awhile to get back to feeling like your body is strong and confident that you aren't going to re-injure this or that if you push a workout. It took me a long time after my Achilles injury to get back to feeling confident and into the competitive mindset of pushing myself to go all out in workouts and races.

Other thoughts on injury prevention or rehabilitation.
If you are injured and the rehab and treatments you are doing are not helping, find new things to try. Different things work for different people. A lot of time can be wasted if you just try the same things over and over that just don't work! Be proactive and always be looking for different ways to get healthy.

Paul McMullen

Eastern Michigan University
800, 1500, Mile

"Patience and a physical therapy regimen. Be committed to it till you strengthen the injured part."

Paul, briefly profiled
Birth Date and Place: Feb. 19, 1972; Cadillac, Mich.
Began running: 16 years old; Began running competitively: 16 years old; Retired: 33 years old
Height/Running Weight: 6'2", 170 lbs.

Eastern Michigan University, B.A., 1995 (Accounting)
College coach: Bob Parks
Cadillac High School, Cadillac, Mich. (1990)
High school coach: Tom Pierson

Current residence: Grand Haven, Mich.
Current occupation: Athlete, Speaker, Painter

Personal records: 800—1:45.71 (2001); 1500—3:33.89 (2001); Mile—3:54.94 (2001)

Notable accomplishments
High School—State champ at 1600.
College/Post-Collegiate—Eight-time All-American...national champ 4x8 (1993) ...runner-up DMR (1995)...runner-up 1500 (1995)...national outdoor champ (1995)...10th at Worlds (1995)...Olympic Trial Champ (1996)...19th at Olympic Games (1996) ...U.S. indoor mile Champ (1998)...3rd outdoors (1998)...6th at Goodwill Games(1998)...3rd in U.S. 1500 (2001)...10th at World Championships (2001).

Worst running-related injuries
Collapsed arch, foot, and hip.

Approximate date of injuries, nature of them and was surgery required?
Collapsed arch October 1990. I had a foot injury in 1997 that did result in a surgery. Hip in December 2002.

What flaw led to the injuries? Or did you do something that caused them?
The collapsed arch was a weight issue. The foot was a trauma injury and the hip was the result of bringing speed work out too fast.

Rehabilitation program that you followed. How long before you resumed "normal" training?
Cycling for all three injuries.

Given that running takes a fair amount of time and that cross training for that same time would probably drive you crazy, what did you do to keep busy?
I went to work immediately to supplement income. I washed dishes in '97. I worked a job as an accountant in '99 and as a salesman in 2000. In 2002 I painted houses.

What was the most difficult aspect of being injured? How did you deal psychologically with missing a season?
It was difficult to re-trust the injured part of the body. I felt like I was the only one injured.

What specifically did you learn from being injured?
Moderation of training, self control, and consistent effort over time.

What advice would you give another elite runner who suffers a season-ending injury?
Go to work, move on until healed, cross train.

When you returned to full-time training, did you alter the type of training you were doing?
Yes, moderation, began on a pace tailored to me. I did not force time of season as it related to workouts. I built from the ground up.

What was the result in your first major competition after returning from injury?
In '98 I ran 1:50, 4:06, and 8:09. In 2001 I ran 3:50, 3:48, 3:44, 3:40, and 3:37 racing pretty much every other weekend.

What advice would you give a high school or young college runner regarding injury prevention and/or rehabilitation?
Patience and a physical therapy regimen. Be committed to it till you strengthen the injured part.

Craig Miller
University of Wisconsin
1500, Mile, 3K, 5K

On being injured: *"I learned how much I like running and how fun and relieving it is to run pain-free. It showed me that I can stay in decent shape through cross training, and that helped my confidence and stress levels when I got less severe injuries and had to take 10-14 days off."*

Craig, briefly profiled
Birth Date and Place: Aug. 3, 1987; Lancaster, Pa.
Began running: 13 years old; Began running competitively: 15 years old
Height/Running Weight: 6'1", 155 lbs.

University of Wisconsin, B.S., 2010 (geographic information systems)
College coach: Mick Byrne
Manheim Township High School, Lancaster, Pa. (2006)
High school coaches: Terry Lee

Current residence: Madison, Wis.
Current occupation: Professional runner
Current affiliation or club:
Current Coach: Mick Byrne

Personal Records: 1500—3:37.81 (2009); Mile—3:58.98 (2010) 3K—7:49.94 (2010); 5K—13:50.40 (2010)

Notable accomplishments
High School—15th at Footlocker Nationals (2004)…3rd at nationals in mile (2004)…2nd at nationals in mile (2005).
College/Post-Collegiate—Seven-time All-American…2nd, NCAA indoor 1500 (2009).

Favorite rehab/cross training workout
My favorite rehab/cross training was the elliptical. I did it 5-6 days a week for around an hour. Some days I did it at a steady pace, and other days I would do intervals on it with a warm up and cool down like 2 minutes fast two minutes slow x20, or a fartlek type of workout. This was in high school, so now if I had to cross train I probably would go longer or twice a day.

Worst running-related injury
Fractured fibula.

Approximate date of injury, nature of it and was surgery required?
April-June 2006, fractured fibula. No surgery healed on its own. I missed 3-4 months.

What flaw led to the injury? Or did you do something that caused it?
The injury started as a bone bruise and I did not take the injury seriously and continued to run on it until it turned into a fracture. The cause was overuse, arrogance, and running in the same shoes for about seven months. I was running the most mileage and the fastest pace I ever had between January and March, all on pavement, which almost everybody advises against.

Rehabilitation program that you followed. How long before you resumed "normal" training?
I took about 6 weeks completely off. Then started biking, and then did the elliptical until I could run again pain-free. Total time was four months, and I was extra cautious because I did not listen to the doctor the first time.

Given that running takes a fair amount of time and that cross training for that same time would probably drive you crazy, what did you do to keep busy?
At first doing a stationary workout seemed to take forever and is very boring, but like anything else, the more you do it the easier it becomes. Doing specific workouts helped to take my mind off the total time and focus more on completing the workout. Also, music or TV helps to draw your attention away from the task.

What was the most difficult aspect of being injured? How did you deal psychologically with missing a season?
The most difficult aspect is not being able to do anything, and the feeling that everybody else it getting faster and you are getting slower. As long as I could cross train, I was fine psychologically because I knew I was getting just as good a workout on the elliptical or bike as when I was running. Cross training can keep runners in really good shape if they want it to. The problem is a lot of runners mentally can't stand sitting on a stationary bike for an hour or longer to get the benefits of cross training. The injury ended my senior year track season, and I did not get to run the state and national meets. At first I was really upset and kept trying to come back too early which prolonged the recovery of the injury, but by May I realized the season was over. At that point I was fine with it because high school was just the beginning and there would be plenty of running in college.

What specifically did you learn from being injured?
I learn how much I like running and how fun and relieving it is to run pain free. Also, it showed me that I can stay in decent shape through cross training, and that helped my confidence and stress levels in college when I got some less severe injuries and had to take 10-14 days off. It gave me confidence in cross training and I could stay in good shape and come back from the minor injury without really missing any training. I also learned a lot about injury prevention. Ice and Advil go a long way in preventing injuries,

and allowing you to keep running when you thought you would not be able to. Those two things allowed me to run through a lot of tendonitis in a variety of areas, such as shins, ankles, Achilles, and knees.

What advice would you give a high school or young college runner regarding injury prevention and/or rehabilitation?
If it hurts too much to run then don't run. Ice can cure a lot of minor stuff that will turn into a major problem if untreated.

Other thoughts on injury prevention or rehabilitation.
It's hard to know when you have some pain if you can run through it or if the injury is going to get worse and become a major problem. You need some knowledge about the human body, running injuries, and prevention so you know what hurts, why, and some treatments without visiting a doctor. Runners should know certain injuries like Achilles problems are slow to heal and can ruin a career, but shin splints may hurt very much but are not serious.

Everybody is different, and has a different experience with certain injuries so, if your teammate tells you "it's just tendonitis," and he ran through it, you might not be able to. You have to listen to your body and know how it reacts to injuries and injury treatment.

Ed Moran
College of William & Mary
5K, 10K, Marathon, XC, Roads

Ed, briefly profiled
Date and Place of Birth: May 27, 1981, Staten Island, N.Y.
Began running: 16 years old; Began running competitively: 16 years old
Height: 5'10", Running Weight: 128 lbs.

The College of William & Mary, B.B.A., 2003 (Finance, government)
The College of William & Mary, M.P.P. (2005)
The College of William & Mary, MBA (2011)
College coach: Alex Gibby
Notre Dame High School, Lawrenceville, N.J. (1999)
High school coaches: Joe Wroboleski, Joe McLaughlin, Paul Vandergrift

Current occupation: student, runner
Current residence: Williamsburg, Va.
Current affiliation or club: Nike
Current coach: Alex Gibby

Personal records: 5K—13:20.35 (2007); 10K—27:43.13 (2007)

Notable accomplishments
Collegiate/post-collegiate—Four-time All-American, twice in XC and track...2007 5K Pan American gold medalist (Pan American Record)....4th, 10K, 2008 Olympic Trials...2nd, 10K, U.S. championships (2010)...two-time world XC team member...

What is your favorite cross training or rehabilitation workout?
I rely mostly on biking for cross training and rehabilitation work. Over the years I've found that biking help maintain the most fitness, especially during an extended period of time off. When cross training on the bike I try to mimic the workouts I would be doing running, but increase the duration.

For example if I am completely off my feet in a given week I will do one threshold effort (20 minute warm-up, 40-60 threshold effort, so 80-85 perceived effort level, 20 minute cool down), one aerobic capacity effort (20 min warm-up, usually a mix of either 3 on/2off x 8-10 or 5 minutes on/3 off X 5-7 with the on segments at 90-95% effort, 20 minute cool down), one long ride 2:30-3 hours, and 4 days of "maintenance rides." The maintenance rides are usually 60-90 minutes.

Worst running related injuries you have sustained
This is a toss- up among three. First, in 2000-2001 I suffered from a bad case of Plantar Fasciitis. The injury presented itself immediately after the NCAA cross country championships in 2000 and gradually got worse until February/March 2001, when I could no longer run on it. Even after months of rehab, cortisone shots, and walking around in a boot I could not shake the injury. Several times I tried to re-initiate training, but each time I was met by debilitating pain. Finally in August 2001, I decided to have surgery on the foot.

The second injury in the running for the worst injury occurred in 2003-2004. Toward the end of cross country in 2003 I began suffering from foot pain. Quickly the pain increased until I realized I probably had a stress fracture. Unfortunately, by this time it was the week of NCAA regionals, so there was no time to take off and recover. Just before mile 6, at the NCAA Southwest Regional, my third metatarsal completely broke and I hobbled to the finish line. This is only half the story. After 6 weeks off, I was able to return to running. Not 2 weeks back to running, I started to suffer from thigh pain and quickly I found out I was suffering from a femoral stress fracture. To this day my coach and I still joke that it probably was the fastest onset of a stress fracture ever documented.

The last injury again was a series of injuries that occurred in 2005-2006. In late 2005 I suffered from a sacral stress fracture on the right side. After 10-12 weeks off, I returned to running only to suffer from another sacral stress fracture on the left side.

Length of time missed
Plantar: about 10 months
Broken foot, femoral stress fracture combo: about 7 months (I took off an extended amount of time with this injury because I thought I was out of eligibility and "retired". I did not found out until the summer of 2004 that I would be granted a 6th year of eligibility because of injuries.)
Double sacral stress fractures: 7 months.

What flaw led to the injuries? Or did you do something that caused them?
After the sacral stress fractures my fracture/fracture total (including high school) reached 6, so I decided to get my bone density tested. The test determined that I suffered from osteopenia (the early stages of osteoporosis.

General rehab program that you followed
As I mentioned above, I tried to mimic what I would have been doing on my feet on the bike.

Given running takes a fair amount of time and that cross training for that same time would probably drive you crazy what did you do to keep busy?
Cross training really kept me busy in that I knew I had to spend more time on the bike to gain the same benefits as running. For example, my long bikes got up to 3-4 hours, compared to my customary 2 hour long run. Because I spent more time cross training than I would have running I always felt busy.

What was the most difficult aspect of being injured? How did you deal psychologically with missing a season? Did you miss a chance to make a U.S. Olympic or World Championship team because of the injury?
The hardest part of being injured is watching others compete. As a competitive individual I yearn for competitive opportunities and quickly miss the "thrill of competition."

What specifically did you learn from being injured?
Patience. I learned more is not always better, and that to be successful at the highest level you need to be in-tune with your body. I've learned to listen to the signals my body is trying to relay.

What advice would you give another elite runner who suffers a season-ending injury?
Stay calm and remember it is not the end of the world. Don't let an injury consume and demotivate you. Rather look at it as an opportunity to grow both mentally and physically. Spend the time finding alternative forms of training you enjoy, so when you return to running you can incorporate it into your routine.

When you returned to training full time did you alter the type of training you were doing?
Again when I first returned to running after the second sacral stress fracture, I learned to listen to the cues my body was giving me. I learned not to push through every ache and pain, and learned that long-term consistency was more important than running every day in the short term. Related to listening to my body more, I also started to take one day off a week.

What was the result in your first major competition after returning from injury?
After 6 weeks of running, I finished 6th in the 5K at the U.S. championships.

What advice would you give a high school or young college runner regarding injury prevention or rehabilitation?
Long-term consistency is the key to success. Don't let short-term goals and volatile emotions govern your training and lead you to poor decision-making. In distance running, there are no short-cuts or quick fixes; success comes with long-term focus and consistent hard work.

After being injured and coming back, did it change your sense of who you are/were as a runner? Did you have more patience or did you find yourself training on the edge again?
It definitely changed my sense of who I was as a runner. I quickly realized I wasn't a "work horse" but rather was more like a "thoroughbred" that needed to approach training more cautiously. Though I did have more patience, I wouldn't go as far to say I took a step from the edge. Instead I re-evaluated the location of my personal "edge," and constructed my training plan to approach it without crossing over.

John Mortimer
University of Michigan
Steeplechase, XC

"Missing big races for my college team killed me...but also made me rush coming back too soon...most of all, after a few months, I just wanted to go for a four mile pain-free run."

John, briefly profiled
Birth Date and Place: March 18, 1976, Lawsdale, Pa.
Began running: 13 years old; Began running competitively: 14 years old
Height/Running Weight: 6'0", 152 lbs.

University of Michigan, B.A., 1999 (Architecture)
College coach: Ron Warhurst
Londonderry High School, Londonderry, N.H. (1995)
High school coach: Larry Martin

Personal records: Steeplechase—8:24.64 (2004)

Notable accomplishments
High School—Twelve-time state champion...three-time national champion...Footlocker runner up.
College/Post-Collegiate—Seven-time All-American...six-time Big Ten champion...two-time national team member.

Worst running-related injuries
Torn meniscus (right knee), which led to three surgeries and three rehabs...finally three months of anti-inflamatories which resulted in a kidney disorder, "membernous neptropathy".

Approximate date of injuries, nature of them and was surgery required?
Spring 1998, I turned my ankle running on the sidewalk, buckled my knee and tore my meniscus.

What flaw led to the injuries? Or did you do something that caused them?
The knee was just bad luck while running on the sidewalk and the three months of anti-inflamatories caused the kidney disorder by scarring the inner lining of the kidney.

Rehabilitation program that you followed. How long before you resumed "normal" training?
Cross training in the knee meant running in the pool and using the elliptical two times a day for two hours. I did rehab two times a day with icing, stretching, etc. I started running after six months off.

Given that running takes a fair amount of time and that cross training for that same time would probably drive you crazy, what did you do to keep busy?
I broke cross training up into two one-hour sessions (TV, music). The harder I cross trained the less boring it became… I went balls out everyday in the pool!

What was the most difficult aspect of being injured? How did you deal psychologically with missing a season?
Missing big races for my college team killed me…but also made me rush coming back too soon…most of all, after a few months, I just wanted to go for a four mile pain-free run.

What specifically did you learn from being injured?
Do not rush coming back…Do not medicate to get better faster.

What advice would you give another elite runner who suffers a season-ending injury?
I would tell them exactly what I learned: Do not rush coming back…Do not medicate to get better faster.

When you returned to full-time training, did you alter the type of training you were doing?
I started running smarter, If I felt any pain I would take a day off to save a week or two of injury.

What advice would you give a high school or young college runner regarding injury prevention and/or rehabilitation?
Same as the advice I'd give an elite athlete.

Billy Nelson

University of Colorado
Steeplechase, 5K, XC

Billy, briefly profiled
Birth Date and Place: Sept. 11, 1984, Bakersfield, Cal.
Began running: 13 years old; Began running competitively: 14 years old
Height/Running Weight: 5'5", 125 lbs.

University of Colorado, B.A., 2008 (Ethnic Studies)
College coach: Mark Wetmore
Taft Union High School, Taft, Cal. (2002)
High school coach: David Dennis

Current residence: Boulder, Colo.
Current occupation: Professional Runner and Assistant XC/Track Coach, University of Colorado
Current affiliation or club: Nike

Personal Records: 1500—3:47; 3K—8:00; Steeplechase—8:21.47 (2008); 5K—13:46

Notable accomplishments
High School—XC state champion…Top 10 Footlocker Nationals…Junior World Team.
College/Post-Collegiate – All-American… three-Time Big 12 champion…NCAA steeple runner-up…XC National team champs…Junior World Team Member…two-time junior national champion.

Favorite rehab/cross training workout
My favorite would have to be the Swim-X machine. I would warm up an easy 15 min of aqua jogging against a mild current, then I would do 3 by 20min against a stronger current with 5 min of recovery jog in between each set, then I would cool down an easy 15 min.

Worst running-related injury
At one time I had three stress reactions in three different metatarsals and a partially torn peroneal tendon.

Approximate date of injury, nature of it and was surgery required?
This particular injury took place in March 2006 right after the NCAA indoor championships. No surgery was required.

What flaw led to the injury? Or did you do something that caused it?
I believe my body wasn't rested enough at certain points, but also in some instances I pushed myself too hard too quickly after a long break.

Rehabilitation program that you followed. How long did before you resumed "normal" training?
Usually cross training lasted 4-6 weeks total including time off.

Given that running takes a fair amount of time and that cross training for that same time would probably drive you crazy, what did you do to keep busy?
The payoff is way more than the craziness that comes with cross training. Just try and stay focused on the task given and, also, teammates would sit and talk or accompany me during my sessions, without hindering workouts, of course.

What was the most difficult aspect of being injured? How did you deal psychologically with missing a season?
The most difficult thing is the lack of competition and frustration knowing the impact that you can make in the sport. Keeping a strong mental state is very important. Family, friends, and coaches helped keep me positive. I only missed out on collegiate meets.

What specifically did you learn from being injured?
To take care of your body on and off the track. Coach Wetmore always says, "Fuel a Ferrari and not a Yugo." He's basically saying that you need to replenish your body with the correct nutrients.

What advice would you give another elite runner who suffers a season-ending injury?
Honestly, I would just be comforting and positive. You can learn from injuries and also use that knowledge to make you a better athlete. Also, in most cases your body is telling you something and it is better to listen. An injury could just mean that you body has nothing left to give. You always come back stronger so stay confident and prepare yourself the best way you can.

When you returned to full-time training, did you alter the type of training you were doing?
Initially you alter a bit, but after you are back in it full swing you tend to do what works to get you back to the top of your game. I usually alter things outside of the hard sessions, such as recovery runs and rest time.

What was the result in your first major competition after returning from injury?
After my injury in 2006, I came back for XC and our team won the NCAA championships and I was a scoring runner. Also, 2007 track season I won my first outdoor Big 12 title and placed 4th at the NCCA outdoor meet.

What advice would you give a high school or young college runner regarding injury prevention and/or rehabilitation?
I would say again to just stay positive during your rehabilitation because stressing out causes stress on the body. To prevent injury listen to your body and take care of the little things before they get bigger.

After being injured and coming back, did it change your sense of who you are/were as a runner? Did you have more patience or did you find yourself training on the edge again?
I felt I still had the same drive to train hard, but I was also aware that I am not Superman. If I push it too hard I will lose the fight with my body. Awareness grew out of my injuries.

Other thoughts on injury prevention or rehabilitation.
Just that people need to educate themselves about injuries, prevention and rehabilitation. It happens so often on all levels of competition and in all sports, that knowledge is so important. Also, one individual's training programs and workouts do not work for everyone. Certain people's strengths are other people's weaknesses so make sure that you are doing what is right for you. Just because someone else can do a drill or run a certain amount of mileage doesn't mean that you need to or have to just to be as good as they are.

Nathan Nutter

Stanford University
5K, 10K, XC

"The most difficult aspect was going down to practice every day and meeting with the team knowing they were going running together and I was going in the pool by myself. That was a bummer and frustrating."

Nathan, briefly profiled
Birth Date and Place: Feb. 13, 1976; Peoria, Ill.
Began running: Since I could walk; Began running competitively: 13 years old; Retired: 25 years old
Height/Running Weight: 5'9", 130 lbs.

Stanford University, B.A., 1999 (Engineering)
College coach: Vin Lananna
Tempe Corona Del Sol, Ariz. (1994)
High school coaches: Sabrina Robinson and Pat Kammerer

Current residence: Scottsdale, Ariz.
Current occupation: Civil Engineer

Personal Records: 1500—3:48 (2000), 5K—13:50 (2000); 10K—28:32 (1998)

Notable accomplishments
High School—State XC champ (1993)…state 1600 and 3200 champ (1994)…#2 U.S. prep 3200m.
College/Post-Collegiate—Six-time All-American…NCAA 10K Champ (1999)…3rd NCAA 10k (1998)…23rd at Olympic Trials 10K (2000)…14th in XC senior nationals 12K (1997)…8th at NCAA XC (1997).

Favorite rehab/cross training workout
Pool running workout (without belt): 15 min warmup, then 5-4-3-2-1-1-2-3-4-5-5-4-3-2-1 mins hard with 1 min rest between each one. 10-15 min warmdown. Caution: Do not inhale water and drown.

Worst running-related injuries:
Two stress fractures, one in the pelvis and one in the femur.

Approximate date of injuries, nature of them and was surgery required?
The first stress fracture was January 1998 and the second in January 2000. No surgery needed.

What flaw led to the injuries? Or did you do something that caused them?
Over mileage, lower than average bone density. I might have been able to hold them off with sufficient strength training, but was unaware of my bones needing extra "help."

Rehabilitation program that you followed. How long did the rehab take before you resumed "normal" training? Pool running, pool running, pool running, pool running. Here's the rundown of week by week improvements for the three months off.
Week 1 – Found out about stress fracture, don't do anything.
Week 2 – Do nothing.
Week 3-10 – Pool workouts every other day (30-60 mins of hard stuff). Long pool run once a week (90-120 mins). Twice a day five times a week. Pool only though!!!
Week 11-12 – Start 5 minutes on elliptical machine. Day off elliptical, then 10 minutes, day off, etc. Build up. Meanwhile, hard pool workouts.
Week 13 – 5 minutes running on grass. Slow build up over next six weeks until first workout on land. Continue pool running and workouts in pool until first land workout.

Given that running takes a fair amount of time and that cross training for that same time would probably drive you crazy, what did you do to keep busy?
I was actually more busy with cross training than regular running! This makes injuries even worse. There was less time for school work...yes, I did study! Two pool runs per day, plus time in the weight room, training room and meeting with the team everyday took up a lot of time.

What was the most difficult aspect of being injured? How did you deal psychologically with missing a season?
The most difficult aspect was going down to practice every day and meeting with the team knowing they were going running together and I was going in the pool by myself. That was a bummer and frustrating. Pool workouts were pretty frustrating too and harder than most land workouts. Another frustration was being in equal or better shape than my teammates prior to the injury, then watching my teammate, Brad Hauser, win the NCAA 5K indoors. Lots of 'what ifs' and 'why me's' came into my mind that I had to deal with.

What specifically did you learn from being injured?
Injuries suck...but they can make you stronger if you stay positive and do what you need to do to take care of yourself. I learned that you can stay in great shape with cross training if you get injured. Within two months of fully coming out of the pool, I set PR's in the 1500, 5K and 10K. I worked HARD in the pool, and the results showed it.

What advice would you give another elite runner who suffers a season-ending injury?
Train your ass off with cross training while staying mentally positive. Get in some quality strength work in the weight room. It will help get you in shape more quickly when you start running again. Also, if you know what caused the problem, change that aspect of

your training. Be proactive with your training approach to avoid the same injury. Be creative and find a regimen that works for you. My change was from high mileage to medium mileage and lots of work in the pool. I believe in the pool!

When you returned to full-time training, did you alter the type of training you were doing?
Yes, more pool and less mileage. I was careful of the surface I was running on, too. I also incorporated some plyometrics for better stability and strength.

What was the result in your first major competition after returning from injury?
First injury, PR in the 5K (14:14) at a dual meet in Fresno. Later that season I shattered my 5K and 10K PR's. After the second injury I ran PR's in my first two races at 5K and 1500.

What advice would you give a high school or young college runner regarding injury prevention and/or rehabilitation?
If you know you're prone to a certain type of injury, regard it and do extra work to prevent the injury. Not only will this increase your chances of a healthy season, you will gain patience, and will benefit from that extra work. Spend time icing, stretching, and massaging your muscles. If you get injured and are rehabbing, stay positive. Your mind is your worst enemy during those times.

Also, if you do get injured and aren't sure the doctor knows what's going on, get a second opinion. My freshman year I developed an IT band injury right after qualifying for the junior world team in cross country. The doctor should have sent me to a masseuse for deep tissue work. Instead, I got acupuncture, cortisone shots, ultrasound, ice and stem work, and five months of frustration. I finally went to a masseuse and was back running in two weeks. By then the world championships had come and gone. This is one of the only regrets I have in my running career...listening to an incompetent doctor. Get a confident and correct diagnosis.

Looking back, would you change any of your cross training?
I believed in my cross training routine and would do it again in a heartbeat. You can work your body harder in the pool because you don't have to worry about your structural system breaking down...there's no impact. One thing I did enjoy and always sought out was someone to do workouts with me. If you can cross train with someone in the same boat as you, do it.

After being injured and coming back, did it change your sense of who you are/were as a runner? Did you have more patience or did you find yourself training on the edge again?
If you aren't going to train on the edge, you shouldn't be competing. However, it does require that you train intelligently! I don't think being injured changed me as a person, but it did change my workout routines.

Other thoughts on injury prevention or rehabilitation
Words of advice: If you're injured and doing cross training, don't get injured again by cross training. Gabe Jennings did this. He got a stress fracture and was cooped up in the

pool. He worked so hard in the pool that he developed IT-band syndrome and was out for even longer.

Use the injury as motivation to kick everyone else's ass when you're cross training. I always shocked my teammates by my ability to "get" in shape so soon after the injury. The truth of the matter is that the three months of pool running increased my cardiovascular strength, which made land training easier. I didn't start workouts huffing and puffing, because I had been killing myself in the pool. When I returned to running all I needed to figure out was how to put one foot in front of the other.

I was generally in "better" shape then everyone else in terms of cardiovascular fitness, but my running muscles were what deteriorated. Luckily, muscles build up quickly. It was only six weeks before I could keep up with everyone on the team. I remember one workout seven weeks after my first steps out of the pool. It included a 9:15 2-mile, 4:24 mile, and some 200's. I shocked everyone, including myself, completing the entire workout. That was when I realized that hard cross training work actually made me stronger mentally and physically.

Don't slack on sleep and nutrition. A quick recovery is a function of this. If you treat your body well, chances are you'll feel better, heal more quickly and be in a better state of mind.

Remember the frustrating times (you'll have them if you're injured). They make future successes sweeter. When I had a mere three months of land training to get ready for NCAA's in '98, no one thought I'd be able to run 28:32 and place 3rd. Knowing that I had been in the pool a dozen weeks earlier made that stand on the medal podium all the sweeter.

Don't run through pain. Assess the situation and be wise about it. And stay positive!

Brian Olinger
Ohio State University
Steeple, 5K, 10K

"...especially at our level, we tend to ignore things for as long as possible so we can keep grinding it out. ...Injuries can be extremely complex and when we do something as repetitive as running every day, the smallest change in gate/biomechanics, etc., if ignored, can manifest into a real problem."

Brian, briefly profiled
Birth Date and Place: June 2, 1983; Coshocton, Ohio
Began running: 12 years old; Began running competitively: 12 years old
Height/Running Weight: 5'8", 125 lbs.

Ohio State University, B.S., 2006 (Human Development and Family Science)
College coach: Robert Gary
Ridgewood High School, West Lafayette, Ind. (2001)
High school coaches: Darrell Ball, Rick Raach, and Chuck McMasters

Current residence: Westerville, Ohio
Current occupation: Professional Athlete and Volunteer Coach at Ohio State
Current affiliation or club: Reebok
Current coach: Robert Gary

Personal records: 1500—3:42.22 (2009); Mile—4:00.19 (2008); 3K—7:51.31i (2009);
Steeple—8:19.29 (2007); 5K—13:31.21 (2008); 10K—28:45.69 (2006)

Notable accomplishments
High School—State XC champion (2000)... state 3200 champion (2001).
College/Post-Collegiate—First-team all-Big Ten cross country (2004)...Big Ten outdoor 5K champion (2004)...Big Ten outdoor 10K champion (2006)...five-time NCAA All-American...4th place in steeple at U.S. nationals (2005)...Olympic Trials finalist in steeplechase (2008).

Favorite rehab/cross training workout
I have been fairly fortunate to avoid major injuries that required an extensive cross training plan. However there have been a couple instances that involved a few weeks in the pool

or on the stationary bike. I really don't have a "favorite" cross training workout but the one that I have performed most often consists of:

30 minute freestyle swim in lap pool (floaty between knees, just using arms), followed by some duration (usually 30 minutes) of pool running with surges. The pool running 30 minutes is broken down into segments of 1:00 as hard as you can go and 1:00 recovery. I usually just cool down for 5-10 minutes of pool running. It should be noted, I also use one of those pool running waist belts made of foam.

Worst running-related injuries
Probably a toss-up between a stress fracture in my sacroiliac joint in low back or an extensive one I am treating presently which stems from twisted disc at C2 in my neck. This has caused a number of nerve related problems that have altered my biomechanics to the point it has been masked by hamstring strains and chronic low back tightness.

Approximate date of injuries, nature of them and was surgery required?
Stress fracture in low back – Winter 2004
C2 Disc problem – Severe onset was February 2009. Actually only missed 2 weeks of running with low back stress fracture. I wore a back brace that conformed to my spine for 6 weeks, however, while walking, sleeping, sitting, etc.

The disc problem hasn't forced me to take time off other than a couple days here and there for some hamstring strains. Instead, though it sent me on a 'wild goose chase' for the better part of 14 months looking for the true cause of my problems.

What flaw led to the injuries? Or did you do something that caused them?
I noticed a weird knot on the right side of my neck at the base of my head back in 2007 but never did anything about it since it didn't seem to be causing any problems. I really have no idea what caused the problem to surface.

Rehabilitation program that you followed. How long before you resumed "normal" training?
Stress fracture in low back required two weeks of pool running regimen. After that I took two weeks to build back up to my normal training load. There wasn't any real 'rehab' that took place during winter-spring 04'. However, coach and I put together a much more structured core routine beginning the following summer that I have performed on a regular basis since the injury.
Disc problem – again, I haven't really missed much training at all….just kept plugging away in a very frustrated manner day in and day out. Since we discovered the mal-positioned disc was triggering problems throughout my kinetic chain, I have been receiving chiropractic treatments/acupuncture/deep tissue massage at least twice a week for the past 10 weeks.

Given that running takes a fair amount of time and that cross training for that same time would probably drive you crazy, what did you do to keep busy?
Anytime I was on a stationary bike I would try to watch TV or at the very least listen to headphones while I worked out. More often than not, though, I was in the pool which obviously eliminates the chances of both, so I would just try to avoid looking at my watch as long as possible and force myself to get lost in the workout.

What was the most difficult aspect of being injured? How did you deal psychologically with missing a season?
In my case, the most difficult aspect was not knowing for sure what the problem was. I'd beat myself up mentally trying to figure things out. Many times I would say I wish I just had a broken leg, because then I would at least know what the problem was and how to specifically fix it.

What specifically did you learn from being injured?
I have learned that, especially at our level, we tend to ignore things for as long as possible so we can keep grinding it out. I also learned that sometimes injuries can be extremely complex and when we do something as repetitive as running every day, the smallest change in gate/biomechanics, etc., if ignored, can manifest into a real problem. I think it's important to 'treat locally, but also think globally' when it comes to complex injuries.

What advice would you give another elite runner who suffers a season-ending injury?
Take a deep breath and gather yourself. You've probably got this far because you're tough and gritty and you'll persevere through it. Make sure you take the proper amount of time off and allow your buildup to progress as slow as you need it to. It seems the older you get, the faster your fitness returns. Listen to your body! Chances are if you think something is 'off', then it probably is.

When you returned to full-time training, did you alter the type of training you were doing?
Usually my return to running was reduced somewhat but never drastically. I never had an injury that required me to start back up running drastically reduced for 5 minutes a day, etc.

This past year, though, I have added 10 minutes of warm-up drills to my training regimen. I usually train at 8:30 a.m. and have now realized the importance of a proper warm-up even before an easy training run. I never just 'head out the door' anymore for a run.

What was the result in your first major competition after returning from injury?
2004 – Mt. SAC 5K – ran a PR of 13:56.

What advice would you give a high school or young college runner regarding injury prevention and/or rehabilitation?
Again, it's a cliché, but listen to your body and take recovery very seriously. Don't be afraid to take a couple days off if need be to try and curb a nagging problem before it develops into a serious one. Eat right! Sleep right! Dress right!

After being injured and coming back, did it change your sense of who you are/were as a runner? Did you have more patience or did you find yourself training on the edge again?
Patience is the perfect word. I used to be insanely meticulous and 'perfectionistic' with my training. I think at this level, we're always training on the edge to a degree. You have to. But, I have learned to allow the training to take effect; allow adaptation to take place!

Stephen Pifer

University of Colorado
1500, 3K, 5K, XC

"BE PATIENT. It seems like the worst thing that could possibly happen, but 90% of injuries happen from overtraining. You should use this time to reflect upon what you were feeling leading up to this injury and what you can do to prevent in or any other type of injury in the future."

Stephen, briefly profiled
Birth Date and Place: Dec. 7, 1984; Maryville, Ill.
Began running: 13 years old; Began running competitively: 15 years old
Height/Running Weight: 6'2", 155 lbs.

University of Colorado, B.A., 2008 (Geography)
College coach: Mark Wetmore
Edwardsville High School, Edwardsville, Ill. (2003)
High school coaches: Timothy Flamer and Jim Price

Current residence: Eugene, Ore.
Current occupation: Professional Athlete
Current affiliation or club: Nike (OTC Elite)
Current Coach: Mark Rowland

Personal records: 800—1:48.17 (2009); 1500—3:38.06 (2009); Mile—3:57.27 (2007); 3K—7:50.43 (2009); 5K—13:33.69 (2009)

Notable accomplishments
College/Post-Collegiate – Four-time All-American in XC…NCAA 5K runner-up (2008)….Big 12 Conference meet record-holder at 1500 (3:40).

Favorite rehab/cross training workout
My favorite cross training regimen is bicycling. I like to warm up for 25-30 minutes. Then I like to do one of two workouts on the bike—(a) a fartlek-type session sometimes with hill climbs in the middle, which can be done by increasing the resistance on the bicycle wheel, or (b) a sustained HR (heart rate) ride around an hour in length with both of these sessions followed by a 20-minute cool down. The second workout requires heart rate

monitor, however, if one is not available you can gauge your effort by cycling at a pace at which you can only respond to questions with short answers.

I enjoy these two rehab workouts the best because of their intensity. I always left the gym feeling a sense of accomplishment and mentally like I was not losing ground to my competition in terms of overall aerobic fitness.

Worst running-related injury
I suffered a bone contusion.

Approximate date of injury, nature of it and was surgery required?
The injury happened the summer before my freshman year at the University of Colorado (2003). Surgery was not required.

What flaw led to the injury? Or did you do something that caused it?
The injury happened on the Mesa Trail in Boulder. The Mesa Trail has a ton of rocks on it and I was running along not paying attention and tripped over one rock and slammed my knee into another. I was running at a pretty quick clip and I remember hitting the ground knees first, rolling onto my stomach, and then my legs were arching back over my body and almost coming up to my head. I was completely covered in dirt and I was thinking of a clever story to tell the guys when I got back from the run. I had no idea it was going to cost me almost my entire freshmen year.

Rehabilitation program that you followed. How long before you resumed "normal" training?
I tried a number of things to stay in shape that did not bother my knee. I would run a day, then cycle a day, run a day, and then take a day off. I would swim often. I would do the elliptical; I did all these things. I needed the variety.

But ultimately a cortisone injection and rest was what healed my injury. Then, coming back after injection is the scary part because you're always worried the pain is going to come back. This part of my recovery I didn't want to do alone, because I would have driven myself crazy every run constantly scanning what I felt in my right knee.

Given that running takes a fair amount of time and that cross training for that same time would probably drive you crazy, what did you do to keep busy?
During my injury I started dating Laura Zeigle who was also a runner at the CU. I spent lots of time with her and she kept my mind off running. Laura and I are now married with two boys now, so I'd say my free time away from rehab and school was extremely well spent.

What was the most difficult aspect of being injured? How did you deal psychologically with missing a season?
The most difficult part of being injured was not being able to compete. There's definitely something in all of us distance runners that needs to push the boundaries and needs to see where you measure up against your classmates, but most of all for me, against myself.

Psychologically, I focused on how this hunger to compete was going to make me a stronger person as well as runner.

What advice would you give another elite runner who suffers a season-ending injury?
BE PATIENT. It seems like the worst thing that could possibly happen, but 90% of injuries happen from overtraining. You should use this time to reflect upon what you were feeling leading up to this injury and what you can do to prevent it or any other type of injury in the future.

When you returned to full-time training, did you alter the type of training you were doing?
When I returned to training I put a lot more emphasis on the weight room. I did this because I was initially afraid of overdoing the mileage and hurting my knee. I think it made a lot of sense looking back at it, because what I had lost in aerobic training I had gained in my strides power, so I was a better runner and more efficient runner in terms of how I came back after building up from the injury.

What was the result in your first major competition after returning from injury?
I helped lead our team to a national championship in cross country, upsetting the heavily favored Wisconsin Badgers in 2004. I placed 44th individually and earned my first All-American honor.

What advice would you give a high school or young college runner regarding injury prevention and/or rehabilitation?
Talk with your school's strength coach. Ask for a balanced weight program. If you are more of an 800/1500/miler type you may want a little more emphasis on explosive lifts. If you don't have someone at your school that can help you in the weight room then go to hour local YMCA and ask for help.

As far as injury prevention goes, take care of yourself. Pay attention to what you put in your body. Your diet can have great effect on your performance or lack thereof. Also, don't be afraid to take days off. For a high school kid, a day off every two weeks is a good investment, especially during your freshman and sophomore years.

After being injured and coming back, did it change your sense of who you are/were as a runner? Did you have more patience or did you find yourself training on the edge again?
Coming back didn't change much about me as a runner. My injury happened as a result of a fall on a rocky trail. What I did learn is that weights are an important part of training for distance runners.

Seth Pilkington

Weber State University
3K, 5K, 10K

"I think it's always important to have your goals in mind; even while you're injured. I've struggled with staying motivated when I've been forced to cross-train for a sustained period of time. I'm able to stay more motivated if I have a goal in mind that I'm working toward."

Seth, briefly profiled
Birth Date and Place: March 15, 1983; Ogden, Utah
Began running: 12 years old; Began running competitively: 12 years old
Height/Running Weight: 5'9", 130 lbs.

Weber State University, B.A., 2008 (Accounting)
College coach: Paul Pilkington
Roy High School, Roy, Utah. (2001)
High school coaches: Paul Pilkington

Current residence: Harrisville, Utah
Current occupation: Financial Auditor/Runner
Current affiliation or club: New Balance
Current Coach: Paul Pilkington

Personal records: 3K—7:59.56i (2008); 5K—13:46.86 (2006); 10K—28:25.56 (2008)

Notable accomplishments
High School—Five-time state champ…Utah state record holder at 1600 and 3200…6th at Footlocker Championships (2000)…Golden West Invitational champion at 3200 (8:55).
College/Post-Collegiate—Five-time Big Sky Conference champion…Five-time NCAA All-American…indoor Big Sky Conference 5K record holder (13:50).

Favorite rehab/cross training workout
I've found that I'm able to best simulate running by either cross-training on an elliptical, or by running in a pool. When I am unable to run, I like to simulate the workout that I would have been doing that day if I were healthy. For example, if the rest of my team was doing 6 x 1 mile repeats, my cross-training workout would simulate mile repeats. I would warm up

and cool down on the elliptical or in the pool for the same amount of time that I would have if I were running. My workout would consist of 6 repeats spanning the duration of time that it would've taken me to complete a mile repeat. My recovery between intervals would also approximate what I would take were I running.

Worst running-related injuries
Plica syndrome

Approximate date of injury nature of it and was surgery required?
I first experienced knee pain and swelling in December of 2006. I was unable to run from December 2006 to June 2007. I was originally diagnosed as having runner's knee (patellofemoral pain syndrome). After several failed attempts at various rehab treatments, I met with an arthroscopic surgeon who diagnosed the injury as plica syndrome. My knee was scoped in May 2007, and I was back running again in June.

What flaw led to the injury? Or did you do something that caused it?
Plica syndrome is a condition that is a result of remnant fetal tissue in the knee. Plica normally diminishes in early fetal development, but if the process is incomplete, plica remains in the knee and can cause irritation in runners. There was really nothing I could have done that would have prevented the injury.

Rehabilitation program that you followed. How long before you resumed "normal" training?
I was able to do some light biking two weeks after my knee was scoped. I began running about four weeks after the surgery. I first began running on a weightless treadmill that uses a harness to reduce impact by reducing body weight. After two weeks of running on the treadmill, I began alternating between running on the treadmill and running on pavement. I was able to get to the point where I was running strictly on pavement within about 10 weeks of the surgery. My knee would often swell up after runs, so I would ice after every run and take anti-inflammatories to help reduce swelling.

Given that running takes a fair amount of time and that cross training for that same time would probably drive you crazy, what did you do to keep busy?
Recovering from an injury can often times be more time consuming than being healthy. The time is takes to cross-train, ice, get massages, see physical therapists etc. is very time consuming. I never found it difficult to keep busy while being injured.

What was the most difficult aspect of being injured? How did you deal psychologically with missing a season?
I missed my junior year of indoor and outdoor track with my knee injury. The most difficult part of being injured is missing out on competing. Had I been healthy in 2007, I would have been the top 10K returner in the NCAA championship. I was at the 2007 NCAA championships as a spectator, and it was difficult to watch the race knowing that had I been healthy, I could have been in contention to win an NCAA title.

What specifically did you learn from being injured?
Whenever I've been injured I've been able to return to running with a renewed motivation and appreciation for when things are going well. Injuries have also taught me to be more aware of my body. Distance runners are always toeing the line between training at their highest level and overdoing it. It's important to be in tune with how you are feeling and to be willing to cut back, if needed, to avoid getting injured.

What advice would you give another elite runner who suffers a season-ending injury?
I think it's always important to have your goals in mind; even while you're injured. I've struggled with staying motivated when I've been forced to cross-train for a sustained period of time. I'm able to stay more motivated if I have a goal in mind that I'm working towards.

When you returned to full-time training, did you alter the type of training you were doing?
I've never had to drastically change my training, but I have had to focus more on preventative measures such as ice, massage, strengthening exercises etc. to avoid sustaining another injury.

What was the result in your first major competition after returning from injury?
After knee surgery I was an all American in cross country.

What advice would you give a high school or young college runner regarding injury prevention and/or rehabilitation?
I think being consistent in your training is key to staying healthy. It's common for runners to get injured after they've taken time off and they try and get back into running high mileage again too fast. It's also important to do the little things like stretching, ice baths, and strengthening exercises that help to prevent injuries.

After being injured and coming back, did it change your sense of who you are/were as a runner? Did you have more patience or did you find yourself training on the edge again?
It's not possible to compete at a high level without "training on the edge," but I've learned that it's important to be in tune with how you are feeling. It's okay to miss a morning run or cut back on a workout if your body isn't feeling recovered.

Steve Plasencia

University of Minnesota
5K, 10K, XC, Marathon

"You can't chase with the owls and be up with the roosters. I also learned that I needed to recover between workouts a little more."

Steve, briefly profiled
Birth Date and Place: Oct. 25, 1956; Minneapolis, Minn.
Began running: 14 years old; Began running competitively: 14 years old; retired: 39 years old
Height/Running Weight: 5'10", 145 lbs.

University of Minnesota, B.A., 1979 (Business Administration)
College coach: Roy Griak
New Hope H.S., New Hope, Minn. (1974)
High school coaches: Jim Fischer

Current residence: Shoreview, Minn.
Current occupation: Men's cross country and track coach at University of Minnesota

Personal records: 13:19.37 (1985); 10K—27:45.20 (1990); Marathon—2:14.14 (1992)

Notable accomplishments
College/Post-Collegiate—Five-time All-American…U.S. national 10K champ (1990)…2nd at U.S. nationals (1987, '91, '93, '94)…World Championships (1987, '91, '93, '95)…Olympic teams (1988 and 1992).

Worst running-related injuries
That's tough. I had one Achilles tendon injury which resulted in surgery. I had five stress fractures. The worst was that I had three of them in a 18 month period.

Approximate date of injuries, nature of them and was surgery required?
I had three stress fractures from March 1983 through September 1984. No surgery.

What flaw led to the injuries? Or did you do something that caused them?
Biomechanical inefficiencies (flat feet), I also took lots of anti-inflamatories for overuse injuries which may have weakened the bone, and overtraining.

Rehabilitation program that you followed. How long did the rehab take before you resumed "normal" training? I cross trained in water, both water-running and swimming, extensively. With one stress fracture (almost a complete fracture of the femur) I was on crutches. During this time I did arm cranking on my stationary bike, turned upside down. After returning to running I gradually phased out the cross training.

Given that running takes a fair amount of time and that cross training for that same time would probably drive you crazy, what did you do to keep busy?
I cross trained equal to what I would have run. It made me tougher.

What was the most difficult aspect of being injured? How did you deal psychologically with missing a season?
I had moved to Eugene, Ore., to run as had many of the best U.S. distance runners at that point. I had no support system in Eugene outside of running. I missed a chance at making some teams but my best chances still came later.

What specifically did you learn from being injured?
You can't chase with the owls and be up with the roosters. I also learned that I needed to recover between workouts a little more.

What advice would you give another elite runner who suffers a season-ending injury?
Develop hobbies in advance that help you cope with the problems.

When you returned to full-time training, did you alter the type of training you were doing?
I made more friends in a full-time graduate school program. Before that I was taking the odd class here and there. By returning to school at the University of Oregon I became more "of the community" and less a transient runner.

What was the result in your first major competition after returning from injury? 4th in 5K at U.S. championships. I then ran 27:59 in the 10K at Stockholm two weeks later.

What advice would you give a high school or young college runner regarding injury prevention and/or rehabilitation?
Listen to your body, communicate with your coach, under-train vs. over-train, and don't continue to train on an injury. Rehabbing is hard work; don't try to treat it as time off. Emotionally, if you are having real difficulties coping then sometimes a break to regain mental stability might be okay.

Ken Popejoy
Michigan State University
1500/Mile, XC

When injured, "Immediately plan for the next season. Turn a negative into a positive mental attitude about how much better prepared you'll be and how you will adjust your training to lessen the chance of a recurring injury."

Ken, briefly profiled
Birth Date and Place: Dec. 9, 1950; Elmhurst, Ill.
Began running: 13 years old; Began running competitively: 14 years old
Height/Running Weight: 5'8", 125 lbs.
Retired: 19__ As a master's runner:

Michigan State University, B.A., 1973 (Pre-Law)
College coach: Jim Gibbard
Glenbard West High School, Glen Ellyn, Ill. (1969)
High school coaches: Jim Arnold and Dave Shinneman

Current residence: Wheaton, Ill.
Current occupation: Circuit Court Judge; DuPage County, Ill.

Personal record: Mile—3:57.0 (1973)

Notable accomplishments
High School—Two-time state champ…All-American (2nd in Golden West mile).
College/Post-Collegiate – Two-time Big Ten champ…Big Ten mile record (3:57.0)…NCAA XC All-American…indoor NCAA mile champ…Track and Field #9 in 1500m/mile (1975) …Olympic trials finalist (1976)

Worst running-related injuries
Bursitis under the knee caps and severe shin splints (possibly a stress fracture in hindsight).

Approximate date of injuries, nature of them and was surgery required?
Summer '69 though fall '69 I had three painful cortisone shots for the bursitis. No surgery. Shin splints in the spring of '69 and again in the fall of '72.

What flaw led to the injury(ies)? Or did you do something that caused it (them)?
I had floating knee caps from poor muscle development in my quads. In fall of 1972 I ran my first cross country race on a rutty course and was injured thereon.

Rehabilitation program that you followed. How long before you resumed "normal" training?
When cortisone shots only provided short term relief I developed a weight regimen for building up the muscle tone around the knee. I did small weights with high reps (leg extensions) to the point where I was doing 300 reps a day. So it took 2-3 hours and had a secondary cardiovascular benefit due to the length of time for the workout and the high level of cardiovascular effort.

Given that running takes a fair amount of time and that cross training for that same time would probably drive you crazy, what did you do to keep busy?
I used 100%, giving normal workout time in the above described weight workout I finished as the team finished their regular workouts. I also did lots of biking but mostly rest. I found that when I was injured my school work suffered. I just wasn't as efficient with my use of time and time management. When injured I had too much time on my hands which led to unnecessary distractions.

What was the most difficult aspect of being injured? How did you deal psychologically with missing a season?
The most difficult aspect was the psychological aspect. You felt unprepared in training, lacked self confidence, and questioned whether you'll be ready for competition.

What specifically did you learn from being injured?
That rest truly is the best cure but you can do alternate cardiovascular cross training and still get the rest to the injury while maintaining a sufficient level of sleep to rebound fairly quickly.

What advice would you give another elite runner who suffers a season-ending injury?
Immediately plan for the next season. Turn a negative into a positive mental attitude about how much better prepared you'll be and how you will adjust your training to lessen the chance of a reoccurring injury.

When you returned to full-time training, did you alter—either somewhat or drastically---the type of training you were doing?
Yes. I did more and better stretching. I did more cardio for my warm-up and cool-down. I incorporated weights as a necessary and vital part of my workout regimen.

What was the result in your first major competition after returning from injury?
After the bursitis, I ran 4:04 in the indoor mile. This was a MSU school record and I had only been running for one month.

What advice would you give a high school or young college runner regarding injury prevention and/or rehabilitation?
Stretch, stretch, stretch. Also, slow building of your base before starting interval workouts.

Looking back, would you change any of your cross training?
Build in more days of less intensity in running and greater intensity in "less-impact" cross training.

After being injured and coming back, did it change your sense of who you are/were as a runner? Did you have more patience or did you find yourself training on the edge again?
Definitely had LESS patience and more intensity to make up for lost time and get back to "the edge" that I loved to train at. The edge is what has the potential to make you great, to be the one who can maintain that edge to the championship races.

Jonathon Riley

Stanford University
1500, Mile, 3K, 5K, 10K, XC

"Train on soft surfaces as often as possible and stretch as much as you can. I don't think it is necessary to have a 30-60 minute stretch routine but just as 'quick limbering up' of most of your muscles a few times a day will have a preventive effect on injuries."

Jonathan, briefly profiled
Birth Date and Place: Dec. 29, 1978, Warwick, R.I.
Began running: 13 years old; Began running competitively: 13 years old; retired: 30 years old
Height/Running Weight: 5'9", 130 lbs.

Stanford University, B.A., 2002 (Studio Art Design)
College coach: Vin Lananna
Brookline High School, Brookline, Mass. (1997)
High school coaches: Jack Reed, Dave Counts, and Mike Glennon

Current residence: Portland, Ore.
Current occupation: entrepreneur

Personal records: 1500—3:38.54 (2004); Mile—3:57.07 (2007); 3K—7:46.84i (2002); 5K—13:19.92 (2007); 10K—28:33.71 (2001)

Notable accomplishments
High School—Five-time state champ…two-time FootLocker finalist…six-time All-American…two-time national champ.
College/Post-Collegiate— Sixteen-time All-American…two-time NCAA champ…3K school record (7:46.84)…bronze medal at junior Pan Am Games (1997)…World University Games (1999 and 2001)…Pan Am Games (1999)… Gold medalist at NACAC (2000)…World XC Championships 4K (2002)…2004 Olympian at 5K

Worst running-related injury
Left femoral neck stress fracture.

Approximate date of injury, nature of it and was surgery required?
My freshman year at Stanford, May 1988. No surgery was required.

What flaw led to the injury? Or did you do something that caused it?
I believe the injury was a result of adjusting to the level of college training. I trained at a very low volume in high school (35 miles a week during the winter and 40-50 miles a week by the end of my senior year). The increase in both intensity and volume at college broke me down.

Rehabilitation program that you followed. How long before you resumed "normal" training?
I really did no cross training and minimal rehab. After an intense freshman year I was ready for a break. I used those three months as a mental and physical break. When I returned to training I was full of energy and fire. I began running on grass for 5 minutes, then 15, 18, and up to 30 minutes. I would run fast though, fast enough where I might have to stop and take a break at half way. I began normal training in early September at our cross country preseason.

Given that running takes a fair amount of time and that cross training for that same time would probably drive you crazy, what did you do to keep busy?
I took a break and worked at a running shoe store in Cambridge, Mass. When I began running, I was ready for it.

What was the most difficult aspect of being injured? How did you deal psychologically with missing a season?
Fortunately I did not miss a season. The break enabled me to be very fresh for the end of my sophomore season in cross country where I had my best finish (9th at NCAA's). I went on to break 4:00 indoors, run 7:58 in my first 3K, and run 13:36 as a sophomore in the 5K (qualifying me for the 1999 University Games). I also finished 5th in the 1500 at U.S. Nationals.

What specifically did you learn from being injured?
What I learned is that you must be smart and prevent injuries, not deal with them when they arise. I do more training on grass and dirt and take time off if something doesn't feel right.

What advice would you give another elite runner who suffers a season-ending injury?
College is a difficult time for an athlete because there are only four chances at each season. This puts pressure on athlete and coaches to come back aggressively and quickly from injuries (often prematurely, in my opinion) to avoid missing valuable opportunities at competing. I believe it is beast to take a little longer to heal to ensure being healthy down the road or during the next season.

When you returned to full-time training, did you alter the type of training you were doing?
I did not alter my training significantly. I was older and more physically mature in addition to having a good year of training under me. I was able to handle the same or even higher levels of training. I did redshirt the spring season after my injury so that I could train at a high level without worrying about becoming injured.

What was the result in your first major competition after returning from injury?
I ran a very small cross country meet and I tied for 1st with Brent Hauser.

What advice would you give a high school or young college runner regarding injury prevention and/or rehabilitation?
Train on soft surfaces as often as possible and stretch as much as you can. I don't think it is necessary to have a 30-60 minute stretch routine but just as "quick limbering up" of most of your muscles a few times a day will have a preventive effect on injuries.

Dathan Ritzenhein

University of Colorado
5K, 10K, XC, Marathon

"I have come back so many times from injury but the one thing that I have found that stands out is the harder I work out when injured, the faster my comeback is."

Dathan, briefly profiled
Birth Date and Place: Dec. 30, 1982; Rockford, Mich.
Began running: 11 years old; Began running competitively: 13 years old
Height/Running Weight: 5'8", 122 lbs.

University of Colorado, B.A., History (2006)
College coach: Mark Wetmore
Rockford High School, Rockford, Mich. (2001)
High school coaches: Brad Prins and Mark Nessner

Current residence: Beaverton, Ore.
Current occupation: Professional runner
Current affiliation or club: Nike
Current coach: Alberto Salazar

Personal records: 1500—3:42.99 (2002); 3K—7:39.03 (2007); 2 Mile—8:11.74 (2007); 5K—12:56.27 (2009); 10K—27:22.28 (2009); Half-marathon: 60:00.0 (2009); Marathon—2:10.00 (2009)

Notable accomplishments
High School—2x Footlocker national XC champion. World XC bronze medalist.
College— 2003 NCAA XC champion. American collegiate 10,000m Record
Post-Collegiate—American Record 5000m-12:56.27. World Half Marathon Bronze Medalist. USA XC Champion. Two-time Olympian.

Favorite rehab/cross training workout
After being injured many times beginning in 2002, my cross training regimen has changed very much. In 2007 a new company called Alter-G invented a treadmill that alters weight. I have been able to train on it almost the same as I would outside through many injuries.

Worst running-related injuries:
I have had eight stress fractures as of 2010, the worst being in the femurs.

Approximate date of injuries, nature of them and was surgery required?
· Large stress fracture in my right femur found on Sept. 1, 2002. 14 weeks completely off.
· Stress fracture in the left femur in April 2003. Recovery was 14 weeks
· Peroneal Tendonitis in left ankle. Recovery four months.
· Stress Fracture in left 4th metatarsal in June 2004. 12 weeks recovery
· Nerve entrapment in May 2005. Two month recovery.
· Stress Fracture in the left 2nd Metatarsal in June 2005. Recovery 6 weeks.
· Stress fracture in left 3rd metatarsal in March 2007. Recovery four weeks.
· Peroneal Tendonitis in September 2007. Recovery two months.
· Stress fracture in left 3rd metatarsal in February 2008. Recovery 12 weeks.
· Achilles Tendonitis in September 2008. Recovery two months.
· Sesamoiditis in right foot in November 2009. Recovery, ongoing.
· Stress fracture in right 3rd metatarsal in February 2010. Recovery ongoing.

What flaw led to the injuries? Or did you do something that caused them?
Biomechanical abnormalities. Leg length difference was a problem for a long time but the biggest problem is what is called Morton's toe. The 2nd metatarsal is longer than the others, causing excessive weight on the midfoot.

Rehabilitation program that you followed. How long before you resumed "normal" training?
My cross training has evolved to the point where now I will workout for 90 minutes to 150 minutes a day! I will try to run on the Alter-G treadmill or the underwater treadmill as much as I would do outside. The muscular effort is the same but the pounding is less. My heart rate ends up being lower due to the decreased weight so I do biking or elliptical at a hard effort to get the extra aerobic training. I also lift weights two to three times a week and try to do that much core training as well. The rehab from stress fractures has been different with each one, but the common thing is to always be pain-free completely for at least one week before beginning easy running outside. Coming off the Alter-G makes the return to normal training much faster.

Given that running takes a fair amount of time and that cross training for that same time would probably drive you crazy, what did you do to keep busy?
I train more when I am injured than when I am healthy. I put in so much more time because it makes my return to good fitness so much faster. I now have a family so I spend the rest of the time with them to keep my mind off the injury.

What was the most difficult aspect of being injured? How did you deal psychologically with missing a season?
Staying positive is the hardest thing about injury. It is easy to think bad thoughts and wonder, "why me?" I try to look at the blessings I have in life and remember the things that are very important like my family. It is difficult to look at the workouts and races you

could be doing, but that attitude is poison and being positive about your comeback makes a huge difference.

What specifically did you learn from being injured?
I learned how much I love running and competing. I try not to take for granted when I don't want to do a double run, because no matter how bad you feel, it is better than cross training.

What advice would you give another elite runner who suffers a season-ending injury?
I would say give yourself goals. It is always easier to take small steps toward the end goal. Do not live by those goals however. If you are not ready to run yet, don't set yourself back by running to early.

When you returned to full-time training, did you alter the type of training you were doing?
With each injury I have changed things afterward. I think learning from every injury is important. We have left no stone unturned and as the next injury happens, as it most certainly will because that is part of competitive running, I will learn from that one too and try to make another change.

What was the result in your first major competition after returning from injury?
I have come back so many times from injury but the one thing that I have found that stands out is the harder I work out when injured, the faster my comeback is.

What advice would you give a high school or young college runner regarding injury prevention and/or rehabilitation?
Don't run through something that is getting worse. You are not indestructible. Take care of it before it becomes a season-ending injury. I have had many other minor injuries other than the ones listed here. These are just the ones that have stopped me from running at some point or seriously hampered training. Pay attention to the progress it makes and stop if it is getting worse. Get on the therapy and cross training right away and the time lost will be minimal.

Looking back, would you change any of your cross training?
The Alter-G is the best tool a runner can use. They are becoming more common and you can almost train through an injury without losing anything. There is a transition period coming off it but it is the best tool out there. I would encourage any runner to see where you can get on one and your comeback will be so much faster.

After being injured and coming back, did it change your sense of who you are/were as a runner? Did you have more patience or did you find yourself training on the edge again?
I have had moments of despair when injured. Just like anyone, I find it is hard to always be optimistic. But I think I found the more important things in life because before I met my wife and had children I was so consumed with running that when it failed me I was lost. I also got the desire back to be great many times. I would be content and then an

injury would happen and I would say to myself, "am I really doing everything I can?" and then I would come back better than ever.

Josh Rohatinsky

Brigham Young University
5k, 10k, Marathon

"I've learned that body maintenance is my #1 priority. If you get hurt, all the hard work you put into it will be for nothing. Getting to the line with 100% health is half the battle."

> **Josh, briefly profiled**
> Birth Date and Place: March 7, 1982, Provo, Utah
> Began running: 10 years old; Began running competitively: 14 years old
> Height/Running Weight: 5'8", 120 lbs.
>
> Brigham Young University, B.A., 2007 (Exercise Science)
> College coach: Ed Eyestone
> Provo High School, Provo, Utah (graduated spring 2000)
> High school coaches: Phil Olsen and Mark Low
>
> Current residence: Beaverton, OR.
> Current occupation: Professional Runner
> Current affiliation or club: Nike/OTC Elite
> Current Coach: Jerry Schumacher
>
> Personal records: 3K—7:49.55i (2009); 5K—13:25.53 (2007); 10K—27:54.41 (2008); Marathon—2:14.23 (2008)

Notable accomplishments
High School—Seven-time state champ...three-time Footlocker finalist (27th, 5th, 4th).
College/Post-Collegiate – Seven-time All-American...NCAA XC champ (2006)...5th in 10k at USA Olympic Trials (2008).

Favorite rehab/cross training workout
I have to be honest, I do not enjoy cross-training one bit. Whenever I got injured for a substantial amount of time as a result of stress fractures, my cross training consisted of pool running (either easy 60-90 minutes per day or 60-120 minutes of 1-minute intervals with 1-minute recoveries) or elliptical training (60-120 minutes per day). Most days it was split up into two workouts. I cross-trained six days per week.

Worst running-related injuries
Four stress fractures, all in approximately same place in fibulas (high in shaft)

Approximate date of injuries, nature of them and was surgery required?
Stress fractures: 2000, 2006, 2008, 2009, no surgery required; just time off.

What flaw led to the injuries? Or did you do something that caused them?
Running on hard surfaces, wearing wrong type of shoes (not enough cushion).

Rehabilitation program that you followed. How long before you resumed "normal" training?
My cross-training habits were described above. Rehab was anywhere from 4-8 weeks, then another month (or often longer) to gain the fitness back that I had lost.

Given that running takes a fair amount of time and that cross training for that same time would probably drive you crazy, what did you do to keep busy?
In college, I could keep busy with school. Afterwards, my stress fractures either came at the end of a season when I was going to take time off anyways, or they came at very inopportune times and basically took my whole season away, so I just gave myself the time to relax and come back slowly. With stress fractures, there's nothing you can do, so as hard as it was to swallow, I needed to accept it and move on with a good attitude.

What was the most difficult aspect of being injured? How did you deal psychologically with missing a season?
The most difficult part was not being able to work as hard as I wanted to, and feeling powerless to do anything about it. Every time it happened I had to evaluate my career and what I wanted to do with it. A few times when big injuries messed up an entire season, I came very close to throwing the towel in for good. However, my stress fracture in the spring of 2006 actually motivated me to work harder than I ever had before, which led directly to my NCAA championship that same fall.

What specifically did you learn from being injured?
Athletically speaking, the importance of body maintenance. Psychologically speaking, the importance of keeping things in perspective and accepting things you have no control over.

What advice would you give another elite runner who suffers a season-ending injury?
Learn from it, because that's the only productive thing you can do. If your injury teaches you to strengthen a certain area of your body, do it; if it teaches you to run on softer surfaces, do it; if it teaches you to run easier on your easy days, do it. The only value a trial has is what you learn from it, and if you learn nothing then you've passed through it in vain.

When you returned to full-time training, did you alter the type of training you were doing?
Yes. I learned to run on soft surfaces more, and to change my shoes and add extra cushioning as well.

What was the result in your first major competition after returning from injury?
Most of the time they were good performances because I gave myself time to come back both physically and mentally instead of rushing things.

What advice would you give a high school or young college runner regarding injury prevention and/or rehabilitation?
I've learned that body maintenance is my #1 priority. If you get hurt, all the hard work you put into it will be for nothing. Getting to the line with 100% health is half the battle.

After being injured and coming back, did it change your sense of who you are/were as a runner? Did you have more patience or did you find yourself training on the edge again?
Definitely. It made me realize that the sport isn't just about working harder than anyone else, but about working smarter too – learning to get as close to the line as you can *without going over it*.

Chris Rombough
University of Minnesota
3K, 5K, 10K, XC

"Young runners need to progressively and incrementally increase their mileage to help prevent injury. When it comes to rehabilitation, too many runners just want to get back to running while ignoring their injuries. It is important to regain the strength and stability in the injured area and to hold off on impact activities until all pain is gone."

Chris, briefly profiled
Birth Date and Place: Dec. 5, 1986, Long Beach, Cal.
Began running: 14 years old; Began running competitively: 14 years old
Height/Running Weight: 6'0", 150 lbs.

University of Minnesota, B.A., 2010 (Coaching and Communication Studies)
College coach: Steve Plasencia
New London High School, New London, Wis.(graduated spring 2005)
High school coaches: Jim Ziegler, Terry Wetzel, and Jim Fischer

Current residence: Minneapolis, Minn.
Current occupation: Athlete
Current affiliation or club: Team USA Minnesota
Current Coach: Steve Plasencia

Personal records: 1500—3:44.49; 3K—7:54.57; 5K—13:48.80; 10K—29:10.67

Notable accomplishments
High School—Two-time state XC Champ…5th at Footlocker Championships (2004)…1600 and 3200 state champ (2005)…3200 Wisconsin state championship record…3rd at NON in 2-mile.
College/Post-Collegiate –Big Ten XC champ (2006)…three-time all Big Ten and All-American in XC…three-time All-American indoor track.

Favorite rehab/cross training workout
Luckily, I have never been too seriously injured where I have had to spend countless hours cross training. However, when I have cross trained, I utilize the pool. I have not done any

workouts in the pool, so my activities in the pool have just been pool running to work my aerobic system.

Worst running-related injuries
At the 2010 NCAA indoor championships, during the DMR, I stepped on the rail with 550 meters to go. At first, it seemed like nothing, but about five seconds after I finished the race, my ankle started throbbing, so I looked down and found my ankle to be swollen about an inch larger than what it should be. I had sprained my ankle, but was able to compete on it the next night in the 3,000 meters.

Approximate date of injuries, nature of them and was surgery required?
March 2004—high ankle sprain. March 2010—ankle sprain. May 2010—Achilles tendinitis. No surgeries were required.

What flaw led to the injuries? Or did you do something that caused them?
March 2004—During a hockey game after getting hit, as I was going down, my ankle turned inward and I pretty much sat on my ankle; I suffered a high ankle sprain.
March 2010- I was bumped coming out of the turn on the banked track, and that momentum took me into the rail.
May 2010- The week of the first round of the NCAA Championships, my left calf was tight, particularly in the posterior tibialis. Throughout the week, our athletic trainer and massage therapist worked on my calf, but the tightness in my calf caused my Achilles to tighten up with 500 meters to go in my race.

Rehabilitation program that you followed. How long before you resumed "normal" training?
The general rehabilitation program that I follow consists of strengthening of and regaining balance in the injured area, as well as cross training. Cross training, however, needs to be at a frequency where I am receiving aerobic benefit. When cross training, I try to remain conscientious of keeping my heart rate above 150 beats per minute.

Given that running takes a fair amount of time and that cross training for that same time would probably drive you crazy, what did you do to keep busy?
When I am cross training, I try to stick with one form for the whole workout. However, depending on the length of the activity, I may break the workout up between two or three different modes. Most times, I use only the pool, but occasionally I will use both the arm crank and the pool. Also, depending on the how many days I am cross training, I will bike so that most the activity is from the legs. I feel that, while pool running, my arms are doing more work than my legs are.

What was the most difficult aspect of being injured? How did you deal psychologically with missing a season?
I think that there are three aspects that make injury difficult. The first aspect is realizing that you are cross training, while all your teammates and competitors are getting better training because they are able to run. Secondly, I think it is very hard to increase the intensity while cross training. When out for a normal training run, I feel very comfortable

running between 150-170 beats per minute; while cross training 150 beats per minute feels like a lot more work. Third, you burn more calories running than you do swimming or biking; therefore, injured athletes need to be conscientious of their caloric intake.

What specifically did you learn from being injured?
I have learned more about myself, more than anything else, during time of injury. I realize how much I actually love running because I am not able to do it. I also learn how strong I am mentally when I am in the pool for an hour by myself with no music; the only thing to think about is my fitness and getting healthy.

What advice would you give another elite runner who suffers a season-ending injury?
While it is very important to regain strength and balance in the injured area, my advice to an elite athlete is to continue working on your fitness. Taking a lot of time to rest will allow your body to decondition. If the athlete continues to work, he can increase or maintain his aerobic capacity rather than letting the body decondition.

When you returned to full-time training, did you alter the type of training you were doing?
Because I have never suffered a serious running related injury (stress fractures, etc.), I have never had to drastically alter my training. Coming back from injury, however, I take the first couple runs easy to ensure that my body is ready to resume the training load.

What advice would you give a high school or young college runner regarding injury prevention and/or rehabilitation?
When it comes to injury prevention, I think young runners need to look at their training. There are too many instances of kids coming into a training program and getting injured. Young runners need to progressively and incrementally increase their mileage to help prevent injury. When it comes to rehabilitation, too many runners just want to get back to running while ignoring their injuries. It is important to regain the strength and stability in the injured area and to hold off on impact activities until all pain is gone.

After being injured and coming back, did it change your sense of who you are/were as a runner? Did you have more patience or did you find yourself training on the edge again?
Coming off injury, I have never found myself a changed runner. I find myself a patient runner; I find myself wanting to come back and hit the training hard, but I am smart enough to know that I would rather be at 90% fitness and healthy than 100% fitness and unable to run.

Galen Rupp
University of Oregon
5K, 10K, XC

"If you cross-train diligently and put in the work, you will be amazed at the fitness you retain. It will take a couple of weeks to get your running legs back under you, but your overall fitness level will still be high after lots of cross-training."

Galen, briefly profiled
Date/Place of Birth: May 8, 1986, Portland, Ore.
Began running: 9 years old; Began running competitively: 14 years old
Height/Running Weight: 5'11", 138 lbs.

Oregon, B.A., Business (expected 2011)
College coaches: Alberto Salazar & Vin Lananna
Central Catholic High School, Portland, Ore. (2004)
High school coach: Alberto Salazar

Current residence: Portland, Ore.
Current occupation: professional runner
Current affiliation: Nike
Current coach: Alberto Salazar

Personal records: 800—1:49.87i (2009); 1500—3:39.14 (2009); Mile—3:56.22i (2010); 3K—7:44.69i (2009); 5K—13:10.05 (2010); 10K—27:10.74 (2010)

Notable accomplishments
High School—Oregon state cross country champ ((2004); 5:18.5 2K national HS record; 13:37.91 national HS record & American Junior record; state record in 1500 (3:45.3) and mile (4:01.8)
College—As a senior in 2008-09, won his first NCAA cross country title and the concluded his college career at home as he won the NCAA outdoor 5K and 10K; at the NCAA indoor meet, he won the 3K and 5K titles and anchored the winning DMR; won the inaugural Bowerman Award as the nation's top male track and field athlete; overall, earned 14 all-American honors at Oregon along with five individual championships and a relay championship while leading Oregon to two NCAA cross country team titles and an indoor track NCAA team title. Finished 8th in 10K at 2007 World Championships in Osaka;

Second in 10K at the 2008 U.S. Olympic trials; finished 13th in the Olympic Games in Beijing in a season-best 27:36.99.
Post-collegiate—Finished 11th at 10K at World Championships in Berlin (2009); won second U.S. outdoor title at 10K in Des Moines, Iowa.

Favorite cross training workout:
Everything we do while injured has to do with pain. I will push things as hard as I can as long as it is not getting more painful. If it is staying the same or getting better I will do as much running as I can, either on a flat, smooth surface or the alterG or Hydroworx treadmill. If I cannot run, I will either aquajog or ride the bike. A workout I will do on the bike is 10 minutes warmup, 10x1 minute hard, 1 minute easy, then a 10 minute cooldown. I will do this every other day when I am hurt. The rest of the time I just go for volume while cross training.

Worst running related injury
Contusion in the navicular bone in my foot

Approximate date of injury, nature of it; was surgery required?
Fall, 2006. I stepped in a hole while running and my foot started to hurt shortly after. I saw a specialist in North Carolina and he was able to construct a brace for my foot that took the stress off of my navicular and I was able to run on the alterG after that. Surgery was not required.

Length of time missed
I trained through the whole thing.

What flaw led to the injury? Or did you do something that caused it/them?
It was a fluke thing where I wasn't paying attention to where I was going and stepped in a hole.

General rehabilitation program that you followed
I cross trained for 2-3 hours per day (combination of bike, elliptical, and aqua jogging), lifted weights (anything that didn't hurt my foot), and eventually was able to resume training on the alterG. I reduced my weight to 70% of normal and slowly increased the weight as long as things didn't get more painful. I would start some of my runs at 9 minute pace and add .1 miles per hour every quarter mile until I got down to 7 minute pace. Needless to say, we would take things slow.

Given that running takes a fair amount of time and that cross training for that same time would probably drive you crazy, what did you do to keep busy?
Listened to my iPod and watched movies/TV

What was the most difficult aspect of being injured? How did you deal psychologically with missing a season? Did you miss your best chance to make a U.S. Olympic or World Championship team because of the injury?
I have been fortunate not to have had any major injuries that have forced me to miss significant time.

What specifically did you learn from being injured?
There are a lot of things that you can train through, but you have to be smart about it. Also, it takes a lot of time trying new things and tinkering with ways to enable you to run when you have an injury. It can be frustrating but you can never stop trying. Also, the two things that you can't really mess around with are Achilles tendons and navicular bones.

What advice would you give another elite runner who suffers a season-ending injury?
Be patient and understand that everyone will get injuries during their career. It is easy to be tough when everything goes well, but the great athletes are those who are able to weather tough times and get through periods of disappointment.

When you returned to training full-time, did you alter the type of training you were doing?
No; we would make adjustments like running on different surfaces if that would make a difference. Coming back from a stress fracture, for example, we would be extra diligent to run on grass or soft woodchips. That may be boring, but if it keeps you healthy it is worth it. After all, it's much better than working out on a stationary bike!

What advice would you give a high school or young college runner regarding injury prevention or rehabilitation?
If you cross-train diligently and put in the work, you will be amazed at the fitness you retain. It will take a couple of weeks to get your running legs back under you, but your overall fitness level will still be high after lots of cross-training.

After being injured and coming back, did it change your sense of who you are/were as a runner? Did you have more patience or did you find yourself training on the edge again?
You always have to walk a fine line when training. Getting hurt should not make you train less or be scared to push things. Just make sure to learn from past mistakes and be smart with training.

Don Sage

Stanford University
1500, Mile, XC

"Practice good injury prevention habits. Many injuries are the result of muscle imbalances and general weakness. Diligently following a good workout routine that includes core strength and ankle/foot stability exercises will eliminate many preventable injuries."

Don, briefly profiled
Birth Date and Place: Oct. 5, 1981, Downers Grove, Ill.
Began running: 12 years old; Began running competitively: 11 years old; Retired: 28 years old
Height/Running Weight: 5'9", 135 lbs.

Stanford University, B.A., 2005 (Economics)
College coaches: Vin Lananna, Andy Girard
York Community High School, Elmhurst, Ill. (2000)
High school coaches: Joe Newton and Charlie Kern

Current residence: Davis, Cal.
Current occupation: Graduate Student

Personal record: 1500—3:39.17 (2001); Mile—3:59.49i (2002); 5K—14:04.94 (2000); 10K—28:40.12 (2002, only time run, in flats)

Notable accomplishments
High School—Five-time state champion (1600 twice, 3200 twice and XC)…4:00.29 at Prefontaine Classic….2nd in FootLocker final.
College/Post-Collegiate – NCAA 1500 champion (2002)…NCAA team XC champs (2002, 2003)…10-time all-American.

Favorite rehab/cross training workout
I enjoyed swimming the most; however, the elliptical was probably the most effective. The elliptical seemed to work well, because the motion is very similar to running. I believe the exercises similarity to running allowed me to get my heart rate up higher than I could biking or swimming.

Though I had my favorite (and least favorite) activities, the key to keeping cross training enjoyable was to rotate among a variety of exercises. Therefore, I often would vary my training sessions to include a combination of biking, swimming, and aqua jogging. For example, I would swim for 30 minutes, aqua jog for 30 minutes, and bike for an hour. I liked to pretend I was training for a triathlon.

Worst running-related injury
Stress fracture in the tibia (inside of right leg).

Approximate date of injury, nature of it and was surgery required?
February through May 2003. I had a "hot spot" on the inside of my leg. Running or walking caused me to feel a sharp pain centered at one spot on my tibia.

What flaw led to the injury? Or did you do something that caused it?
My body was very durable throughout most of my running career which, unfortunately, led me to think I was impervious to stress fractures. Looking back on the two months leading to my injury, there were many things I could have done to save my track season.

My lack of preparation for the 2003 indoor season definitely contributed to the stress fracture. I ran inconsistently over winter break. When I came back to school, I should have been forthright with my coaches about my lack of preparation. Instead, I tried to jump into workouts and ramp up my mileage very quickly.
During the weeks leading up to my injury, I had a lot of soreness in my shins. I have always had problems with tendonitis and general soreness in this area. The resulting weakness in the muscles occasionally causes my foot to slap against the ground when I am running. At this point, I become susceptible to injury because my foot is hitting the ground very hard. Instead of taking it easy, I tried to run through the soreness and tendonitis.

I can pinpoint the two days which caused my likely two-week stress reaction to turn into a year-ending stress fracture. Surprisingly, given my poor winter break, I was feeling better than ever. My shin was starting to bug me, but I was excited about the season and did not want to pay attention to my body's signs. I remember my shin feeling very sore after a track session. I thought about taking a day or two off from training. Instead, the next day I went for a hilly run at Arastradero Park. After that run, I could not walk without feeling intense pain.

Rehabilitation program that you followed. How long before you resumed "normal" training?
My coaches drew up a great rehabilitation program that consisted of numerous different cross training activities. Coach Lananna had me run in place on the pole vault mats, which was actually a great workout (it's hard). Mike Reilly, our assistant coach, was very generous with his time in administering pool workouts. Once we realized that it was going to be a while until my injury healed, I settled into a rotation that consisted of

aquajogging, swimming, and using the elliptical/exercise bike. I would try to do 90 to 120 minutes of cross training per day. Overall, my injury lasted around three months, which was the duration of my rehabilitation program.

Given that running takes a fair amount of time and that cross training for that same time would probably drive you crazy, what did you do to keep busy?
Cross training is actually more time-consuming than running. Running is such an efficient form of exercising. Most of my training runs ranged from 45 to 60 minutes. To get what I felt was an equivalent workout on the bike and elliptical, I would spend at least 2 hours exercising.

What was the most difficult aspect of being injured? How did you deal psychologically with missing a season?
The toughest part about being injured was missing the competition season. I enjoyed competing and helping out the team. While I was injured, I tried hard to cheer and support the guys, but it wasn't the same as being out there with them.

What specifically did you learn from being injured?
My injury taught me about both injury prevention and rehabilitation. With regard to injury prevention, I learned to listen to my body. It is incredibly hard to take a few days off during an important training cycle. However, taking a little downtime is preferable to missing an entire track season.

From a rehabilitation standpoint, I learned to be patient. Injuries need time to heal. Certainly, the stress fracture would have recovered sooner if I had not been constantly testing it by running, jumping up and down, or pushing on it to see if it still hurt.

More specifically, I learned that some injuries still hurt even after they have healed. During the last month of my injury, there was substantial evidence that I had recovered. Two of the main indications were that I felt fine walking around campus and the doctor's tests showed that my bone had healed. Unfortu-nately, my leg still hurt when I tried to run.

Eventually, the coaches, training staff and I decided to start running despite the pain. I started a schedule of running every other day. If the injury did not get worse during the day off, I would run again for a slightly longer period of time. Within a week or two, I began running every day. I had not realized that the residual pain from the injury would be so intense. It is likely that I could have started the process a few weeks sooner. It turned out that I was too anxious to return during the first month of my injury and too conservative during the last month!

What advice would you give a high school or young college runner regarding prevention and/or rehabilitation?
I would give the following two pieces of advice to any competitive runner:

· Practice good injury prevention habits. Many injuries are the result of muscle imbalances and general weakness. Diligently following a good workout routine that includes core strength and ankle/foot stability exercises will eliminate many preventable injuries.

· Understand your own body. Every ache and pain represents an opportunity to learn more about yourself.

A thoughtful athlete seeks answers to the following questions:
—Which aches and pains require rest and which can be run through?
—Which injuries are recurring and how are they best treated/prevented?

Brett Schoolmeester

University of Colorado
3K, 5K, 10K, XC

"I think most runners end up associating their self worth with their most recent... performances, so to not even be able to have good training to reflect on...makes your self-esteem fluctuate greatly, and finding other ways to feel good about yourself becomes very important. ...these experiences end up making you a better person and (with)... proper perspective...will make you a stronger athlete."

Brett, briefly profiled
Birth Date and Place: Orange, Cal.
Began running: 7 years old; Began running competitively: 10 years old
Height/Running Weight: 6'1", 143 lbs.

University of Colorado, B.A., 2006 (Spanish Language and Literature)
College coach: Mark Wetmore
Denver Christian High School, Denver, Colo. (2002)
High school coaches: Dale Schoolmeester

Current residence: Cornelius, Ore.
Current occupation: Brand Marketing, Nike Inc.
Current affiliation or club: Bowerman Athletic Club
Current Coach: Chris Cook

Personal Records: 3K—7:49; 5K—13:39; 10K—28:34

Notable accomplishments
High School—Footlocker Finalist
College/Post-Collegiate—Six-time All-American...5th at NCAA XC (2004)...5th in 10K at USATF championships (2005).

Favorite rehab/cross training workout
I've only recently had to deal with a cross training program but have found the ElliptiGo machine (recently released) to be the only method I can use that gives me a significant workout, fairly close to the running motion without too much impact and yet I can mentally sustain the effort and get out the door.

It's basically an elliptical machine with wheels so you can perform the exercise outdoors and enjoy actually moving rather than sitting still in the gym.

I've tried the alter-G treadmill and had some success with it but I also feel it becomes too much of a crutch and can be resorted to too quickly, rather than addressing the real issue.

Worst running-related injury
I recently underwent surgery for a labral tear in my right hip due to femoralacetabular impingement. Basically the way my hip capsule is shaped created increased pressure and caused a large cartilage tear, most likely made worse by running the Chicago marathon after the tear had started.

Approximate date of injury, nature of it and was surgery required?
The injury was initially sustained in late September 2009 and went undiagnosed until March 2010; I had surgery on May 17 and have a 12 week rehab protocol which should put me at full strength 6 months post-surgery.

What flaw led to the injury? Or did you do something that caused it them?
The impingement in my hip is part congenital and it's also seen more often in hockey players or those with an equine history because it creates strength in the hip flexors which pulls the hips into a forward lean. I spent many of my formative years on a horse's back and this probably led to the injury.

Rehabilitation program that you followed. How long before you resumed "normal" training?
12 weeks of physical therapy, general strength exercises, now jogging VERY lightly.

Given that running takes a fair amount of time and that cross training for that same time would probably drive you crazy, what did you do to keep busy?
Fortunately or unfortunately, I have a very busy job that keeps me busy, along with a wife and 2-year-old daughter. I'd never taken more than a coupe of weeks off of running since I was very young, so I enjoyed the first half of my hiatus, but then I realized that on top of it being a compulsion of mine, I actually enjoyed running and being fit and desperately wanted to be healthy again.

What was the most difficult aspect of being injured? How did you deal psychologically with missing a season?
I think most runners end up associating their self worth with their most recent running perfor-mances, so to not even be able to have good training to reflect on, that makes your self-esteem fluctuate greatly, and finding other ways to feel good about yourself becomes very important. In the end I think these experiences end up making you a better person and if the proper perspective is taken will make you a stronger athlete.

What specifically did you learn from being injured?
To enjoy the feeling of running a hard 10 miles whether it's getting ready for a race or just taking advantage of being healthy and fit.

What advice would you give another elite runner who suffers a season-ending injury?
See the right doctors, get a plan to get better as soon as is safely possible. Take the time to get some perspective, and don't be afraid to pursue other things. Too much introspection is unhealthy.

When you returned to full-time training, did you alter the type of training you were doing?
Ask me in 4-5 months but I'm guessing it will be a yes.

What advice would you give a high school or young college runner regarding injury prevention and/or rehabilitation?
Running is a great source of fitness but if you're only running, your body's imbalances will become worse and by the time you realize they're there it will take way more work to correct them than if you had started addressing them from the beginning. Well-rounded core work is fantastic for preventing these issues.

After being injured and coming back, did it change your sense of who you are/were as a runner? Did you have more patience or did you find yourself training on the edge again?
I think it will—let's hope so anyways!

Jerry Schumacher
University of Wisconsin
1500

"The key to success after an injury is to return 'intelligently.' We all know and want to work hard, but if you rush it...more injuries are certain."

Jerry, briefly profiled
Date/Place of Birth: Aug. 6, 1970
Began running: 15 years old; Began running competitively: 15 years old; retired: 25 years old
Height/Running Weight: 6'1", 140 lbs.

University of Wisconsin, 1993
College coach: Martin Smith
Catholic Memorial High School, Waukesha, Wis. (1988)
High school coaches: John Gabelbaur

Current residence: Portland, Ore.
Current occupation: Coach
Current affiliation or club: Nike Oregon Project

Personal records: 1500—3:39.46 (1993)

Notable accomplishments
College—XC All-American (1992)...1500 All-American (1992 and 1993)...two top-10 U.S. championship finishes.

Worst running-related injury
Plantar Fasciitis.

Approximate date of injury, nature of it and was surgery required?
I dealt with this from November 1992 through February 1993 and missed about two months. No surgery required.

What flaw led to the injury? Or did you do something that caused it?
I didn't do enough flexibility exercises.

Rehabilitation program that you followed. How long before you resumed "normal" training?
Lower leg strength exercises and flexibility exercises were built into my program. This helped a lot. After two months of "NO" running I was able to begin running again.

Given that running takes a fair amount of time and that cross training for that same time would probably drive you crazy, what did you do to keep busy?
I really enjoyed my Christmas break...too much (gained 12 lbs.)!

What was the most difficult aspect of being injured? How did you deal psychologically with missing a season?
The most difficult thing for me was dealing with it mentally. The idea of not being fit is often unacceptable for a distance runner and I hated to take time off.

What specifically did you learn from being injured?
Take your time and come back "intelligently."

What advice would you give another elite runner who suffers a season-ending injury?
The key to success after an injury is to return "intelligently." We all know and want to work hard, but if you rush it...more injuries are certain.

When you returned to full-time training, did you alter the type of training you were doing?
No.

What was the result in your first major competition after returning from injury?
I ran 3:40 for 1500.

What advice would you give a high school or young college runner regarding injury prevention and/or rehabilitation?
Flexibility and strength exercises can save a season from injury and add years to your competitive time.

Steve Scott

University of California-Irvine
800, 1500, Mile

"Do all the little things properly. Stretch, warm-up well, warm down, take your time coming back, be healthy first. Also, make sure you cross train; it will keep you fit physically and mentally."

Steve, briefly profiled
Birth Date and Place: May 5, 1956, Upland, Cal.
Began running: 15 years old; Began running competitively: 15 years old; retired: 33 years old
Height/Running Weight: 6'1", 160 lbs.

University of California Irvine, B.A., 1978 (Criminal Justice)
College coach: Len Miller
Upland High School, Upland, Cal. (1974)
High school coaches: Bob Loney

Current residence: Carlsbad, Cal.
Current occupation: Track and cross country coach, Cal State-San Marcos

Personal records: 800—1:45.05 (1982); 1500—3:31.76 (1985); Mile—3:47.69 (1982); 2 miles—8:22.2i (1980); 5K·—13:30.39 (1987)

Notable accomplishments
High School—2nd in 800 at state championships.
College/Post-Collegiate— U.S. Olympic Teams (1980, 84, 88)...5th in OG 1500 in 1988...silver medalist at World Champs (1983)...ten-time U.S. champion....held American record in mile (3:47.69) for 25 years...NCAA 1500 champ (1978)...2nd in NCAA 1500 (1977)...nine-time All-American.

Worst running-related injuries
Strained hamstrings.

Approximate date of injuries, nature of them and was surgery required?
Injury began in May 1987 and lasted four weeks. No surgery was needed.

What flaw led to the injuries? Or did you do something that caused them?
Too much speed work and not enough recovery. I came back too soon. The injury lingered all season and eventually became bursitis in the upper hamstring.

Rehabilitation program that you followed. How long before you resumed "normal" training?
Cross trained in the pool for two weeks. I felt better but still felt it in the upper hamstring. I got ultrasound, ice, heat, and massages.

Given that running takes a fair amount of time and that cross training for that same time would probably drive you crazy, what did you do to keep busy?
I spent a lot of time in the gym cross training and in rehab.

What was the most difficult aspect of being injured? How did you deal psychologically with missing a season?
The worst part is knowing that every day you miss puts you further behind the competition. Also, with a big meet coming up, there's the pressure of time. Money lost from no racing is also a factor.

What specifically did you learn from being injured?
Take all the time you need to properly recover before you begin training.

What advice would you give another elite runner who suffers a season-ending injury?
Don't come back too soon.

When you returned to full-time training, did you alter the type of training you were doing?
I altered it slightly, did more stretching and drills to strengthen the muscle.

What was the result in your first major competition after returning from injury?
Bad result! Was technically still injured so couldn't run freely.

What advice would you give a high school or young college runner regarding injury prevention and/or rehabilitation?
Do all the little things properly. Stretch, warm-up well, warm down, take your time coming back, be healthy first. Also, make sure you cross train; it will keep you fit physically and mentally.

Jeff See

Ohio State University
1500, Mile, 3K, 5K, XC

"...trust your training to the point that it's ok to back off to prevent further injury, training is a long process and a few days off is no problem. Also, when doing rehab you just need to take things one step at a time and not try to predict your level of fitness."

Jeff, briefly profiled
Birth Date and Place: June 6, 1986; Dayton, Ohio
Began running: 13 years old; Began running competitively: 13 years old
Height/Running Weight: 6'1", 162 lbs.

Ohio State University, B.A., 2010 (Marketing and Economics)
College coach: Robert Gary
Middletown High School, Middletown, Ohio (2005)
High school coaches: Dave Fultz

Current residence: Columbus, Ohio
Current occupation: Student
Current affiliation or club: Current coach: Robert Gary

Personal record: 1500—3:40.46 (2009); Mile—3:58.70 (2007)

Notable accomplishments
High School—National champion (4:04.8).
College/Post-Collegiate – Six-time NCAA All-American...USA championship finalist.

Favorite rehab/cross training workout
5 min. warm, 5 min. cool down
20 min. pool run: 1 min. hard, 1 min. easy followed by 20 min. free swim, followed by 15-20 min. pool run: 1min. hard, 1 min. easy.
60 total (max of 70 min.)

Worst running-related injury
Stress fracture in right tibia (lower inside region).

Approximate date of injury, nature of it and was surgery required?
Feb. 1, 2009, after Boston Indoor Games, no surgery required.

What flaw led to the injury? Or did you do something that caused it?
Winter weather forced me to run all my miles on the roads, didn't back off soon enough.

Rehabilitation program that you followed. How long before you resumed "normal" training again?)
Altering pool run/swim with stationary bike (60 min.) 7 days a week.

Given that running takes a fair amount of time and that cross training for that same time would probably drive you crazy, what did you do to keep busy?
To trust your training to the point that it's ok to back off to prevent further injury, training is a long process and a few days off is no problem. Also, when doing rehab you just need to take things one step at a time and not try to predict your level of fitness.

What was the most difficult aspect of being injured? How did you deal psychologically with missing a season? The expectation was that this was a small stress fracture that would heal in 6 weeks, 8 at the most. The hardest part was dealing with the fact that it would affect me all season and wouldn't go away until I rested in the summer. I feel that I could have been much more competitive at NCAAs and USAs where I was 8th and 9th, respectively.

What specifically did you learn from being injured?
To trust your training to the point that it's ok to back off to prevent further injury, training is a long process and a few days off is no problem. Also, when doing rehab you just need to take things one step at a time and not try to predict your level of fitness.

What advice would you give another elite runner who suffers a season-ending injury?
Be patient, take your time, and use it as a break and then recharge.

When you returned to full-time training, did you alter the type of training you were doing?
The main difference in my routine is the peripheral aspects… doing more of the small things like ice massage, ice bath, small strength exercises, better stretching.

Did just as much road running this winter but as a result of a great fall build up, my body handled the stress much more easily.

What was the result in your first major competition after returning from injury? Big 10s – 3rd in the 1500, did not score in the 5k.

What advice would you give a high school or young college runner regarding injury prevention and/or rehabilitation?
It's very easy to prevent injury, pay attention to your body… in my experience it's rarely an acute injury, most of the time your entire body needs a break and a couple days can do the trick. Don't be afraid to back off your training to get healthy.

After you were injured and then coming back, did it change your sense of who you are/were as a runner? Did you have more patience or did you find yourself training on the edge again?
Trust your training to the point that it's okay to back off to prevent further injury, training is a long process and a few days off is no problem. Also, when doing rehab you just need to take things one step at a time and not try to predict your level of fitness.

I think I have a better balance of being patient and aggressive. I can identify things that I should push through and things I should take a step back for. My training is much more intense this year but I've also felt that it's much easier. I think this is mainly because I can read my body better because of what happened last year.

Chris Siemers

Western State College
5K, 10K, XC

"Setbacks can lead to long interruptions if they get the best of you mentally. When you suffer from injury setbacks, let them set you back but not derail you. Keep positive and when you get back you get better!"

Chris, briefly profiled
Birth Date and Place: Jan. 10, 1981, Chicago
Began running: 13 years old; Began running competitively: 16 years old
Height/Running Weight: 5'8", 125 lbs.

Western State College, B.A., 2004 (Business Administration)
College coach: Duane Vandenbusche and Michael Aish
Fenton High School, Bensenville, Ill. (1999)
High school coaches: John Kurtz

Current residence: Gunnison, Colo.
Current occupation: assistant coach, Colorado School of Mines
Current affiliation or club: strands.com/Mizuno
Current Coach: Michael Aish

Personal records: 5K—14:18; Marathon—2:21.22

Notable accomplishments
High School—Footlocker XC All-American, 10th place (1997).
College/Post-Collegiate— NCAA D-II All-American (2001, 2002, 2003). 15th, U.S. XC champs, 12K race (2004); 2007 Glass City marathon winner (2008 Olympic trials qualifier), 2009 Denver marathon winner, 2009 USA mountain running champion (Mt. Washington hill climb)

Favorite rehab/cross training workout
My core routine is my favorite.

Worst running-related injuries
I've had many running injuries and missed lots of time due to them; my worst running injury has yet to be properly diagnosed. I first noticed it back in high school and am still dealing with figuring it out. When I'm running fast I experience left leg weakness and

eventually lose control of the left leg when my stride is repetitive. There is actually no pain associated with the problem, however; running through the loss of control has caused two sports hernias which both were very painful. I can be running very relaxed and the next mile I can be dragging my leg and slowing rapidly.

Approximate date of injuries, nature of them and was surgery required?
April 1998 to current day. I was misdiagnosed in 2002 which led to unsuccessful surgeries for compartment syndrome and peroneal nerve entrapment in 2003, 2004 and 2005. In 2006 and 2007 I had sports hernia operations which I believe were related to my loss of coordination problem. In 2006 I ran the Chicago Marathon and had to limp through most of it; that led to my first sports hernia. Soon after the operation in December 2006 I qualified for the 2008 Olympic Trials marathon by winning the Toledo Glass City marathon by 13 minutes. Not long after that the sports hernia reoccurred on the same side and the second procedure was done in summer of 2007 which kept me out of the Olympic Trials.

What flaw led to the injuries? Or did you do something that caused them?
After all these years I'm realizing the problem is most likely coming from my hip. When I run my left leg turns in, which means I was probably born with my hip rotated in the socket. I feel the problem has to be related to all internal rotation from my hip when I run.

Rehabilitation program that you followed. How long before you resumed "normal" training?
I have been in very great shape numerous times over the years and yet sometimes I would get nothing out of my hard work. In college the symptoms were not as noticeable in cross country, because of grass and uneven surfaces. I was a three time NCAA-II all-American in cross country but could never run track.

My best runs post collegiately were accomplished due to left glute/core exercises and changing my training to help the muscles around my hip/glute fire. I learned that the glute/core routine helped me compensate for whatever the problem is. I was doing lots of core/glute in 2007 and 2009 when I ran my two decent marathons.

Given that running takes a fair amount of time and that cross training for that same time would probably drive you crazy, what did you do to keep busy?
I was never good at this. Now I resort to video games and NetFlix when I go through the periods of "giving up." Luckily I'm currently employed and that keeps me busy most of the time.

What was the most difficult aspect of being injured? How did you deal psychologically with missing a season?
This certainly caused me to be depressed. In high school I only noticed it in longer training runs but because the longest race was 3 miles I never had to deal with it in competition. I was successful, placing 10th at FootLocker my junior season, and a good college career looked promising.

However, I would learn how bad this was when I couldn't get through a lot of training sessions in college. Most of my teammates and college coach didn't understand why I could keep up or be ahead during intervals but in most tempo runs I would fall off early and usually never finish. They eventually understood what I was dealing with but the thought of them thinking I had a mental problem for sure caused me a lot of psychological pain.

What specifically did you learn from being injured?
To control what I can and still run because I love it. I still deal with periods of having my head stuck up my butt. But for the most part I'm doing better because I control what I can, and being in a routine helps me keep confident. I've yet to give up, I entered this year's USA mountain running champions not in very good shape. It ended up being the easiest run of my life because I didn't have to deal with my problem. The uphill slow pace (8 min pace) allowed no problems. I won and qualified for the world mountain championships but decided to pull out because I'm not interested in mountain running yet. But the Mt. Washington race along with running 223:03 at 5,500 feet shows I have talent to be very competitive if I didn't have to deal with this injury.

What advice would you give another elite runner who suffers a season-ending injury?
This sport is very hard and to be your best you have to be 100% confident all year long. Setbacks can lead to long interruptions if they get the best of you mentally. When you suffer from injury setbacks, let them set you back but not derail you. Keep positive and when you get back you get better! Try not to gain weight because that only makes things harder.

When you returned to full-time training, did you alter the type of training you were doing?
I certainly had to alter my training to help compensate for this problem. I tried to make my training repetitive so when the leg fatigued I could make the muscles fire better. An example of this is long progression runs where I can't stop. Also, the problem is worse when the glute is fatigued so doing less speed work and going in rested into the few races I've run has helped. In 2006 I switched to training in racing flats full time and that also helped compensate.

What was the result in your first major competition after returning from injury?
Still have the injury

What advice would you give a high school or young college runner regarding injury prevention and/or rehabilitation?
When you're young you think everything has to happen now. It's really not true; your best running will come between the ages of 27 and 32 if you have your mind right and can train right when older.

Looking back, would you change any of your cross training?
I hate cross training, never did any for this problem.

After being injured and coming back, did it change your sense of who you are/were as a runner? Did you have more patience or did you find yourself training on the edge again?
After qualifying for the world mountain championships I was full of confidence and went crazy in my training. I was excited that I had found something I could do well. However, my 6 weeks of training following the race were way too much. I should have listened to those around me and trained smarter.

Other thoughts on injury prevention or rehabilitation.
I've talked to a few people who have been diagnosed with hip labral tears and this is something I might look into, considering they have dealt with a lot of similar issues.

Patrick Smyth
University of Notre Dame
3K, 5K, 10K, XC

"I learned how easily running could be taken away from me. That was a real 'Eureka' moment, that it could all be gone in an instant. Patience was definitely something I took away from the experience. The only way to achieve greatness is through consistent hard work, the best way to consistency is patience, it's all an organic process. Whenever I've thrown that notion to the wayside is when I've run into problems with training, racing, and injuries."

Patrick, briefly profiled
Birth Date and Place: 8/6/1986; Rock Springs, Wyo.
Began running: 16 years old; Began running competitively: 16 years old
Height/Running Weight: 5'9", 135 lbs.

University of Notre Dame, B.A., 2009 (History)
College coach: Joe Piane
Judge Memorial Catholic High School, Salt Lake City, Utah (graduated spring 2005)
High school coaches: Daniel Quinn, Mike Kirk, Bob Thompson

Current residence: Minnesota
Current occupation: Professional Runner
Current affiliation or club: Team USA Minnesota (Nike)
Current Coach: Dennis Barker

Personal records: 3K—7:55.4; 5K—13:39.5; 10K—28:25.85; Half-marathon: 1:02:01

Notable accomplishments
College/Post-Collegiate—2nd at World Cross Country Trials (2010)... 2nd at Aramco Houston Half Marathon (2010)... 1st at Emerald Nuts/NYRR Midnight Run (2010)... 2nd at Manchester Road Race (2009)... 3rd at USA Men's 10 Mile Championships (2009)... 5th USA Men's 10k Championships (2009)... seven-time NCAA All-American... two-time USTFCCCA Great Lakes Region Athlete of the Year (2007, 2008)... 10 sub-14:00 5K races, most in Notre Dame history... (five sub-13:50 performances)

Favorite rehab/cross training workout
Cycling is my primary mode of cross-training. Favorite workout (on road bike hooked to trainer) is 10 min warm up at 80-90 rpm at
med. resistance, 5x5min hard (as close to lactic threshold as possible, so 170-175 bpm on hr monitor) at 110 rpm and high resistance with 5min easy between reps. 15 min cool down at 70-80rpm.

Worst running-related injury
Severe Achilles tendonitis.

Approximate date of injury, nature of it and was surgery required?
Summer 2008 and again fall 2008, tried to resume training/build up after break too quickly (too much too soon) and the right tendon became severely inflamed sidelining me for about two weeks time. It became inflamed again that fall during early season cross country preparations. No surgery required.

What flaw led to the injury? Or did you do something that caused it?
Too much too soon from the original onset. During cross country I just had the intensity of workouts and training runs at an unsustainable level and it flared up again. My easy days were never easy back then, something I rectified after it flared up again.

Rehabilitation program that you followed. How long before you resumed "normal" training?
One of the best things I did was to see a well known orthopaedic doctor in Salt Lake (Dr. David Petron) who specializes in overuse injuries that lead to tendonitis and non-operative solutions for such problems. He immediately put me on a stretching and strengthening program and suggested that I keep a light running regimen in addition to supplementary cycling/cross training as that had been shown to reduce time to recovery more so than time off completely from running. This regimen combined with daily icing and consistent use of ibuprofen (no more than 800mg per day) helped to bring inflammation down and eliminate the problem in both instances.

Given that running takes a fair amount of time and that cross training for that same time would probably drive you crazy, what did you do to keep busy?
The cross training/light running, icing, stretching etc kept me just as busy, if not more so, than my previous running-only routine.

What was the most difficult aspect of being injured? How did you deal psychologically with missing a season?
I've been extremely lucky. No injury has caused me to miss a major championship or even a significant block of training. But with the Achilles injury, it wore on me psychologically because in the early going because there were days when I thought it would never get better, ever go away. The specter of possibly having to miss a season or even just a race wore on me; but luckily the problem went away before it affected any of my racing plans or seasons.

What specifically did you learn from being injured?
To do the little preventive things. I incorporated a proper warm-up, ancillary strength, icing and general recovery routine into every single run/workout and even cross training days. Also, to be extremely careful in building up after and significant time off as that seems to be when a lot of injuries crop up and if not tended to quickly then you run the risk of the 'one time' issue become a 'chronic' issue.

What advice would you give another elite runner who suffers a season-ending injury?
I think I would be out of place giving advice to another runner who'd suffered a season ending injury, as I've never experienced that hardship. I would simply remind them to make a two-columned list of all the things they love about the sport and all the things they sacrifice for the sport, compare, and make an informed decision as to where ones priorities should lie.

When you returned to full-time training, did you alter the type of training you were doing?
I didn't alter the actual training significantly other than to make my build ups after time off a lot more gradual (30mpw-40mpw-50mpw etc). I incorporated a more substantial general and ancillary strength routine into my overall regimen and took the warm up (active and static stretching, proprioceptor stimulation) as well as the recovery process (icing, massage, chiro, sleep, diet) more seriously.

What was the result in your first major competition after returning from injury?
5th Place at the Notre Dame Invitational (8k cross Country) 23:35.

What advice would you give a high school or young college runner regarding injury prevention and/or rehabilitation?
Do all the little things: active and static stretching, proprioceptor stimulation (ie hurdle drills, leg swings, marches, agility ladder), general and specific strength, icing, massage, chiro, sleep, diet. Even if time/cost factors must be taken into consideration (and 99% of the time they do) then choose a few of these 'supplemental' things to focus on/invest in, as it will pay dividends in the long run.

After being injured and coming back, did it change your sense of who you are/were as a runner? Did you have more patience or did you find yourself training on the edge again?
I learned how easily running could be taken away from me. That was a real 'Eureka' moment; that it could all be gone in an instant. Patience was definitely something I took away from the experience. The only way to achieve greatness is through consistent hard work, the best way to consistency is patience, it's all an organic process. Whenever I've thrown that notion to the wayside is when I've run into problems with training, racing, and injuries.

Other thoughts on injury prevention or rehabilitation.
Remain a well-rounded individual. Keep touch with all the social factors (family, friends, academics, religion) that kept you grounded during the highest of times and pulled you up during the lowest. Isolation and obsessive tendencies of all kinds lead to the creation of an environment where the physical recovery process is hindered.

Josh Spiker
University of Wisconsin
1500

"Just be smart. DO NOT try to be tough and run through anything. It does not work. Take days off if you need to. Ice, get massages, get sleep, eat correctly, stretch, deep your coach informed if anything hurts.

Josh, briefly profiled
Birth Date and Place: March 8, 1982
Began running: 6 years old; Began running competitively: 6 years old
Height/Running Weight: 5'8", 125 lbs.

University of Wisconsin, B.A. (Business Marketing and Management)
College coach: Jerry Schumacher
Ventura High School, Ventura, CA. (graduated spring 2000)
High school coaches: John Kurtz

Current residence: Mammoth Lakes, Cal.
Current occupation: Runner

Personal record: 3:40.36 (2004)

Notable accomplishments
High School—Three-time All-American
College/Post-Collegiate – 9th at NCAA XC (2001)...ran on second-place DMR at indoor NCAA (2002)...3rd in 1500 at NCAA outdoor (2002)...Verizon All-American...Junior National Team XC (2001).

Worst running-related injuries
Stress fracture in tibia twice and a stress fracture in pubic ramus.

Approximate date of injuries, nature of them and was surgery required?
First stress fracture was freshman year of high school and lasted about six months. The second tibia fracture was my senior year of high school and I missed about four months. The pubic fracture occurred in my third year of college and I missed 10 weeks.

What flaw led to the injuries? Or did you do something that caused them?
Basically, training on hard roads, not taking enough easy days, and training too hard.

Rehabilitation program that you followed. How long before you resumed "normal" training?
For the first six month injury I did about 10-12 spinning classes. Each was 45 minutes and I also rode my road bike a lot. For the second four month injury I did about 1.5-2 hours of cross training a day with the elliptical trainer, swimming, aqua-jogging, biking, and the stair stepper. For the last injury, I rode my bike a little and that was it.

Given that running takes a fair amount of time and that cross training for that same time would probably drive you crazy, what did you do to keep busy?
A lot of web site stuff and just lived like a normal college student.

What was the most difficult aspect of being injured? How did you deal psychologically with missing a season?
The most difficult part was knowing that you were going to miss a cross country season for the team or that you were going to be out of shape when you raced. I tried to block running from my thinking process…pretend I wasn't a runner.

What specifically did you learn from being injured?
Be smart and think before you do anything. Take easy days of off days when you need them.

What advice would you give another elite runner who suffers a season-ending injury?
Don't be too hard on yourself. It probably happened because you were working too hard, which isn't a bad thing in a sense. Just live like a regular person and try to enjoy it.

When you returned to full-time training, did you alter the type of training you were doing?
No. I came back slowly but once I was back to running my normal mileage and I did the same type of training.

What was the result in your first major competition after returning from injury?
After my injury during senior year of high school, I ran a 4:17 my first race back in a relay, but a 4:06 later that year.

What advice would you give a high school or young college runner regarding injury prevention and/or rehabilitation?
Just be smart. DO NOT try to be tough and run through anything. It does not work. Take days off if you need to. Ice, get massages, get sleep, eat correctly, stretch, and keep your coach informed if anything hurts.

Jim Spivey

Indiana University
1500, Mile, 3K, 5K, 10K, XC

"When you work out in the pool, approach it like you will be competing in the Olympic pool running contest. Have your coach hold you accountable for getting in your cross-training."

Jim, briefly profiled
Birth Date and Place: March 7, 1960, Franklin Park, Ill.
Began running: 15 years old; Began running competitively: 15 years old; retired:
Height/Running Weight: 5'11", 140 lbs.

Indiana University, B.A., 1983 (Business)
College coach: Sam Bell
Fenton High School, Bensenville, Ill. (1978)
High school coaches: John Kurtz

Current residence: Wheaton, Ill.
Current occupation: ASICS representative

Personal records: 800—1:46.5 (1982); 1000—2:16.54 (1984); 1500—3:31.01 (1988); Mile—3:49.80 (1986); 2K—4:52.44 (1987-AR); 3K—7:37.04 (1993); 5K—13:15.86 (1994)

Notable accomplishments
High School—Three-time state runner-up …state champion at 880 (1978)…#1 ranked U.S 880…#2 ranked mile.
College/Post-Collegiate—Thirteen Big Ten titles…12-time All-American…two-time NCAA champion…1st ever Big Ten athlete of the year award…U.S. Olympic Teams (1984, 1992, 1996)…five-time World Championship qualifier….bronze medalist at World Champs (1987)…silver medalist at Pan Am (1987)…2K American record-holder.

Worst running-related injuries
Left Achilles tendonitis, plantar fasciitis, stress fracture, low back spasms, solas muscle and hamstring, and hip muscle tear.

Approximate date of injuries, nature of them and was surgery required?
Had an injury most years from 1986-1991. I never needed any surgery but did have cortisone shot for both the Achilles and the hip injury to remove scar tissue.

What flaw led to the injuries? Or did you do something that caused them?
Injuries were the result of a number of factors, such as training too fast indoors, mileage, shoes, training too hard while tired, and hips not in balance. The solas muscle and hamstring attachment injury was actually the result of a root canal that got infected from dental work which led to gland spasm and tendonitis in the hamstring.

Rehabilitation program that you followed. How long before you resumed "normal" training?
I did intervals in the pool with an aquajoger on Monday, Wednesday, and Friday. Tuesday and Thursday were recovery days in the pool. I had weights on Monday, Wednesday, and Friday, physical therapy on Tuesday and Friday and I god deep tissue massage on Monday and Thursday. I also rode an exercise bike each morning. Returning to "normal" training depended on the injury and was anywhere from one week to six months.

Given that running takes a fair amount of time and that cross training for that same time would probably drive you crazy, what did you do to keep busy?
I cross-trained far more time in rehab than I would have run. Also, driving to and from place of rehab, waiting at the office, scheduling appointments, all took major amounts of time.

What was the most difficult aspect of being injured? How did you deal psychologically with missing a season?
It was difficult not knowing when I could resume training. I missed out on cash that could have been earned by racing in Europe. In 1988 I pulled training back and my confidence was shaken. I was in shape for the Olympic Trials but I did not fully believe in my abilities. I missed the 1991 world championships despite having made the team.

What specifically did you learn from being injured?
I needed to have a massage once a week regardless of cost. Dr. John Durkin told me, "You are not a Ford or Chevy, and just drive everyday. You are a Ferrari, you run one day, then come see me to get adjusted and checked."

What advice would you give another elite runner who suffers a season-ending injury?
Seb Coe said to me, "You have to approach your injury in cross-training like it is the Olympics of running in the water." When you work out in the pool, approach it like you will be competing in the Olympic pool running contest. Have your coach hold you accountable for getting in your cross-training.

Matt Tegenkamp

University of Wisconsin
5K, XC

"Take a little time to regroup, give your body so time to heal, and rest mentally. Then do what you have to so you can keep yourself focused as you work towards your goals."

> **Matt, briefly profiled**
> Birth Date and Place: Jan. 19, 1982, Kansas City, Mo.
> Began running: 13 years old; Began running competitively: 13 years old
> Height/Running Weight: 6'2", 147 lbs.
>
> University of Wisconsin, B.A., 2005 (Human Ecology)
> College coach: Jerry Schumacher
> Lee's Summit High School, Lee's Summit, Mo. (2000)
> High school coach: Dave Denny
>
> Current residence: Portland, Ore.
> Current occupation: Professional Athlete
> Current affiliation or club: Nike Oregon Project/KIMbia
> Current Coach: Jerry Schumacher
>
> Personal records: 1500—3:34.25 (2007); Mile—3:56.38 (2006); 3K—7:34.98 (2006); 2-Mile—8:07.07 (2007--AR); 5K—12:58.56 (2009)

Notable accomplishments
High School – 5th at Footlocker XC championships (1999)…USA junior XC champion (2001).
College/Post-Collegiate – American Record holder at 2-miles (8:07.07)…Beijing Olympic 5K finalist (2008)…USA 5K champion (2009)…two-time U.S. indoor 3K champ…4th in 5K at 2007 world outdoor.

Favorite rehab/cross training workout
Honestly, I have only crossed trained two or three time in my career; I may be completely wrong but I feel that my fitness comes back just the same whether I cross train or not. My belief is that if your body is injured it could use the rest and heal up. As bad as injuries are they allow me to get away from the stress of the sport and refresh, not only physically, but mentally.

Worst running-related injuries
Stress fractures in right femur and in left tibia.

Approximate date of injuries, nature of them and was surgery required?
Spring 2003, stress fracture in femur; fall 2003, stress fracture in tibia. No surgery needed.

What flaw led to the injuries? Or did you do something that caused them?
One reason I believe is the simple fact that I was growing/maturing. I grew about 4 inches from my freshman to my junior year in college. That combined with the intense training combined with not listening to my body (warning signs) led to the fractures. I now realize that if the body needs it and you need a few days of not running/down time you are not going to lose fitness. I am not saying that I don't push training to the red line and that I still don't go too far but more times then not I am able to read the warning signs and keep myself healthy.

Rehabilitation program that you followed. How long did the rehab take before you resumed "normal" training? Nothing from the past. But now that I am living in Portland and have access to the Alter-G, I use that to start training back up. When I feel I am out of the woods and feeling healthy I will utilize the Alter-G for about 10 days to 2 weeks to get the legs moving again and make sure everything is 100%.

Given that running takes a fair amount of time and that cross training for that same time would probably drive you crazy, what did you do to keep busy?
During college I would still show up to the locker room and be a part of the team. I wanted to be there to support the team and help out however I could. Now that I am married and have a family and house I have plenty to do to keep me busy. I love projects!!

What was the most difficult aspect of being injured? How did you deal psychologically with missing a season?
I would say the hardest season was the 2003 fall cross country season because I was not able to help out the team. Every thing else was individual and while I could have accomplished more I have had plenty of great moments to consider my career a success.

What specifically did you learn from being injured?
A little rest here and there will not hurt your fitness.

What advice would you give another elite runner who suffers a season-ending injury?
Take a little time to regroup, give your body so time to heal, and rest mentally. Then do what you have to so you can keep yourself focused as you work towards your goals.

When you returned to full-time training, did you alter the type of training you were doing?
After the stress fracture I started adding a second run 3 or 4 days a week. This allowed me to still run the mileage but do it in a short burst. After I graduated college, I got serious about core training and that has become an integral part of my training routine.

What was the result in your first major competition after returning from injury?
I don't know what my first result was but I competed in the 2004 indoor season and after missing two straight season I ran a 13:44 5K and 13:30 outdoors.

What advice would you give a high school or young college runner regarding injury prevention and/or rehabilitation?
For most athletes pushing the limits of training, injuries are going to happen. The difference in the athlete who takes the next step is one that can learn from their injuries so they don't continue to make the same mistakes.

After being injured and coming back, did it change your sense of who you are/were as a runner? Did you have more patience or did you find yourself training on the edge again?
I am a patient person and know if I stick to the plan and see the big picture injuries are only a bump in the road and I can still achieve everything I want.

Edwardo Torres
University of Colorado
5K, 10K, XC, Marathon

"After each injury...I learned different things... In some cases I became a little more cautious on how far I pushed my training. It kind of took away the innocence of just going out and training hard.... I did become more patient with my building phase..."

Edwardo, briefly profiled
Birth Date and Place: Aug. 22, 1980; Chicago, Ill.
Began running: 13 years old; Began running competitively: 13 years old; retired: 30 years old
Height/Running Weight: 5'7", 117 lbs.

University of Colorado, B.A, 2003 (Economics)
College coach: Mark Wetmore and Jason Drake
Wheeling High School, Wheeling, Ill. (1999)
High school coaches: Greg Fedyski

Current residence: Chicago, Ill.
Current occupation: owner, medal engraving systems

Personal records: 5K—13:59.84 (2002); 10K—28:16.87 (2009); Marathon—2:17.54 (2008)

Notable accomplishments
High School—Four-time all-state in XC ...three-time FootLocker qualifier...state runner-up in 3200 (1998, '99).
College/Post-Collegiate—Three-time XC All-American...3rd at USA XC championships (2003)...World XC qualifier in Switzerland ...NCAA All-American 10K (2003).

Favorite rehab/cross training workout
Aqua jogging fartlek workouts 20x1 min on and 1 min off. Plus a 1/2 hr swim after the workout.

Worst running-related injuries
I had two stress fractures on the inside of my shins. I fell on a run on a trail my left knee sustained a rock in it. Had IT band issues.

Approximate date of injuries, nature of them and was surgery required?
Freshman year of high school in right shin and sophomore year of high school in left shin. My sophomore year of college, I had a left knee injury; a rock stabbed me, major tissue damage.

What flaw led to the injuries? Or did you do something that caused them?
Stress fractures were caused by too much cement running and part of it was that I was growing. The knee injury was a freak accident. With the IT band, I ran a snowy run and strained it and then I continued to push through it.

Rehabilitation program that you followed. How long before you resumed "normal" training?
Rehab for stress fractures: Ultra sound, ice massage for 20 minutes, two times a day; swimming 60 minutes a day. I did this for one to one and a half months. When I started running again it felt like I still had a stress fracture for the first week. Treatments went on for three weeks and after that I felt good.

Rehab for knee injury: one month off. Then first week back running I did 20 minutes of running and added 5-10 minutes everyday that week till the end of the week. The second week I ran 60 miles and I would ice twice a day. I also did exercise for my knee and did ultrasound twice a day. This went on for two months.
Rehab for IT band: ultra sound, stretching sessions twice a day for 20 minutes, strengthening exercises, and ice massages. I missed a season with this one.

Given that running takes a fair amount of time and that cross training for that same time would probably drive you crazy, what did you do to keep busy?
I would become a regular civilian for a couple weeks. Give that I was a student, school would take up most of the time.

What was the most difficult aspect of being injured? How did you deal psychologically with missing a season?
Watching my base go to hell. Missing a season was painful because I would watch my brother win all these races. I wanted to be out there having the same fun he was.

What specifically did you learn from being injured?
To be patient; if something isn't feeling good, listen to your body.

What advice would you give another elite runner who suffers a season-ending injury?
Don't try to be superman and try to come back to fast. Build yourself to be stronger at that weak spot where injury occurred.

When you returned to full-time training, did you alter the type of training you were doing?
No, running mileage and workouts did not change after any injury. I just went back to the woodwork.

What was the result in your first major competition after returning from injury?
After knee injury I finished 27th at NCAA cross country championships.

What advice would you give a high school or young college runner regarding injury prevention and/or rehabilitation?
I would say stretch a lot, keep hydrated, and get your rest sleep straight not five hours at night and five during the day. Listen to your body.

Looking back, would you change any of your cross training?
I would add more sprint drills and plyo stuff to my cross training. I lacked this very much in my youth and it's what gets you stronger and keeps you healthy. I would also add more bike riding to my workouts. Swimming didn't get all the cardio I needed.

After being injured and coming back, did it change your sense of who you are/were as a runner? Did you have more patience or did you find yourself training on the edge again?
I learned different things after each injury. In some cases I became a little more cautious on how far I pushed my training. It kind of took away the innocence of just going out and training hard. I did become more patient with my building phase and would learn to bring in faster stuff later and shorter time of it before my big races.

Other thoughts on injury prevention or rehabilitation
I would advice any young runner reading this to incorporate sprint drills and weights you're your training regimen as early as possible. It is key to building strong core and keeping healthy. Every year you build on this it will only make you stronger as you get older. The results don't show immediately but it's money in the bank that matures at a later time.

Jorge Torres

University of Colorado
5K, 10K, Marathon, XC

"I think one thing that most professional runners can do to prolong their careers is to take more easy or rest days. The recovery days are just as important as the workout days."

Jorge, briefly profiled
Birth Date and Place: Aug. 22, 1980; Chicago, Ill.
Began running: 12 years old; Began running competitively: 12 years old
Height/Running Weight: 5'7", 120 lbs.

University of Colorado, B.A., 2004 (Economics)
College coach: Mark Wetmore
Wheeling High School, Wheeling, Ill. (1999)
High school coaches: Greg Fedyski

Current residence: Boulder, Colo.
Current occupation: Athlete
Current affiliation or club: Reebok
Current Coach: Steve Jones
Personal records: 1500—3:41.29 (2004); 3K—7:51.15 (2003); 5K—13:20.57 (2005); 10K—27:42.91 (2007); Marathon—2:13 (2009)

Notable accomplishments
High School—Three-time state XC champ… four-time Footlocker qualifier…four-time all-American…Footlocker national champion.
College/Post-Collegiate— Nine-time all-American…NCAA XC champion…2nd at U.S. XC championships 4K (2002)… 11th at IAAF World Champs (2002)…USATF 10K track champion (2006)… 3rd in 10K in Olympic Trials… 2008 US Olympian….7th in 2009 NYC Marathon (2:13, debut)

Worst running-related injuries
Left Achilles tendonitis; stress fracture, right hip, and IT Band issues on both left and right side.

Approximate date of injuries, nature of them and was surgery required?
I pulled my Achilles tendon in March 1998; this then turned to tendonitis. I injured the Achilles again in January 2001. I ran with a blister on my Achilles in the ice for two hours

and that became tendonitis as well. The stress fracture in my hip in March 1999 came from running too much. No surgeries were needed.

What flaw led to the injuries? Or did you do something that caused them?
The first Achilles injury came from running too much and lack of stretching. The second time it came from running two hours in slippery conditions with a blister already on the Achilles. The stress fracture simply came from too much mileage and eventually my body broke down.

Rehabilitation program that you followed. How long before you resumed "normal" training?
I did ultrasound and a lot of stretching on the Achilles. It took me two months to run normally again but I did run through it. The second Achilles injury was different. I wore a night splint and a boot during the day. I did no running or cross training for five weeks. I did a lot of ultrasound, stem, cross-friction massage, and stretching every day. I saw a chiropractor and did both ultrasound and stem for the stress fracture. I couldn't run for 10 weeks.

Given that running takes a fair amount of time and that cross training for that same time would probably drive you crazy, what did you do to keep busy?
When I get hurt, I just turn into a civilian. I play golf, ride my motorcycle (if weather permits), or take my dogs for hikes.

What was the most difficult aspect of being injured? How did you deal psychologically with missing a season?
Realizing that I was injured was the most difficult aspect. At first I didn't know how to take it. Then I realized that there was nothing I can do about healing it in that moment, so I decided to act like a normal person would and enjoy the extra free time.

What specifically did you learn from being injured?
With every injury I have learned how to recover my body. I've learned what my body's limits are and I make sure to pay attention to that.

What advice would you give another elite runner who suffers a season-ending injury?
Reflect on the mistakes you made. Make a mental note and learn from those mistakes.

When you returned to full-time training, did you alter the type of training you were doing?
The first couple of weeks I always took it really easy. I wouldn't feel comfortable training on until I felt my body was fully recovered from the injury.

What was the result in your first major competition after returning from injury?
I've never really won a big race after returning from injury. I was only 5th in the 5K outdoor NCAA and 13th in the 5K at the U.S. championships in 2001. I attribute the bad showings to a lack of base training.

What advice would you give a high school or young college runner regarding injury prevention and/or rehabilitation?
Aches and pains are signs from your body. If you can rest once you feel these aches and pains then you will more than likely escape a season-ending injury.

Looking back, would you change any of your cross training?
I would probably do some cross training to keep the weight off. But I tend to just take time off during my injuries.

After being injured and coming back, did it change your sense of who you are as a runner? Did you have more patience or did you find yourself training on the edge again?
While being injured I often asked myself if running was worth it. My answer would always be "yes." I would also reflect on my life and career goals, so that when I resumed training I would have a sense of what I wanted to achieve. I learn a lot about myself while injured. Patience was up there on my list.

Other thoughts on injury prevention or rehabilitation.
I think one thing that most professional runners can do to prolong their careers is to take more easy or rest days. We tend to push our bodies pretty hard and never really give them a chance to recover. The recovery days are just as important as the workout days.

Ryan Vail

Oklahoma State University
5K, XC

"There is no point in being in great shape if you can't toe the line when it's important. I learned to not be so focused on counting mileage and focus more on the signals my body was providing."

Ryan, briefly profiled
Birth Date and Place: March 19, 1986, Portland, Ore.
Began running: 14 years old; Began running competitively: 17 years old
Height/Running Weight: 5'9", 138 lbs.

Oklahoma State University, B.A., 2009 (Spanish Political Science; M.S., International Studies)
College coach: Dave Smith
Centennial High School, Portland, Ore. (2004)
High school coaches: Gregg Letts and Julie Hilsenteger

Current residence: Gresham, Ore.
Current occupation: Professional Runner
Current affiliation or club: Brooks
Current Coach: Dave Smith

Personal Records: 3K—7:52.17i (2009); 5K—13:37.02 (2009); 15K—44:37 (2010)

Notable accomplishments
College/Post-Collegiate –Three-time NCAA XC All-American…Two-time NCAA track All-American…captain of 2009 NCAA XC national championship team…Member of the three USA cross country teams (2005, '09, '10)…33rd at World XC Championships (2009).

Favorite rehab/cross training workout
With a stress fracture there is not much rehab that can be done. I was staying off my feet as much as possible, wearing a boot, and taking a calcium supplement. This was before Oklahoma State was equipped with an Alter-G treadmill, so staying in the pool was important.

Worst running-related injury:
Stress fracture

Approximate date of injury, nature of it and was surgery required?
In the fall of 2007, I suffered a stress fracture on the tibia of my right leg. Surgery was not required. I missed 6 weeks which included the 2007 cross country season.

Rehabilitation program that you followed. How long before you resumed "normal" training?
I took 2 weeks with no training. I was wearing a boot, and limiting my walking. After 2 weeks, I spent 4 weeks aqua jogging 2 hours a day (usually two workouts a day). As I got stronger in the pool I moved to fartlek and interval aqua jogging sessions. Eventually I rid myself of the flotation belt and was able to aqua jog for a complete 2 hour session without one.

Given that running takes a fair amount of time and that cross training for that same time would probably drive you crazy, what did you do to keep busy?
I actually tried to cross train for more time than I was running. Thinking back, I don't know how I stayed in the pool for 2 hours per day, and I'm not sure I could do it again. I had a teammate who had also suffered an injury in the pool with me many of the days, which helped tremendously.

Anybody who has every tried aqua jogging knows how lonely and horribly boring the task can be. Cross training this much helped me stay focused on fitness rather than taking up my time with other unproductive distractions that can be found on a college campus.

What was the most difficult aspect of being injured? How did you deal psychologically with missing a season?
The worst part about this stress fracture was the timing. I was in the best shape of my life, and we had a great cross country team during the 2007 season. This was one of the many letdowns facing the team that year, and I felt helpless. I tried to run through the pain for as long as possible and even had myself convinced I could still contribute at NCAA cross country nationals which were 5 weeks away.

After putting in a great summer of training, having a great opening race, and being surrounded by the best team Oklahoma State had seen in many years, it was heartbreaking to be getting soggy in the pool every day rather than helping my team.

What specifically did you learn from being injured?
TAKE DAYS OFF. Whenever I feel any sort of hot spot anywhere on my body, I take two days off or two days in the pool right away. Taking a couple of days off a few times during a season will not significantly impact your fitness, and it might keep you healthy. There is no point in being in great shape if you can't toe the line when it's important. I learned to not be so focused on counting mileage and focus more on the signals my body was providing.

This is a difficult but important lesson for every runner to learn. There are the select few runners who can run for years at very high volume with a day off and stay injury free, but this doesn't apply to many people. Listen to your body.

What advice would you give a high school or young college runner regarding injury prevention and/or rehabilitation?
Stress fractures are difficult to diagnose in the early stages. It can feel like only muscle tightness at first and quickly transition into a throbbing bone pain, and by this time it is too late. Localized pain near a bone is a warning that should be heeded and accounted for. Take a few days in the pool, or off completely, and let it cool down. Even if the pain was not at all bone-related, your chances of feeling fresh and remaining injury-free are then greatly increased.

Micah VanDenend

University of Iowa
3K, 5K, 10K, XC

"I always tell people that I have a love/hate relationship with cross training. I hate cross training but I love the mental toughness that is developed as a result. Some things you can't learn by simply running on the roads."

Micah, briefly profiled
Date/Place of Birth: Feb. 23, 1984, Hinsdale, Ill.
Began running: 10 years old; Began running competitively: 10 years old
Height/Running Weight: 5'9", 130 lbs.

Iowa, B.A., 2006 (History, Religious Studies); 2008 (Health & Sport Studies)
College coach: Larry Wieczorek
Glenbard South H.S., Glen Ellyn, Ill. (2002)
High school coaches: Andy Preuss and Terry Artman

Current residence: Kenosha, Wis.
Current occupation: Men's & Women's Track/Cross Country Coach, University of Wisconsin-Parkside Current affiliation or club: unattached
Current coach: Larry Wieczorek

Personal records: 3K—8:00.81 (2007); 5K—13:49.31 (2007)

Notable accomplishments
High School—Class AA Illinois state cross country champ as a senior in 2001, leading team to state title... won 3200 in track as a senior in only third meet of season... placed eighth in 3,200 at Golden West... set school records in 1600 (4:11.9) and 3 miles in XC (14:19)... other best time was 9:04 in 3,200 meters.
College—2007 Big Ten 10,000-meter champion in only race at that distance... 2006 NCAA Midwest Region cross country champion... 2006 NCAA Midwest regional cross country runner of the year... three-time cross country all-region honoree... four-time NCAA cross country national qualifier... set Iowa 3,000 (8:00.81) and 5,000-meter (13:56.46) records indoors, and 5,000-meter (13:49.31) record outdoors.

Favorite rehab/cross training workout:
One of my favorite workouts on the stationary bike. Each bike is different and you need to find what kind of RPMs and what levels work for you. I try to do 80-85 RPMs for my warm-ups, cool downs, and rest intervals. I try to keep the hard intervals between 100-110 RPMs.
—Start with 15 minutes of a gradual warm-up.
—The workout: 1-1-2-2-3-3-4-4-5-5-4-3-2-1 (Each of these is a hard segment and should be followed by easy pedaling at half the length rest. Therefore, after the 1 minute hard you get 30 seconds rest. After 2 hard you get 1 minute rest, 3 hard gives you 1.5 minutes rest, and so on).
—15 minute cool down!
This workout gives you 1.5 hours of work and usually leaves me drenched in sweat and ready to throw up.

Worst running-related injuries:
· Numerous stress fractures in right fibula and other overuse injuries.

Approximate date of injuries, nature of them and was surgery required?
· Stress fracture in right fibula that began in September 2000 and lasted through April of 2001. I nearly lost a chunk of bone from my leg. (8 months)
· Had tendonitis in right Achilles in 2002. (2 months)
· A quad injury that began in November my freshman year of college and led into an Achilles injury that kept me from running the winter and spring (indoor and outdoor track season) of 2003. (5 months)
· Stress fracture in right fibula began in the summer of 2003 and lasted through most of the winter of 2004. (6 months)
· Hip and IT Band issues that kept me from running the spring of 2004. (3 months)
· More IT band problems and a stress reaction in right fibula again in the spring of 2005. I once again missed the indoor and outdoor track seasons (this was the third year in a row that I didn't run a single indoor or outdoor track race). (4 months)
· Stress reaction in right fibula in late spring of 2006. Qualified for NCAA outdoor championships but couldn't run. Lasted from early May to late July 2006. (2-3 months)
· Stress fracture in right fibula beginning in January 2008. This is still my ongoing injury and has resulted in four surgeries over the last two years.
· Stress fracture in right foot occurred in early November 2009 and lasted through March 2010. This stress fracture popped up after only about two weeks of jogging after two years off from the previous injury. I'm dealing with a lot of muscle weaknesses and imbalances as a result of all that time off.

What flaw led to the injuries? Or did you do something that caused them?
I'm still searching for the answers here. I don't believe that it was one thing that led me to these injuries but a combination of things, e.g., overtraining, going above my training ceiling, lack of prehabbing (strengthening done before you get hurt and have to rehab). I wasn't able to build a base because I was always getting ready for something. I was doing

too much, too fast, too soon. This is a different story with my most recent stress fracture in the fibula which had a lot to do with the surgery I underwent.

Rehabilitation program that you followed. How long before you began "normal" training?
I'm not sure that "normal" training after began again. I had to find a "new normal" that worked for me.

Given that running takes a fair amount of time and that cross training for that same time would probably drive you crazy, what did you do to keep busy?
I crossed trained anyway. In fact, I cross trained more than I would have run. I tried to do some mixture of biking, pool running, and elliptical training for 30-45 min each morning and 75-120 min each afternoon. I didn't cross train this extensively through my early injures (probably an hour a day through the early ones) but over time, I learned that you have to work even harder when you are on the sideline.
I spent hours with the athletic trainer getting massages, doing lower leg strengthening exercise, and doing modalities. I saw deep tissues therapists, acupuncturists, and all kinds of doctors.

I lifted weights more rigorously, I iced multiple times a day, and I stretched like crazy.

What was the most difficult aspect of being injured? How did you deal psychologically with missing a season?
The toughest part is the "what ifs." It's always wondering what could have been if only you were able to stay healthy, train consistently, and compete. It's difficult to watch everyone else around you go out the door for a run or to hear them talk about upcoming races when you are relegated to the pool or bike and you have no sight of running in the future. Sometimes it's difficult to hear people try to give you advice or encouragement when you know that they are merely giving you empty words and promises. They typically don't know if and when you will run again any more than you do. As runners, we love to run. It's always hard to deal with losing something that you love. It's like losing a part of yourself.

Psychologically? It's important to have the right people around you. I had a coach who would always remind me that I was writing my own story and that it was shaping up to be a good one. He would tell me that it is better that this be happening to me than anyone else because I was tough enough to get through it. Really, he was just feeding me crap but it was what I needed to hear.

You have to remind yourself over and over again that you are the toughest guy out there and that you will eventually get through this injury and show everyone just how tough you are.

I also had a lot of support, encouragement, and prayers from my family, friends and teammates. I wouldn't have made it without this support system.

What specifically did you learn from being injured?
First of all, I learned that being injured sucks. I also learned that when injured, you really only have two options: roll over and die or fight like hell. I take pride in being a fighter. I learned how much I loved running. I learned that I was willing to do things that most other people are not willing to do (cross train for 2+ hours a day). I learned to persevere; I learned to never back down from a challenge; most importantly, I learned a lot about encouragement and humility. As I said, I have been blessed to have a great core of individuals around me who encouraged me and made it easy for me to keep after it.

What advice would you give another elite runner who suffers a season-ending injury?
Don't back down from the challenge at hand. You became an elite runner by being both mentally and physically tough, being fearless, and tackling each running challenge that was thrown at you. Embark upon this challenge with the same fearlessness, desire, passion, toughness, and courage. "Never be broken" is a phrase I try to train by.

When you returned to full-time training, did you alter the type of training you were doing?
Each time I was hurt, I learned something new. I altered the training that I was doing by beginning to incorporate more and more cross training into my daily workouts. I learned that 60-70 miles was probably the top end of mileage that my body could handle. So instead of continuing to push the envelope and reach for those 80-mile weeks, I supplemented. I still ran 60-70 miles but continued to cross train for 30-45 minutes each morning.
I also began taking each Monday completely off from running and I used that day as only a cross training/recovery day.

What was the result in your first major competition after returning from injury?
I've had mixed results depending on the injury and the length of time of the injury. Also depends on the length of training I had done before being thrown back into racing. I'm still expecting big results from my next comeback.

What advice would you give a high school or young college runner regarding injury prevention and/or rehabilitation?
As to injury prevention, take pride in doing the little things (icing, stretching, core strength, etc.). As runners, it is easy to get out the door and run. Every runner does that part because as runners, we love to run. But it is all of the other little things that take the real commitment. All of the other things are not fun, they are not easy to do, and they take time. It is also these things that set you apart from everyone else. If all it took to be great was running, everyone would be national champs and Olympians. It's the person who goes above and beyond who gets the well deserved glory.

Listen to your body. As distance runners we often think that we can run through anything. We have this no pain, no gain attitude. But it is better to take a day or two off from running than to find your self missing weeks and months on end. You can look at these days off as planned recovery days that keep you healthy and consistent in training. When you are forced to take unplanned recovery days (because of injury) that's when you are in real trouble. It took me a long, long time to learn this lesson.

Looking back, would you change any of your cross training?
I wish I would have known through my early injuries what I had found out the hard way and applied to my later injuries. I don't think that it is the kind of cross training that you do that matters. It is the consistency, the intensity, and the duration.

After being injured and coming back, did it change your sense of who you are/were as a runner? Did you have more patience or did you find yourself training on the edge again?
In a lot of ways, I think it is important to not let the injury change you. It may change some of the things you do. Hopefully it makes you listen to your body more, makes you think more about prehabbing, icing, strengthening, etc. That being said, you will never be any good if you aren't willing to walk the edge. Ken Popejoy told me when I was in high school that there is a fine line between a record and an injury. He's absolutely right. You've got to find the right balance and you've got to walk along the edge; just don't fall off.

Other thoughts on prevention/ rehabilitation
Train hard, recover hard.

Don't think that you have all the answers and don't be afraid to seek out advice from others.

Stay optimistic; keep the faith. It is not a matter of if you will get through it but a matter of when. Cross train like crazy so you are ready when opportunity knocks.

A final comment: I have heard from a lot of injured athletes who have cross trained for a very long time (months) that there is eventually a breaking point, a point when you feel fed up and feel as if you can no longer continue on cross training. I've had these moments— where 20 minutes into a cross training session I have just stopped, taken a shower and gone home. I've even been to the point where for a couple days I wouldn't even get on the bike because I could no longer see the point. I believe that that is normal. But your desire to be great will eventually get the best of you. I can never stay away from the bike/ elliptical for too long (more than a couple days) because I always have to prove to myself how tough I am.

I always tell people that I have a love/hate relationship with cross training. I hate cross training but I love the mental toughness that is developed as a result. Some things you can't learn by simply running on the roads.

Luke Watson

University of Notre Dame
Mile, 3K, steeplechase, 5K, Marathon, XC

"Be diligent in prevention; this is the first step to being injury-free. Focus on the future when injured. Try to avoid rushing back to training and competition. Know your body! Listen to it. Sometimes it says do more, sometimes less. Try not to force anything."

Luke, briefly profiled
Birth Date and Place: Aug. 20, 1980; Minneapolis, Minn.
Began running: 12 years old; Began running competitively: 14 years old
Height/Running Weight: 6'0", 150 lbs.

Penn State University, Ph.D. Candidate, 2013 (Accounting)
University of Notre Dame, B.A., 2002 (Accounting); M.S., 2003 (Accounting)
College coach: Joe Piane
Stillwater High School, Stillwater, Minn. (1998)
High school coaches: Scott Christensen

Current residence: State College, Pa.
Current occupation: Athlete and graduate student

Personal records: Mile—3:57.0; 3K—7:49; Steeple—8:36; 5K—13:38; Half—1:03.51; Marathon—2:15.29

Notable accomplishments
High School—Five-time Minnesota state champion. Gatorade Midwest Track Athlete of the Year. 1:53.0, 4:12 1600, 9:08 3200
College/Post-Collegiate— 5th NCAA XC (2001), 7th (2000)…six-time All-American …six-time Big East champion… Drake Relays champ (4x1600)…U.S. Junior XC champion (1999)…32nd at World Junior XC.
Three-time Olympic Trials qualifier (2004, 5K; 2008, 3000mSC; 2012, Marathon).

Favorite rehab/cross training workout
Road biking.

Worst running-related injuries:
IT Band friction syndrome in right hip and knee.

Approximate date of injury, nature of it and was surgery required?
January 2001 was the worst time of it. It reoccurs once in a while but now I know how to fend it off.

What flaw led to the injury? Or did you do something that caused it?
I was in Minnesota over Christmas break. It was a particularly cold winter with lots of snow and ice. I probably ran on city, hard pavement too much. Also, the slope of the roads when always running on the left side probably contributed. I also may have jumped into speed work too quickly.

Rehabilitation program that you followed. How long before you resumed "normal" training?
One week of swimming only with one day off. One week of swim, bike, run, and then one day off. Two weeks of limited running with one day of each week. Then I transitioned into some easy, slower speed work gradually building back to full speed work after two weeks.

I also did chiropractic care two times each week during the first month then one time each week after that. I did electric stim 1-2 times per day during the first two weeks. I also did lots of stretching, some ultrasound, and heat before activity and ice after.

Given that running takes a fair amount of time and that cross training for that same time would probably drive you crazy, what did you do to keep busy?
I cross-trained approximately the same volume (in minutes) as I would have run. Plus, it wasn't a long period, so the cross training was not that bad. Because it was my redshirt season, we did not rush getting me into shape or into racing. This was definitely better than if we had rushed things because I'm certain it would have returns.

What was the most difficult aspect of being injured? How did you deal psychologically with missing a season?
Being at track meets and not racing and being at the track while missing out on workouts were the worst parts. I was, however, glad that it allowed me to focus on the outdoor season. Really, I don't feel like I missed too much, because I was redshirting anyway.

What specifically did you learn from being injured?
Importance of stretching, varying running surfaces, and not jumping into speed work too quickly.

What advice would you give another elite runner who suffers a season-ending injury?
Forget about it; it's "water under the bridge," as they say. Focus on what is ahead, getting ready for the next season. Have the courage to take a day off.

When you returned to full-time training, did you alter the type of training you were doing?
Not much, I just avoided roads more and did more IT Band and glute stretching.

What was the result in your first major competition after returning from injury?
I ran 13:49, then a PR at 5K, on May 4, 2001.

What advice would you give a high school or young college runner regarding injury prevention and/or rehabilitation?
Be diligent in prevention; this is the first step to being injury-free. Focus on the future when injured. Try to avoid rushing back to training and competition. Know your body! Listen to it. Sometimes it says do more, sometimes less. Try not to force anything.

Looking back, would you change any of your cross training?
I think it was appropriate. If anything, I would do less. The body needs the chance to recover.

After being injured and coming back, did it change your sense of who you are/were as a runner? Did you have more patience or did you find yourself training on the edge again?
I feel that I was always pretty aware of how my body was feeling, and that was a gift that allowed me to go uninjured for virtually all my career. I know the feeling of the IT band syndrome now and I know when I need to address it.

Other thoughts on injury prevention or rehabilitation.
Many injuries are symptoms of something that is going wrong elsewhere in the body, so you often must treat the source of the imbalance, which is different than the part of the body that hurts.

Alan Webb

University of Michigan
800, 1500, Mile, 3K, 5K, XC

"Running is a contact sport with every step a force of 3-5 times your body weight is being placed on your legs. If you can look at running in this way then you and your coach will become more aware of the risks of intense training and therefore plan this training in a more precise manner which will lead to fewer injuries and, most importantly, to faster running."

Alan, briefly profiled
Birth Date and Place: Jan. 13, 1983, Ann Arbor, Mich.
Began running: From Birth; Began running competitively: From Birth
Height/Running Weight: 5'9", 140 lbs.

University of Michigan (2001-02 school year)
College coach: Ron Warhurst (one year); and Scott Raczko
South Lakes H.S., Reston, Va. (2001)
High school coaches: Marc Hunter and Scott Raczko

Current residence: Portland, Ore.
Current occupation: Professional runner
Current affiliation or club: Nike
Current Coach: Alberto Salazar

Personal records: 800—1:43.84 (2007); 1500—3:30.54 (2007); Mile—3:46.91 (2007); 2 mile—8:11.48 (2005); 5K—13:10.86 (2005); 10K—27:34.72 (2006)

Notable accomplishments
High School—FootLocker finalist...broke Jim Ryun's H.S. mile record with a 3:53.43 in the Pre meet at Eugene...
College/Post-Collegiate–ran at Michigan for one season before turning pro...won Big Ten XC title and was 11th in NCAA XC...won Big Ten outdoor 1500 and was 4th in NCAA...won 2004 Olympic Trials 1500, ran in Athens...won U.S. 1500 titles in 2005 & 2007, placing 9th and 8th, respectively, in World Champs...

Worst running-related injuries
Right perriformis (hip) and right Achilles strains.

Approximate date of injuries, nature of them and was surgery required?
Both were caused by simple training overload and both were season/year ending injuries.

Rehabilitation program that you followed. How long before you resumed "normal" training?
Water-running and weight training at first but only thing that really healed both injuries was TIME OFF!!!

Given that running takes a fair amount of time and that cross training for that same time would probably drive you crazy, what did you do to keep busy?
Try my best to concentrate on school more.

What was the most difficult aspect of being injured? How did you deal psychologically with missing a season?
The hardest part was only when I was actually taking the time off. Once I got back running I made a conscious decision to put the past behind me and look towards my goals in the future.

What advice would you give another elite runner who suffers a season-ending injury?
Since your season is over anyway, take whatever appropriate time off to heal injury (this obviously depends on the injury). Whatever that recommended time off is, add a week to it just in case. That way once you do start to run again you will be 110% confident that everything is healed up and you will probably have built up a nice healthy gut.

I find this a rededicating experience because when I look at myself in the mirror the morning before that first run, after eaten McDonalds everyday for the last month and a half, see that pot belly, and realize what it is like to be "normal." It makes me want to work that much harder to eat right and run hard (but smart).

What advice would you give a high school or young college runner regarding injury prevention and/or rehabilitation?
TAKE IT SLOW on the way back. There is no need to rush things. It is hard and having a coach that you trust is a big part of this and I should probably go back and read what I have just written and try to take some of my own advice because I have made the mistake of trying to come back after an injury too soon and too fast only to have to take more time off, which was the situation with my Achilles injury.

Other thoughts on injury prevention or rehabilitation.
Running is a contact sport with every step a force of 3-5 times your body weight is being placed on your legs. If you can look at running in this way then you and your coach will become more aware of the risks of intense training and therefore plan this training in a more precise manner which will lead to fewer injuries and, most importantly, to faster running.

Larry Wieczorek
University of Iowa
Mile, 5K, XC

"Many injuries stem from the 'too's'—too much, too soon, too fast, etc. Be progressive and consistent."

Larry, briefly profiled
Birth Date and Place: Sept. 11, 1946; Chicago, Ill.
Began running: 15 years old; Began running competitively: 15 years old
Height/Running Weight: 5'8", 135 lbs.
Retired: 1970

University of Iowa, B.A. (1968)
College coach: Francis Cretzmeyer
Proviso East High School, Maywood, Ill. (1964)
High school coaches: Bob Polson and Don Green

Current residence: Iowa City, Iowa
Current occupation: Head Track and Cross Country Coach, University of Iowa

Personal records: Mile—4:04; 5K—13:56.0

Notable accomplishments
High School—state mile record (4:14)…state mile champ (1963, '64).
College/Post-Collegiate – Big Ten champion…All-American…U.S. international team (1968).

Favorite rehab/cross training workout
I swam, rode the stationary bike, and did body weight strength training.

Worst running-related injuries
Stress fracture in the tibia, Achilles tendonitis and a ruptured Achilles tendon.

Approximate date of injuries, nature of them and was surgery required?
Stress fracture in the fall of 1965. Dealt with Achilles tendonitis from 1968-70 and in 1970 I ruptured my Achilles and had to have it surgically repaired.

What flaw led to the injuries? Or did you do something that caused them?
Overuse injuries.

Rehabilitation program that you followed. How long before you resumed "normal" training?
I did swimming workouts—swimming laps, not aqua jogging. I rode the stationary bike and simulated running workouts. I did body weight strength training, pull-ups, pushups, dips, and sit-ups.

Given that running takes a fair amount of time and that cross training for that same time would probably drive you crazy, what did you do to keep busy?
I cross trained to stay physically fit and mentally tough and strong. I stayed engaged with my teammates and coach. I also spend a lot more time on academics.

What was the most difficult aspect of being injured? How did you deal psychologically with missing a season?
None. However, my post collegiate career ended prematurely because of chronic Achilles tendon injuries and I started teaching P.E. and coaching in high school.

What specifically did you learn from being injured?
Perseverance!! Greatness delayed is not greatness denied.

What advice would you give a high school or young college runner regarding injury prevention and/or rehabilitation?
Don't just run miles. Work on core muscle strength, lateral movements, explosive motions, and balance.

Other thoughts on injury prevention or rehabilitation.
Many injuries stem from the "too's"—too much, too soon, too fast, etc. Be progressive and consistent.

Lex Williams

University of Michigan
1500, Mile, 3K, 5K, 10K, XC

"Try to stay connected to your support group. It doesn't benefit anyone if you seclude yourself when you're injured. People like to see you making an effort to get better and really respect that you want to be a part of something bigger than yourself. Even if you think you're doing the right thing by "staying out of the way" and doing your own thing, it projects selfishness."

Lex, briefly profiled
Birth Date and Place: March 21, 1987; Ann Arbor, Mich.
Began running: 7 years old; Began running competitively: 10 years old
Height/Running Weight: 5'9", 140 lbs.

University of Michigan, B.A., 2010 (Economics)
College coach: Ron Warhurst
Dexter High School, Dexter, Mich. (2005)
High school coaches: Greg Meyer, Jaime Dudash, Nick Stanko, Todd Snyder

Current residence: Hanover, N.H.
Current occupation: Athlete
Current affiliation or club:
Current Coach: Tim Broe

Personal records: 1500—3:42.38 (2007); Mile—4:01.72i (2007); 3K—7:55.59i (2008); 5K—13:47.57i (2008); 10K—30:03.89 (2009)

Notable high school, collegiate and post-collegiate accomplishments
High School—3rd at NIN in mile run (2005)…4th at NON in 2 mile run (2005).
College/Post-Collegiate – Big Ten champion indoor 5000m (2007)…All American DMR (2007).

Favorite rehab/cross training workout
I absolutely hate training inside, but most of the time it's the best way to get your heart rate up, which should be the main goal in cross training or a rehabilitation workout. I stole this from Nate Brannen, but I've simulated the "Michigan" workout in the pool with aqua jogging and on a bike.

On land, the standard Michigan is a 1600m, 1200m, 800m, 400m step down on the track with a 2k loop at tempo pace around Michigan Stadium in between each interval. We typically run a 3 mile warm-up and cool-down. To simulate that in the pool/on the bike I started with 20 minutes easy, then converted each of the hard and moderate intervals into minutes (1600 = 4:30, 1200 = 3:20, 800 = 2:10, 400 = 1:00 and 2k = 6:00). After each hard interval there is about 400m of easy running before the 2k loop around the stadium and then another 400m from the end of the 2k to the track, so I inserted 1:30 of recovery in-between each. The pool or bike "Michigan" would look something like this:

    20:00 min easy
    4:30 min hard
    1:30 min easy
    6:00 min moderate
    1:30 min easy
    3:20 min hard
    1:30 min easy
    6:00 min moderate
    1:30 min easy
    2:10 min hard
    1:30 min easy
    6:00 min moderate
    1:30 min easy
    1:00 min hard
    20:00min easy

Total workout: 78 minutes

On off days, my favorite thing to do is get on a bike outside and ride.

Worst running-related injuries
The only stress related injury I've sustained from running occurred my freshman year of high school when I was playing soccer, hockey, and running cross country all at the same time. I broke completely through the 2nd metatarsal in my right foot during the middle of a cross country race. It happened around 1.5 miles in, and I was able to finish the race, but with a crap time and a lot of pain.

I also had an inflamed iliolumbar ligament in my lower back during my senior year of cross country at Michigan, which made for some up and down training and performances. It was probably already bothering me quite a bit, but was really set off by a deep tissue massage performed by a masseuse I had never worked with before. I could barely walk the next day and had pain even walking for a couple weeks after. I had to be very aggressive with treatment because we were already in-season. I was going 2x a day to the training room to get ice, stim, and laser treatment and to have my alignment checked. I also visited a D.O. who did some manipulations to my back to make sure everything was in balance. I was unable to run for about 3 weeks and was on the bike or in the pool every day. When I came back to running I stayed almost completely on soft surfaces and did workouts as I felt comfortable. This was probably the most urgency I've ever felt with an injury, because it was right at the beginning of my senior season. Everything felt rushed, which is the last thing you want to do with an injury, but is necessary in most instances for a competitor.

Also, probably worse than any injury was my problems with sickness, which I believe all started with mononucleosis, which I got at the end of my sophomore year; I felt like it really knocked down my immune system. I was a kid who rarely got sick, and for the next year and a half or so it seemed that I was catching something new every couple of months. I'm not sure if there is any medical evidence for that.

It could have also been attributed to a college lifestyle and living in a house with 8 other college guys, or some combination of those things! I was out for about 4 weeks with mono, those were weeks where I couldn't do anything at all. Just rest. Then as soon as I got the OK, I went down to the track and ran an all-out mile. Pretty stupid in the scheme of things, but a kid who had mono the year before had done it and I wanted to see if I could beat his time.

I was already done for the season, so I thought "why not?" and ran a 4:24. I had run 3:42 (my PR) for the 1500 five weeks before that, and a 4:04/4:03 double for the anchor of the DMR and second leg of the 4xmile at Penn the week later when I started to really feel symptoms.

Was surgery ever required?
Never needed surgery.

What flaw led to the injuries? Or did you do something that caused them)?
As I already stated with mono and other sickness to follow, it was most likely a college lifestyle. That is to say too little sleep while balancing running 85-90 miles per week with a fairly challenging class schedule and maintaining some sort of a social life. I also just started to cook for myself so I probably wasn't on the ideal diet at the time either. I lived directly across from a pizza place that I ordered from 2-3 nights per week.

Rehabilitation program that you followed. How long before you began "normal" training?
Rehabilitation time is a case by case thing that depends completely on the injury. My back was the trickiest because it was in the middle of the season and my entire running form was thrown off by the pain I was feeling. It was impossible to run through at the beginning, and even after I had gotten to the point where I was able to run with pain I started having hip problems because I was compensating.

With any injury I've had, I've been able to get on a bike or in the pool every day. I even did some training on an alter-G treadmill when I was coming back from my back injury, which allowed me to run below my full weight before coming back to running outside normally.

Every injury is different, with a different time frame. For example, you can't really put a time frame on an ankle sprain. I've had minor sprains where I can run the next day through pain, and I've had ankle sprains where I've taken weeks off and continued with minor pain up to 6 months to a year after the injury. I listen to doctors and trainers and then make my own judgments according to how I feel and what I can handle.

Given that running takes a fair amount of time and that cross training for that same time would probably drive you crazy, what did you do to keep busy?
When I'm injured I put more time into running. I'm in the training room seeing what I can do to get better twice a day, then work out in the pool or on a bike, and then ice on my own another 1-2 times a day. It works out to be a bigger time commitment than just going for a healthy 1-hour run and stretching, doing core, and everything that comes with an everyday training routine.

What was the most difficult aspect of being injured? How did you deal psychologically with missing a season?
The most difficult time I had was my junior year of college. I got sick during indoors and performed very poorly at my conference meet and at NCAAs. I entered the NCAA meet with the 2nd fastest time in the 5K and finished either last or second to last. For whatever reason, the virus I caught had completely wiped me out. I was feeling tired every day and could not get through workouts.

I met with my coach and we decided that the best thing for me to do would be to redshirt my outdoor season. That would give me a chance to rest up for the remainder of that year and just focus on getting my body physically and mentally prepared for cross country the next year.

The hardest part about the experience was the fact that we had a great team and ended up winning the Big Ten title. I really wanted to be there competing and celebrating with my teammates, but was unable to because of the decision to redshirt.

The most frustrating thing about that season was that doctors were unable to diagnose what was wrong with me and therefore unable to prescribe a cure. I saw team doctors, my family doctor, cardiologists, allergists, etc. went through a ton of tests and had blood work done and still don't know exactly what was going on with me that season. It would've been nice to hear that I could just take a pill and get better, but instead I just had to wait it out. I felt powerless and still don't have a ring for winning a Big Ten team title.

What specifically did you learn from being injured?
The biggest thing that I took away from everything is patience. I learned that I have none. You really have to give injuries time; otherwise you will drag them out longer than necessary. Don't be anxious. Whenever you think you're ready, wait another day.

What advice would you give another elite runner who suffers a season-ending injury?
Try to stay connected to your support group. If you're on a team, get down to practice every day, travel everywhere within reason to cheer them on. It doesn't benefit anyone if you seclude yourself when you're injured. People like to see you making an effort to get

better and really respect that you want to be a part of something bigger than yourself. This is a huge problem I had to overcome. I felt like I was of no use to the people around me if I wasn't able to compete at full capacity. Even if you think you're doing the right thing by "staying out of the way" and doing your own thing, it projects selfishness.

When you returned to full-time training, did you alter the type of training you were doing?
I had to learn to alter my expectations whenever I was starting to come back. Almost always, you aren't going to come back exactly where you left off. You have to realize that besides coming back from the injury, there is still a timeline to being "fit" again. You can't expect too much too soon. Be patient.

What was the result in your first major competition after returning from injury?
I've never had a great race the first time back from injury. I like to race a couple times to get fit. I think the key, again, is altering your own expectations of what you're going to be able to do. Probably the most effective thing is to eliminate expectations completely and enter a race where you can be competitive. Even if it means entering a "slow" heat, sometimes just racing people—no matter what level they are at—can aid in confidence when you're coming back to racing.

What advice would you give a high school or young college runner regarding injury prevention and/or rehabilitation?
The best thing you could ever do for yourself is never get injured. As my coach Ron Warhurst says, "an ounce of prevention is worth a pound of cure." It is definitely worth it to take 30 minutes each day to stretch, use a foam roller, and ice. Even if you think you're invincible—which is incredibly easy to think if you're young and talented and have never been injured before. Even if you don't think this stuff will benefit you, I guarantee it cannot hurt you.

After being injured and coming back, did it change your sense of who you are/were as a runner? Did you have more patience or did you find yourself training on the edge again?
One of the biggest things I've seen injuries do to runners is make them scared to train at the same level again. I've seen a lot of "injury-prone" runners look back at what they did to get injured, instead of looking at what they didn't do to prevent it. You need to look at what you weren't doing to recover after your workouts and on your off days. Running hard in training is how you get better and make improvements to get to the next level. How you treat the recovery process will determine how much you can do before getting injured.

Dan Wilson
University of Connecticut
1500, Mile, XC

"Be smart and get ready for next season. Do all of the little things that need to be done so when you do finally come back you're ready to take it to another level."

Dan, briefly profiled
Birth Date and Place: Feb. 19, 1979; Milford, Conn.
Began running: 14 years old; Began running competitively: 14 years old
Height/Running Weight: 6'1", 148 lbs.

University of Connecticut, B.A., 2002 (Communication Sciences)
College coach: Greg Roy
Notre Dame High School, West Haven, Conn. (1997)
High school coaches: Bill Parkinson and Bob O'Brien

Current residence: Lenoir, N.C.

Notable accomplishments
High School—Three-time All-American...6th at indoor NSI...3rd at outdoor NSI...ran the Melrose Games mile...six-time state champ.
College/Post-Collegiate – Five-time All-American...five-time Big East Champ...14th at NCAA cross country championships (2001) ...ranked 1st in collegiate 1500 (2001)...4th in mile at U.S. indoor championships (2001)...6th in 1500 at U.S. outdoor championships (2002) ...ranked 5th in U.S. 1500m (2002).

Worst running-related injuries
Torn ligaments in ankles.

Approximate date of injuries, nature of them and was surgery required?
November 1995, September 1996, and September 1999. All three were severe ankle sprains where the entire foot blew up. I missed two months the first two times and missed six weeks the last time. No surgeries were needed.

What flaw led to the injuries? Or did you do something that caused them?
Chronic weak ankles. The first sprain was from running on trails, the second from playing basketball, and the third from stepping in a pothole while on a run.

Rehabilitation program that you followed. How long before you resumed "normal" training?
For all three I did extensive pool running. These were so bad that I could not even put a shoe on the foot for over a month each. While in high school I went to the public pool and did 45-60 minutes three times a week. In college I was in the pool six times a week. I couldn't put pressure on it so I didn't bike.

Once I started running again it was a slow process. After a few weeks I could resume normal training. More than once I tried running only to have the ankle/foot blow up again and be back in the pool.

Given that running takes a fair amount of time and that cross training for that same time would probably drive you crazy, what did you do to keep busy?
In high school I would imagine the state meet course (wickham) and try to take a good 15 minutes to go over every part of the course. I would work harder up the hills, relax down them, etc. I tried to come back for the state meet but it was way too soon. First day running was race day and I was very tentative. I ran 22 minutes and limped home. I had to take another three weeks off because the foot swelled really badly after.

What was the most difficult aspect of being injured? How did you deal psychologically with missing a season?
The worst part about being hurt was missing my senior year of cross country. Most colleges stopped recruiting me. I missed the chance to be a FootLocker finalist as both a junior and a senior. I was hurt before the qualifying meets both years. I am convinced that I could have made it once if not twice.

What specifically did you learn from being injured?
It's part of athletics. Although being injured feels like the worst thing in the world, all athletes have gone through it.

What advice would you give another elite runner who suffers a season-ending injury?
Be smart and get ready for next season. Do all of the little things that need to be done so when you do finally come back you're ready to take it to another level.

When you returned to full-time training, did you alter the type of training you were doing?
I just made sure to watch where I ran. Certain trails became off limits.

What was the result in your first major competition after returning from injury?
At indoor NSI as a senior I finished 6th in a PR 9:14, winning the slow heat. I spent the majority of the season getting my fitness back and I actually won two events at the state open (3200m and SMR).

What advice would you give a high school or young college runner regarding injury prevention and/or rehabilitation?
Rehab is probably the most tedious of all aspects in track and field but it can keep you on your feet. Whenever I feel any sort of ache or pain I'll ice it 7-10 times a day. You've got to do what's necessary to stay healthy.

Matt Withrow

University of Wisconsin
5K, XC

"Be honest with your coach about where you are at with your injuries. Do the best you can to stay positive, you'll be surprised how much it helps. And remember, the sun is still going to rise tomorrow."

Matt, briefly profiled
Birth Date and Place: Dec. 26, 1985, Chicago, Ill.
Began running: 11 years old; Began running competitively: 13 years old
Height/Running Weight: 5'9", 140 lbs.

University of Wisconsin, B.A., 2010 (History and Political Science)
College coaches: Jerry Schumacher and Mick Byrne
Victor J. Andrew High School, Tinley Park, Ill. (2004)
High school coaches: Joe Mortimer, Bob Matz, and Mark Luttrell

Current residence: Hanover, N.H.
Current occupation: professional runner
Current Coach: Tim Broe

Personal records: 5K—13:35.32 (2005)

Notable accomplishments
High School –Footlocker National Champion (2003)…state champ in XC, 1600 and 3200.
College/Post-Collegiate –Four-time All-American; Big Ten XC champ (2007); made U.S. senior team for 12K race in World XC in 2005 as red-shirted freshman and was top U.S. finisher in 60th place.

Favorite rehab/cross training workout
Mixture of mobility based physical therapy, fascia release, with intense strength training.

Worst running-related injuries
Hip/Groin/Back.

Approximate date of injuries, nature of them and was surgery required?
2005 to present. I had structural and muscular issues. No surgery was needed.

What flaw led to the injuries? Or did you do something that caused them?
Imbalances with spine and tailbone, hip and core muscles.

Rehabilitation program that you followed. How long before you resumed "normal" training?
I think I redefined what "normal training" meant. I tried pretty much everything you can think of rehab-wise. If it was legal, I tried it. As far as cross training, I was pretty restricted there as well. The pool actually did more harm than help for me. Same as the Alter-G. The only effective cross training for me was my road bike, but there is no real substitute for running.

Given that running takes a fair amount of time and that cross training for that same time would probably drive you crazy, what did you do to keep busy?
I tried to take my mind off things by taking on hobbies. I started to cook a lot.

What was the most difficult aspect of being injured? How did you deal psychologically with missing a season?
Not being able to run everyday.

What specifically did you learn from being injured?
To enjoy the pain free days, because you don't know how many of them you have.

What advice would you give a high school or young college runner regarding injury prevention and/or rehabilitation?
Find someone you trust and believe in your therapy. You are your own worst enemy when it comes to rehab. If you don't have faith in the rehab you are doing, it won't work, no matter what it is.

Other thoughts on injury prevention or rehabilitation.
Be honest with your coach about where you are at with your injuries. Do the best you can to stay positive; you'll be surprised how much it helps. And remember, the sun is still going to rise tomorrow.

Rick Wohlhuter
University of Notre Dame
800m

"Prevention is the way to go. My coach once said that all injuries are predictable and therefore avoidable. Injuries often result from changes in training; a weak point is suddenly exposed. This means knowing your body and listening to what it tells you."

Rick, briefly profiled
Birth Date and Place: Dec. 23, 1948
Began running: 14 years old; Began running competitively: 14 years old; Retired: 1978
Height/Running Weight: 5'9", 135 lbs.

University of Notre Dame, B.A., 1971 (Economics)
College coach: Alex Wilson
St. Charles High School, St. Charles, Ill. (1967)
High school coaches: Paul Bergeson

Current residence: Jacksonville, Fla.
Current occupation: financial analyst and trader

Personal records: 800—1:43.5 (1974); 1000—2:13.9 (1974, U.S. record); Mile—3:55.3 (1974)

Notable accomplishments
High School—Two-time Illinois state 880 yard champion.
College/Post-Collegiate –NCAA indoor 600 yard champion…AAU national indoor 1000 yard champion…AAU national outdoor 800 champion…U.S. Olympic Team (1972 and 1976)…U.S Olympic Team Co-Captain (1976)…U.S. Olympic 800 bronze medalist (1976)…world record in 880 yards…world record in 1K…world record in 2-mile relay …Ranked first in world at 800 by Track & Field News…named Athlete of the Year by Track & Field News…Sullivan Award winner.

Worst running-related injuries:
Left Achilles Tendonitis and a pulled left hamstring muscle.

Approximate date of injuries, nature of them and was surgery required?
Achilles tendonitis sophomore year in college (April 1969) and junior and senior years of college (September 1969 and '70). Pulled hamstring muscle my senior year of college (March 1971).

What flaw led to the injuries? Or did you do something that caused them?
I have limited flexibility in both Achilles tendons that caused me to run up high on the ball of my foot rather that heel-toe. This style of running placed additional stress on my Achilles tendons.

I missed a week of practice before racing over 600 yards at the indoor IC4A Championships at Princeton due to an Achilles problem. The early pace was very fast (22 point at 220 yards). I pulled my hamstring muscle just after the 220-yard mark.

Rehabilitation program that you followed. How long before you resumed "normal" training?
I began rehab by rubbing ice directly on the Achilles tendon for 10 minutes two or three times per day until I returned to running. After several days of icing, I began mildly stretching the tendon. No cross training, rest only. Generally, I would miss 10 days to one month before I could return to practice.

After my hamstring pull, I was on crutches for one week. I could walk normally after two weeks; however, the muscle remained tender. This type of injury required rest for three weeks followed by mild stretching and weight lifting to strengthen the muscle. I resumed modified training in about one month. No cross training. The leg was far too weak.

Given that running takes a fair amount of time and that cross training for that same time would probably drive you crazy, what did you do to keep busy?
I was a college student then so I filled my time with studies and college life.

What was the most difficult aspect of being injured? How did you deal psychologically with missing a season?
The most difficult aspect of being injured is dealing with the loss of something that has become a defining part of your life. A big hole in your life emerges and the challenge is to fill that hole with rehabilitation and other activities or school. I tried to stay focused on the future.

What specifically did you learn from being injured?
Injuries can humble you very quickly. You can abruptly go from being a hero to an also-ran. You must look beyond the injury period when you can not compete and focus on the future. You will be back training and competing again.

What advice would you give another elite runner who suffers a season-ending injury?
Find advice on how to rehab your injury. Most importantly, learn how to avoid injuries; seek out qualified help. When at large relay meets such as the Drake Relays, I would ask

several trainers for advice about injuries, even though I was not hurt at the time. Always educate yourself.

When you returned to full-time training, did you alter the type of training you were doing?
When I returned to training after pulling a hamstring muscle, I wanted to regain my competitive form quickly. I made a major change in my training program. I went to the track and ran many short-rest intervals at a quick pace. Each day I would run intervals on the track and add a long run on the weekends. After a month of this routine, I ran a personal best at 880 yards and won a major college championship. This chance in my training routine eventually propelled me to world class.

What was the result in your first major competition after returning from injury?
After a month of intense interval training, I ran a personal best at 880 yards and won the IC4A outdoor championships.

What advice would you give a high school or young college runner regarding injury prevention and/or rehabilitation?
Prevention is the way to go. My coach once said that all injuries are predictable and therefore avoidable. Injuries often result from changes in training; a weak point is suddenly exposed. This means knowing your body and listen to what it tells you. The best way to remain uninjured is to learn how to overcome your physical limitations.

Use flexibility exercises or weight training to correct any weak areas. In my case, every day I would stretch my Achilles tendons and calf muscles. I stretched hard. I also did isometric exercises to strengthen my hamstrings. In addition, I changed my running form when doing long runs to minimize leg problems. I never suffered a season-threatening injury again during my career.

Appendix A—Injuries Incurred by Responding Athletes

Achilles tear
Achilles tendonitis
Achilles tendonosis/paratendonitis
Bone bruise/contusion
Bursitis of foot
Collapsed arch, foot, hip
Eversions of ankle
Fractures
- Osseos
- Sesmoid
- Stress

Groin problems & sports hernia
Haglund's deformity
Hamstring strains
Hip disorders
Inversions of ankle
IT Band tendonitis
Knee tendonitis
Ligament strains and tears
Low back syndrome
Muscle strains and tears
Necrosis of Achilles
Nerve disorders
Osteochondral fracture
Osteocondritis Desicans
Plantar fasciitis
Plica syndrome
Pubitis
Sacroiliac joint disorders
Shin splints
Strain of right TFL
Stress fracture(s)
Stress reaction
Torn ligaments
Torn meniscus
Vertebral disorders

Appendix B—Half-decade started running competitively

1960-64	1985-89	1990-94 (continued)	2000— (continued)
Popejoy	Appenheimer	Schoolmeester	Fernandez
Wieczorek	Baker	Torres, Ed	Jager
Wohlhuter	Chorny	Torres, Jorge	Miller
1965-69	Dobert	VanDenend	Pifer
Brown	Downin, Andy	Watson	Rombough
1970-74	Gary	Wilson	Rupp
Brahm	Graff	**1995-99**	Smyth
Plasencia	Herman	Huling	Vail
Scott	Jimmerson	Keller	
Spivey	Johnson	Lincoln	
1975-79	McMullen	Mobley	
Atkinson	Nutter	Moran	
Culpepper	Schumacher	Nelson	
Deady	Siemers	Olinger	
DeHaven	Spiker	Pilkington	
Diemer	**1990-94**	Ritzenhein	
Frerker	Bethke	Rohatinsky	
Hacker	Broe	See	
1980-84	Downin, Matt	Tegenkamp	
Bailey	Hauser	Williams	
Coogan	Luchini	Withrow	
Cordes	Mortimer	**2000—**	
Kennedy	Riley	Derrick	
Webb ("from birth")	Sage	Eagon	

Appendix C—U.S. Olympians Profiled in This Book

Jeff Atkinson—1988 (1500)

Terry Brahm—1988 (5K)

Tim Broe—2004 (5K)

Doug Brown—1972, 1976, 1980 (Steeplechase)

Mark Coogan—2000 (Marathon)

Alan Culpepper—2000 (10K); 2004 (Marathon)

Mark Deady—1988 (1500)

Rod DeHaven—2000 (Marathon)

Brian Diemer—1984 (Steeplechase—bronze); 1988 (Steeplechase); 1992 (Steeplechase)

Pascal Dobert—2000 (Steeplechase)

Robert Gary—1996, 2004 (Steeplechase)

Brad Hauser—2000 (5K)

Bob Kennedy—1992, 1996 (5K)

Daniel Lincoln—2004 (Steeplechase)

Paul McMullen—1996 (1500)

Billy Nelson—2008 (Steeplechase)

Steve Plasencia—1988, 1992 (10K)

Jonathan Riley—2004 (5K)

Dathan Ritzenhein—2004 (10K); 2008 (Marathon)

Galen Rupp—2008 (10K)

Steve Scott—1980, 1984, 1988 (1500)

Jim Spivey—1984 (1500); 1992 (1500); 1992 (5K)

Matt Tegenkamp—2008 (5K)

Jorge Torres—2008 (10K)

Alan Webb—2004 (1500)

Rick Wohlhuter—1972 (800); 1976 (800—bronze; 1500)